Your Essential
SELF

© Toni Bonet

About the Author

Richard Harvey, the founder-director of Therapy and Spirituality, a personal and spiritual growth center in the Sierra Nevada Mountains in Spain, is a psychotherapist, author, and spiritual teacher. For over thirty-five years he has helped thousands of people find greater peace and fulfillment in their lives through his workshops, trainings, and private therapy practice.

You can visit him online at www.therapyandspirituality.com.

RICHARD HARVEY

The Inner Journey to Authenticity
& Spiritual Enlightenment

Your Essential
SELF

Llewellyn Publications
Woodbury, Minnesota

FIRST EDITION
First Printing, 2013

Cover art: Woman: iStockphoto.com/Aleksandar Nakic
Cover design by Lisa Novak

Llewellyn is a registered trademark of Llewellyn Worldwide Ltd.

Library of Congress Cataloging-in-Publication Data

Harvey, Richard, 1952–
  Your essential self : the inner journey to authenticity and spiritual enlightenment / Richard Harvey. — First edition
      pages   cm
  Includes bibliographical references and index.
  ISBN 978-0-7387-3470-5
  1. Self—Religious aspects. 2. Spiritual life. I. Title.
  BL65.S38H37 2013
  204'.4—dc23
                            2013002525

Llewellyn Publications
A Division of Llewellyn Worldwide Ltd.
2143 Wooddale Drive
Woodbury, MN 55125-2989
www.llewellyn.com

Printed in the United States of America

Other Books by This Author

The Flight of Consciousness:
A Contemporary Map for the Spiritual Journey

To Xanthe, Skip, Lily, and Gabriel, for their love, their lessons, and their freedom. Always remember your essence is divine.

Acknowledgments

My gratitude and deep respect go to those committed souls who have sought the unknown with me. I write this out of respect and admiration to them and in awe of the mystery that guides us in the endeavor to realize our potential, our truth, and our divinity.

To those seekers and friends whose dreams, narratives, and anecdotes have been drawn on for this book, thank you.

To my reader's group, who examined, commented, and contributed to the manuscript over many stages of change—particularly, Duncan Bell, the late Aspen Edge, Julie Kaloczi, and Eric Krohn—and to my friend and collaborator Rev. Robert Meagher for invaluable fine-tuning at the end. Their time and attention has given invaluable and inspiring support in the shaping of *Your Essential Self.* Also to my wife, Nicky Harvey, who tended this book from conception to realization and who has contributed to it and to my life in more ways than I can express.

To my vigilant and well-informed editor, Brett Fechheimer, who gave such careful comments and attention and through whose guidance I was able to create a more approachable, accessible book; to Angela Wix; and to all the team at Llewellyn, my heartfelt thanks.

To this wonderful reflection of the Divine—ordinary life in the world of thought and feeling, past and future, loss and rebirth, reflections of light, unselfconscious beauty and luminosity... I cannot stay here long, but how much I learned while I was here!

To my teachers, alive and dead: may the resonant truth of their wisdom, insight, and understanding reverberate long after this book is dust. For not leaving us to wander, I extend deep gratitude and reverence to them all. And, finally, to the great silence, *mouna,* the sense of presence, the Divine within.

Contents

Prologue

What Is Your Essential Self?

Awakening to your essential self is an idea that has been around since human history began. It can be found in most or all religious and spiritual traditions, as well as modern New Age thinking. Simply put, it's the idea that human birth is a paradoxical experience. On the one hand we grow, mature, and adapt to become part of the human world; on the other, through the indoctrination of conditioning, we forget where we have come from and who or what we really are. So being born is awakening into this world, but falling asleep to a deeper reality.

This book is about how we can awaken to our essential self in this lifetime and live to our full capacity and potential as a human being. Human beings are animalistic, compassionate, and divine—infinitely more splendid, amazing, and diverse than we can imagine. Most of us spend our lives in the first level—the animalistic level. Sometimes we rise to the second level and truly love, and feel compassionate. Fewer still make the heart the abiding center of their lives and even rarer is the human being who longs for the truth, for the eternal, and for the divine, and sees human life as a unique and precious opportunity for discovering the divine being that inheres within the psychic body-form.

Human beings mostly live at a fraction of their full potential. Try as we might, money, relationships, possessions, and prestige cannot fill the inner void. Potential and fulfillment, like satisfaction and joy, must be authentic and real. In fact, they must be *inner*. We have a deep integrity about life and a great curiosity. Human beings have been questioning and questing for thousands of years. At the forefront of their field of interest is the search for their true nature, for something that is deathless. Some call it God, or Brahman, Allah, YHWH, or Great Spirit; it is changeless, omnipotent, omniscient, and immanent—more here than we are—and it is our human destiny to awaken to it.

This book charts the course of awakening to your essential self in three stages. The fulfillment of these three stages of human development is within our innate capacity, and it is attained through *a single, connected process of awakening*.

The first stage, *The Process of Self-Discovery*, describes how we explore, understand, and finally transcend our small sense of self through identifying and shedding restrictive life conditioning and emotional and behavioral patterns, becoming whole, and fulfilling our personal potential.

The second stage, *The Transformation into Authenticity*, describes how we can reach the state of permanent change and personal authenticity by stabilizing in the personal changes we made in the first stage and empowering ourselves to relate authentically and compassionately to other people and the outer world. This stage is the flowering of personal inner work.

The third stage, *The Source of Consciousness*, describes the experience of living in the world when we have touched transcendent reality and understand who we really are. Through shedding illusion, living in the present, and re-centering in the true Self, we at last live our divine nature.

Each stage includes abundant exercises and practices for your ongoing growth and development. You may simply wish to read *Your Essential Self*, but you will get far more out of it if you engage with the book as an interactive experience, because above all, awakening is an experiential event. In short, you must practice. You cannot think your way to your essence.

Starting at the beginning is advisable, but if you scan the sections of this book and feel a strong impulse to go straight to a certain topic, please do so. I have found as I grow older that when I read books in a chaotic order, sometimes they yield a greater wisdom. Having said that, I have arranged the book in sequential order and I have yet to meet anyone who genuinely reaches any one of the three stages before the previous ones.

The introduction is about how we come to inner work, and it is important because how you start out is intimately related to the outcome of your inner search. In chapter 1, I give you the basis for an inner-work practice, via a clear model of how to approach inner work for maximum effectiveness and success.

The purpose of this book is to introduce you to an integrated, innovative, practical, and real model of the inner spiritual journey for self-understanding, growth, and healing. *Your Essential Self* helps you see where you're at in your personal journey, where you've been, what you've accomplished, and where you're headed, and to prepare you, in some cases, for what lies ahead. It also helps you to recognize what stages you may have skipped over and how you might remedy that, often through the exercises found at the end of each chapter.

Spiritual inner work is now a crucial activity for the modern world. *Your Essential Self* clearly connects personality and ego to true nature and enlightenment. It acts as a map for the inner journey and guides you through the stages of the process for inner work, discovering authenticity, and Self-realization.

In addition to teaching stories, ancient and modern, I have used case histories to amplify and illustrate. Because these accounts are real, they do not always have "fairy-tale endings" (although sometimes they do). Names, gender, and specific details have been changed or adapted, and the stories are sometimes a composite of different experiences in order to make individuals and events completely unrecognizable and preserve privacy and confidentiality.

Who Is This Book For?

Ashrams, churches, yoga schools, monasteries, temples, and convents may be centers of religious life, but for an increasing number of people the practical, day-to-day world has become the center of spiritual life and practice. These are the new gnostics, the modern mystics, worldly *sannyasi*. But they are more, for they are forging a new way to the life of the soul and the spirit. This way is largely self-directed, and seeks guidance from within. If you fall into this growing demographic, you are aware that spiritual knowledge or wisdom is inner and that only a unique inner journey will lead you to it.

Establishing a spiritual life in the world today is fraught with difficulties. But spiritual life has always thrived on difficult circumstances and tests. The great challenge to the complete fulfillment of human life today is, first, the challenge of defeating the ego forces that have become so insidious and powerful and, second, establishing an open and informed attitude to spirituality that is as unpolluted by modern populist ideas, which are shallow and misinformed, as it is unhindered by the authoritarian prejudices of many religious traditions. The essential self can only be awakened—individually and collectively—when the foundation for the undertaking to attain the ultimate treasure is based firmly in reality and truth, and made relevant to our contemporary milieu.

So, this book is for people who are interested in truth, reality, and the invisible realms—spiritual seekers, personal-growth adherents, therapists, healers of all kinds. More broadly it is for those who feel that we are approaching a new era, a spiritual age.

Many people today are disappointed by their experience of inner work. Psychotherapy, group workshops, meditation, or other spiritual practices have not brought about the results they had wished for, or fulfilled their desires or expectations. People are inclined toward remaining blindly supportive of the alternative (or in some cases ancient) practices, or carrying off the consolation prize of temporary rewards, or turning into cynics and becoming detractors, or—and this is most common amongst the spiritual practitioners—settling for the ego compromise that suits them. But finding a spiritual context for the ego will never work.

I hope this book can remedy this. I will explore with you the path of personal and spiritual unfolding, with all its challenges and joys, from initial stages to Self-realization. *Your Essential Self* is a comprehensive guide to the process of the psycho-spiritual journey, or to put it more simply, *how we discover who we really are.* Rather than being an unattainable fantasy, I will try to show you how spiritual attainment is the logical extension of human development and exactly how the personality, the authentic self, and the transcendent Self[1] are connected.

If you are interested in human psychology; the identification with a separate ego self; the way in which our early life experience, the creation of character, and the expression of personality have dictated how we live; and particularly if you feel the impulse to release yourself from the constraints of self-contraction and penetrate through the egoic process, then this book is for you.

The flowering of a human life leads to untold wonders and joys too intense and precious to describe. If you are interested in this— the life of authenticity and compassion, of living as if you and the other events, people, and life forms of all kind and circumstances are not separate from you and how life could be lived in such a generous, open, resonant, and empathetic way joining emotionally, mentally, and spiritually with the world—then this book is also for you.

Finally, if you are genuinely intent on rising to the challenge of a human life and finding what it means to realize the true Self— through spiritual, transcendent, and divine stages of liberation and realization—then this book is most certainly for you.

---

1. At the heart of this book is the relationship between the relative and the absolute, the human and the spiritual, the earthly and the transcendent. To distinguish between them I use lowercase and uppercase words; for example, *self* and *Self*, *truth* and *Truth*, *love* and *Love*. The lowercase *love* refers to love in the relative world, while the uppercase *Love* refers to transcendent love. The essential point is that, while love has its opposite in hate or fear, Love has no opposite, because it is absolute. Sometimes I have made exceptions where a word is made obvious by description—for example, divine love, since it is self-explanatory.

The inner seeker today has an obligation to discover and heal the personality and ego as a prelude to spiritual processes. To act as an unobstructed conduit of divine energy, the modern spiritual seeker must seek resolution in character habits and defenses.

Living in the age of holism we can no longer talk of the physical, emotional, or mental, without including the spiritual. All of these aspects make up the complete human being, the total blessing of a human life. Each one *inheres* in the others.

Spiritual attainment has been presented directly and simplistically in the past. The great profundity of such a simple statement as *be as you are*, for example, still carries weight. But today ego forces are so complex and powerful, and human beings are so extraordinarily conflicted and multilayered, that we are required to persist in an ordeal of unwinding character that has no precedent in human history.

Unwinding character or shedding the ego, the flowering of human personality, and the full realization of what it means to be a human being are what these three stages are all about. This book guides you through them sequentially and initiates and encourages you in establishing an effective, inspiring inner-work practice for your awakening.

How to Use This Book

As you read through this book, you may identify inner places you have already become familiar with or passed through. At other times you will intuit the places you have yet to reach. In Taoism it is said that knowledge of the future is merely a flowery trapping. I do not mean to preempt your unique experience. But sometimes we fall into temporary despair or dejection, and at those times the guidance in this book may prove invaluable to you. Then you will know that there is more and that the path is long and hard, but also joyful and wonderful.

At the end of each chapter is a selection of questions for you to work through. These questions will provoke your inner-work practice and inspire you to devise further questions and tasks for inner inquiry that are personal to you. For uninterrupted reading simply glance over them, but when the time is right (and the time is always *now* in healing and awakening), respond to these questions and use them to explore your inner realms.

Hence *Your Essential Self* is both a book to read and a book to work through. No one can do your inner work but you. It is arguably the most important, necessary, and indispensable activity of your life. Through inner work you can awaken and discover yourself, your life purpose, and your path to Self-realization. If you are already convinced of this, you will surely take your inner-work practice seriously. If you are doubtful, try it for a short period, say a month, but be consistent and then see how you feel.

Throughout this book, I will guide you through the inner journey, clarify and/or inspire you if you have already begun it, and present a clear and accessible model of how you can realize your psychological and spiritual potential. I have tried to present profound ideas in an accessible way without cheapening the subject matter or patronizing you, the reader. May it illuminate, inspire, and encourage you to awaken to a most welcome stranger, your deeper self; to a life of empowerment lived out of your authenticity; and to a dazzling light beyond anything you could ever think possible, your true Self.

ℰℴ

I am a psychotherapist and spiritual teacher. My background is in humanistic and transpersonal psychologies, Taoism, and Zen. I lead workshops, trainings, and retreats, and run a private practice for individuals and couples. I am the founder-director of Therapy and Spirituality, a personal and spiritual growth center situated in the Sierra Nevada Mountains in southern Spain. For over thirty-five years my work has consistently attracted and fascinated me. Each human being has a depth and a uniqueness that is enriched by familiarity and deepening... and found through self-discovery.

For me, inner work has been a means of self-development and spiritual insight, a way to reach personal liberation from psychological conditioning, a journey to reality, present real happiness, understanding, and spiritual illumination.

My personal journey took me through work with eminent psychologists, psychotherapists, meditation teachers, and spiritual masters, through Europe and India to an intensive period of training in a Zen monastery. But most of all, developing the practice of awareness has returned me to my essential self, empowered me, and led me forward into deepening understanding and expanded freedom.

After twenty-one years in practice, I felt compelled to write an account of the spiritual journey. In *The Flight of Consciousness*,[2] I mapped the stages of spiritual development as simply and directly as I could without dishonoring the sacredness of the material. It was a work of direct intuitive insight, drawn from my experience of spiritual unfolding in myself and others. I wanted to dispel the confusion many felt from the ready availability of spiritual texts from different traditions that seemed to conflict in meaning.

Over the years I have distilled my psycho-spiritual approach. Some time ago I began to notice and wonder how our personality connected to our spirituality and exactly how we developed through one into the other. My observation and personal experience has led me to propose a third connective layer of authenticity, or the flowering of the human soul and personality in its true nature. I believe that this middle stage serves as a testing ground for the soul and heart in the process of transformation, not unlike "proving" in bread rising or the alteration of substances in a crucible.

I believe this middle stage of inner growth, which comprises Stage 2 of this book, is an original and important discovery in the field of psycho-spiritual psychology, modern-day mysticism, and spirituality. As I have integrated the three-stage model described in *Your Essential Self* into my workshops and trainings, I have been amazed at how it has proved accurate, accelerative, and insightful as a framework and a method.

As ever, the clinical findings of a single practitioner, particularly in the realms of psychology and spirituality, will have to be confirmed by the rational mind reasonably over time. For now I encourage you to take the ideas in this book, work with them, and see what emerges as a result. Before that, however, consult your innermost heart and see if what you read here "rings true" and resonates with your essential self.

---

2. Richard Harvey, *The Flight of Consciousness: A Contemporary Map for the Spiritual Journey* (Ashgrove Publishing, 2002).

*Realization of the Self is the greatest help
that can be rendered to humanity.*

—RAMANA MAHARSHI [3]

Introduction
to Your Essential Self

How We Come to
Self-Exploration and Inner Work

In times of trauma—depression, anxiety, sorrow, confusion, and despair—our personalities are not enough. We are challenged to go beyond our normal limitations. We are forced to look inward, to journey to a deeper reality. Those of us who do not experience trauma or crisis, but nonetheless want to grow, may also choose to journey inward. It is a more circuitous route: crisis is given, it cannot be chosen. This is how we discover who we truly are. For those who have gone deep enough, the truth proves to be so far removed from the personality that the swells and troughs of life in the so-called "real" world take on the appearance of play, lightness, and detachment.

For most of us, however, our physical health, relationships, finances, fears, and desires are all there is and all we have time for. Our daily lives are spent in an obsession with ourselves either directly or indirectly through our projections and concerns for others. The loop-tape of our

---

3. Ramana Maharshi, *Talks with Sri Ramana Maharshi* (Inner Directions Foundation, 2000), 12 (30 January 1935, Talk 20).

life compels and distracts and shows us how we live through cycles of repetitive dynamics of action and reaction. Our frustration is as certain as our satisfaction, our happiness as predictable as our misery: one invariably follows the other. When we are honest with ourselves, we see that we are not as free as we think we are.

Even when we entrust our freedom to Eastern teachings and practices and the distant likelihood of enlightenment, our culture may pose a terminal caution to our aspirations to freedom. The Sufi leader Pir Vilayat Khan said that of all the great spiritual teachers he had met in the East, if you brought them to the West and gave them a family, a mortgage, insurance, taxes, a job, children, and a spouse, they would all have a hard time.

Though his remark is simply a caution, it could be construed as supporting a limited assumption made by many: the idea that enlightenment lives in the East, while neurosis lives in the West. What if we say instead that, if you were to bring a Western teacher to Asia and ask them to adapt to an Eastern culture, they too would have a hard time? The point is that enlightenment and the spiritual are not confined by form, as much as we tend to dress them in certain clothes to give the appearance of holiness and serenity. Who says that we cannot be neurotic *and* spiritual at the same time? One is a symptom of our humanness, the other of our divinity. This is one of the overriding themes in this book: finding the way, in a modern Western milieu, to wisdom and illumination. But we'll get to that later; for now we start with change—personal change.

Everyone who looks within wants, consciously or unconsciously, to change. Change may be brought about by effort, through an act of will, but that kind of change is relatively superficial because it reverts when the will weakens. A deeper transformation comes about when we tap into the change that flows through all of existence and learn to surrender to it through the deep acceptance of *how things are.*

How things are is tricky to experience. We habitually bring our prejudices and assumptions to bear on direct experience and cease to be aware. The goal of self-discovery is to become aware of who we are and to truly experience the world *as it is*. We get there through explor-ing our inner world.

But first there must be a break, a tear, a crack in the fabric of our complacency; it is something negative, some event or feeling that upsets our contentment, but it is also a call to reality and to our deep-est self.

A Crack in the Fabric

It is the potential of every person to grow into a whole human being. Human beings strive for wholeness or completion by looking for a mate, acquiring material possessions, and pursuing worldly accom-plishments. The idea of completing ourselves drives us unconsciously in everything we do.

Those of us who make the commitment to inner work are look-ing for completion, too. Something gives us the courage to take up self-reflection and attempt to know ourselves intimately and discover who we really are. Some of us have an implicit trust that the way will be revealed; others of us come with openness and faith, or a deep response to the urge to grow. Each of us has suffered a crack in the fabric that protects us from the world.

The personality is a mass of conflicts and competing urges. In inner work we work with our attachments and obstructions to clar-ity and change. Our unrealistic hope is that we can change without personal loss, which is never possible, or that we can manipulate our situation to bring about change, but such change by its very nature is never lasting. Yet the mind unwinds its plans and intrigues, spin-ning a web, producing mock solutions and bogus resolve. A terrific wrestling match goes on between the self that deeply desires to heal and change and the self that wishes to be healed but unchanged. But successful self-exploration heals through inner changes that require our surrender to loss: the release of attachment and the shedding of emotional patterns.

These patterns originate in early childhood beyond our conscious memory. They are held together by powerful emotions and rein-forced by reaction. Inside us, reactive emotions force our unconscious, spontaneous, natural feelings down and substitute a superficial, habitual, mechanical self for our real nature. We inhibit the expression of our deeper feelings because we like to think that we are in control. But our life is out of our control, as anyone who has suffered a mental breakdown, bankruptcy, or the death of a loved one will readily confirm. By denying our feelings and their expression, we reject ourselves.

We cannot reject ourselves without creating an inner tangle of doubts, desires, aversions, and attachments. We are beings of overriding feeling. Wrapped in conflict, unable to find resolution, and tied in the knots of reactive emotions, we become inwardly divided and in conflict with ourselves. We project this inner conflict onto the outside world as opposition to people or events. We develop layers of protection, false persona, and distrust, and defend ourselves from others with often-concealed antagonism and separation. Averse to real meeting, we prefer to remain uncommunicative and unconnected. When this happens, our inner conflict becomes an outer reality.

Often we are trapped in reaction to our early life circumstances—our family, how we were treated, who we have become. We may suffer from guilt, shame, negative judgments, and self-criticism, which result in pain, frustration, denial, and withdrawal. We practice inner work to discover the ghosts and dark shapes in our unconscious, to feel our forbidden needs and desires, our deep fears, and the awe-inspiring rage and sadness of our existence.

Secretly we are embarrassed at our lack of self-knowledge. We may try to compensate by demonstrating our awareness or communicating our suffering. But we deeply crave an atmosphere of allowing, permission, and containment, a safe space in which we can unravel the tangled cord of reaction and held emotion, and lessen the inner pressure that re-creates resentments.

As our inner journey continues, we pass through the layers of appearance to subconscious layers of deception and avoidance. We think we know ourselves, but we are hidden beneath defenses and resistance. We may imagine that we are open to self-discovery, while we are really in a fog of conflicts, apologies, justifications, and unconscious urges. When challenged, we may not know who we are. One inner seeker recalls:

> I had always thought of myself as a nice guy—polite, thoughtful, considerate. I rarely got angry or lost my temper. But my inner work changed all that. I found that underneath the "niceness" there were feelings and passions I would never have guessed at. Jealousy, rage, fear, need, desires—they all poured out of me. I found out that I had left so much of me behind. It was as if I had met life's challenges by pruning off pieces of myself that were unacceptable until what remained was nothing like who I really was. It took a huge amount of soul-searching, honesty, courage, and persistence. But eventually I got there. Now, I have never felt more like myself. Behind the niceness was my rage, my need, and my sadness, but behind *that* I discovered my capacity for joy, love, and fulfillment.

Most of us come to inner work wanting to add to ourselves—to make things better, to be happier or more fulfilled. We would rather be happy than discover what has made us unhappy. But while happiness remains out of reach, we are unclear and unfocused, and the distance allows us space for excuses, regrets, and dissatisfaction. The more we let go in our inner work, the clearer we become. Everything we express, verbalize, and give form to is diminished in its intensity and its hold on us, as we release our attachment to it. As thoughts and feelings are expressed, they immediately begin to die and give way to new experience. One of the deep lessons of inner work is that *we have to lessen ourselves to find ourselves*. We have to relinquish all that is false in us to reveal our real Self.

Unexpressed feelings create a psychic cage around our spirit. We are unable to release ourselves until we have cried, raged, felt pain and sadness. Releasing negative emotions allows feeling to flow within us and takes us to deeper levels of experience and fulfillment. When we integrate these experiences in the psyche, we can begin to live with newfound freedom and expansion, as if a great weight has been lifted off of us.

On one level, inner work is an examination of the instability of life: how things manifest and dissolve in a seemingly endless state of fluctuation. Our emotions create endless scenarios of desire, of pleasure and pain. On another level, inner work is like polishing coal until it turns into a diamond—a metamorphosis of substances that were always within. This metamorphosis is possible because we are both human and divine. Our humanness is apparent, but often we conceal our divinity.

In inner work we explore our personality in all its aspects until the chinks—those little gaps between the tightly packed content of personality and personal drama—appear, and light enters into the darkness through the crack in the fabric of our façades. Personality is a thin layer around the soul. It is *how* we appear, to ourselves and others—not *who* we are. The word *person* is derived from the Latin *persona*, meaning the mask we wear to play a character. Each one of us is wearing a mask, but what is beneath it? To find out—to know ourselves—we must journey within.

People begin the inner journey to awakening for a variety of reasons—ill health, relationship issues, career crisis, a sense of meaninglessness, lack of purpose, challenges of aging, coping with emotions, anxiety, spiritual inquiry. Some come through choice; some through necessity. The way in which we come to therapy and inner work indicates the quality of our intention and may even predict the outcome of our efforts. The end is inherent in the beginning.

Everyone's path to inner work is unique, but broadly speaking there are two ways—curiosity and desperation, the way of the dilettante and the way of despair. The desperate seeker comes out of crisis; the curious seeker comes out of dissatisfaction. Both represent some shattering of our picture of how things are, some form of disenchantment, disappointment, or disillusionment. The difference is in how we come to inner work: dissatisfaction is like distant rumbling thunder; crisis is like a bolt of lightning.

Dissatisfaction

Sometimes, for no conscious reason or for many reasons, we are dissatisfied. We feel an inner turbulence that torments us with worry, anxiety, and unnameable fears. By day we are nervous, preoccupied, and unable to concentrate; at night we suffer from insomnia, fearing to sleep, or longing for sleep, full of imaginative forebodings. Sometimes our existence is "coated" in a vague feeling of dread. Outwardly, things may be going well for us—or not—but it doesn't seem to matter; the dread stays with us regardless, and, inwardly disturbed, we can find no peace.

When deep dissatisfaction falls upon us, we are faced with a choice. Either we make a conscious decision to go *in*, or we try to find a way *out* as soon as we can, at any price. Our friends may try to "help" by cheering us up or advising us to "snap out of it." But without uncovering the cause of our dissatisfaction, it may continue or return. Snapping out of it usually means that we snap back into it soon afterward.

By turning inward to meet our dissatisfaction and explore our inner world, we deepen in our experience, usually with surprising results.

Straightaway we feel more whole, because when we stop fighting against deep dissatisfaction by resisting it, we are more at ease. Since the dissatisfaction is part of us, when we fight against it, we split into two selves: the dissatisfied self and the self that resists the experience of dissatisfaction. Only one side can win, but we lose either way. By accepting the experience, we create the conditions for opening and discovering what is happening in our inner world.

Next, through opening to our experience and not judging our feelings, dissatisfaction turns out to be not as "bad" as we thought. We see that it is the thought of dissatisfaction, rather than the experience itself, that creates our aversion in the first place. When we stop fueling our dislike of dark or negative feelings, it is as if a door opens inside us and we deepen into ourselves naturally. This natural in-turning is comforting and grounding. We find a way to be with ourselves, and the dissatisfaction offers us the means to do it. Instead of considering our feelings a distraction, we acknowledge and accept our feelings as a part of us.

Then we discover the unknown within. If we ask, "What am I dissatisfied about? What is my unease?" it is most likely that many things—some known and some not known to us—will be encouraged to rise to the surface. Issues that were previously buried beneath layers of conditioning become clear, and from this deeper centering in ourselves we are motivated to make more authentic decisions.

When we choose the way out, dissatisfaction is likely to return. The way out is an avoidance or, at best, a delaying tactic. The way out appeals more to those who are afraid, reluctant, or resistant to inner reflection.

So, although it may be the harder option, when we choose the way in, we become unified, embrace our rich emotional lives, and discover new depths. The way in involves going through our dissatisfaction to emerge in a more expansive state. The dissatisfied seeker chooses to practice inner work out of an inner conviction that there is more to life and this is his or her response to the inner call.

Crisis

Crisis comes about through the action of forces beyond our control that may defeat us utterly and propel even the most unlikely of us into inner work. Whereas dissatisfaction usually contains an element of choice, crisis generates an acute feeling of urgency. It is as if something is forcibly urging us toward change.

Crisis occurs in dramatic, painful, and often unexpected ways such as a mental breakdown, the breakup of a relationship, the loss of a career, the death of a loved one, serious physical illness, or spiritual descent. The traumatic effects include shock, profound apathy, depression, suicidal thoughts, unpredictability, or extreme shifts in personality and behavior. Crisis shatters our complacency, disrupts the routine of our lives, and plunges us into uncertainty, confusion, and bewilderment.

When the outer fabric has collapsed, crisis propels us deeply within, because there is nowhere else to go. When a person responds to crisis by simply taking medication or fighting against it, they deny the inner calling to self-exploration. When they listen to the call, their crisis turns into an opportunity. In inner work, feelings and experience may be uncontained and transparent. There is little or no gap between feeling and expression.

Crisis is not always personal; it may be spiritual. When it is, the veil between ourselves and others turns out to be surprisingly thin. Sometimes entirely unbidden and with no personal preparation, we are plunged into an awareness of our interconnectedness and experience a spontaneous "awakening."

My early personal inner work was essentially a period of self-absorption. I was on a journey of self-discovery and personal change. From my perspective, those people who were concerned with the "terrible state of the world"—politically, sociologically, and ecologically—were simply projecting their unresolved personal issues onto a wider canvas. But one day, while moving into a new house, I was overcome with genuine compassion for the world and the beings that inhabited it. This feeling was tremendously powerful and came entirely unexpectedly. No one could have been more surprised than me. I experienced a crisis of heart-opening and compassion that propelled me into new activities. I spent time in a peace camp on an air force base, read feminist literature in an attempt to understand the plight of women in Western society, and undertook a deep descent of conscience and soul searching. The experience has never left me. Through it I expanded and became a bigger human being, and my inner work proceeded in the wider context of my appreciation of collective humanity.

This experience was a spiritual descent that left me in no doubt of the reality of compassion. I touched it, tasted it, lived it, and knew that compassion is present when we are not separate, when we transcend our small sense of self. We may only see the negative connotations when our life falls apart, but if we can respond positively it can be a powerful catalyst for growth and change. The decisive factor is openness. If the heart can open sufficiently, the crisis of a major breakdown propels us toward positive change. When the heart remains closed, we fall into an abyss that only intensive work on powerful emotions can liberate us from. Personal crisis is a deep call from the heart to embrace inner wisdom; this is why major breakdowns can be seen as golden opportunities for change.

To view crises, defeats, and failures as opportunities for change is a wise gift of the soul. Life is composed of negative and positive experiences ranging from the delightful to the excruciating. We never know when our lives will change in such a way that we will never be the same again. To live as if our lives will never change is foolish; to live as if our lives are in a constant process of change is wise. On the path of personal and spiritual discovery, we often learn most from openly acknowledging our failures and mistakes.

In a dramatic scene from the Arthurian legend, an old crone riding a decrepit, limping mule rides in to King Arthur's court, where a great feast is being held. The feast is in honor of the celebrated knight Parsifal, who has tried and failed to find the Holy Grail but has nevertheless attained a high degree of fame for his chivalry and courage. Pointing her crooked finger at Parsifal, she recounts all the embarrassing, shameful failures and misdeeds of his career, just at the point in his life when he is most admired and revered. This moment of shame puts him back in line with his life's purpose, and with renewed commitment he sets out once again to search for the Grail.

Though it may be hard to see at the time, crisis works like the crone, giving us the opportunity to get back to what we need to do to further our inner unfolding. Crisis brings with it experiences of loss and suffering, the feeling of being out of control, uncomfortable shifts of reference points, and the challenge of surrendering to forces greater than our individual selves. If we can rise to meet it, crisis is the unexpected twist of fate that opens us up to the process of personal transformation.

The attachment to self distinguishes the dissatisfied seeker from the seeker in crisis. The seeker in crisis is fully ready to work on herself, while the dissatisfied seeker still holds back. It is a question of commitment and resolve. The dissatisfied seeker may take months or even years to get to the place where his façade has peeled away and his sense of self is as thin and fragile as the client in crisis, whereas the seeker in crisis has already arrived. Stripped of character and attachment, she can only open to the exploration of the self—there is simply nowhere else to go.

We can never manufacture the crisis that leads to desperation and despair. We can only ever start from where we are. Dissatisfaction or crisis may motivate us to start the inner journey, perhaps a mixture of both. Either way they represent a call to journey to the inner world … and how we respond to the call is vital for the outcome.

A Life-Changing Moment

My entry into inner work was essentially unselfconscious. In retrospect I can see that dissatisfaction with my life commingled unconsciously with a crisis that manifested out of the ignorance of my emotions, repeated bad relationships, and an attachment to my personality. The culmination of all aspects of my life was a habitual state of chronic fear. It was seemingly by accident, a simple twist of fate, that I was precipitated into the circumstances that orchestrated change in my life.

I was in my early twenties. Some of my friends were converts to "therapy," but I was cynical. In heated discussions I countered their arguments in support of self-exploration with intellectual objections. I am sure they could see through my defensive stance. I felt vulnerable and threatened. Eventually they persuaded me to attend a group workshop. I went partly to justify my cynicism and partly to meet their challenge.

On the day of the workshop, Lyn, a young hippyish social worker, picked me up in a battered old station wagon. We drove into the countryside to a converted village school building owned by a middle-aged couple who kept goats and chickens and lived an alternative lifestyle. I still remember the smell of mint tea; the curious sight of goat cheeses hung in muslin bags dripping onto the kitchen counter; the bohemian ambience of worn sofas, ethnic ornaments, and cushions on bare wooden floors; and the pungent smell of Indian incense. This was mid-1970s England, and therapy workshops were becoming an underground fashion. New healing methods sprouted up alongside whole-food shops and a dawning of alternative life-styles. Everything was questioned—diet, health, emotions, behavior, spirituality, television, media, politics.

Others arrived until there were about fifteen of us. The group was composed of social workers, a teacher, a young mother, and a student, plus Simon the therapist. I seemed to be the youngest. In a hushed and reverent silence, each of us took a floor cushion and sat in a circle. People began by saying why they had come and their expectations of the day ahead. I was impressed and embarrassed by the unrestrained honesty and lack of inhibition. One had a broken relationship; another had a problem with sexual impotence; another complained he couldn't feel his emotions; another anger; another need; another felt useless; one young woman wanted to "allow her energy"; another confessed to feeling overwhelming frustration in his life.

Gazing intently at the carpet before me, I tried desperately to disappear into its involving intricacies and swirling patterns. They reflected the inner contortions I was going through, as I listened to all this naked revelation. I realized that I felt inadequate for not having a problem. I passionately wished that I had any of the problems the others had and that I could feel some strong emotion, so I could fit in. But I kept telling myself that I was fine and simply in the wrong place. I felt withdrawn and tiny, and I prayed that nobody would notice me and that I would be mercifully overlooked if I kept quiet.

"What brought you to the group, Richard?"

It was Simon's voice. Everyone was looking at me and I felt faintly sick, but I couldn't risk drawing more attention to myself by delaying my reply.

In a weak, thin voice I announced, "I'm just curious about groups."

A resounding, blank silence settled on the room. More than any-thing else in the world, I wished I was somewhere—anywhere—else. No one, I reasoned silently, had ever come to a therapy group for such a feeble reason.

After a lengthy pause, the group acknowledged me with affirming, sage-like nods. Simon proposed some group exercises, and the tremen-dous tension of the sharing circle was dissolved. We warmed up with some Bioenergetics—deep breathing, shaking our limbs, and focusing on feelings and sensations. Then we did the Bus Stop exercise.

Everyone got into a line, and the person at the end turned, faced the person behind, and said, "Get out of my way!" The idea was to move away only when you could *feel* the other person's energy. The aim was to reach the end of the line.

The exercise was a revelation to me. Everyone was so different. An apelike man with a booming voice roared through the line. A timid woman with a whiny voice couldn't budge anyone. Others seduced, manipulated, apologized, intimidated, bargained, or pleaded their way through—it was a fascinating parade of human character.

When my turn came, I took the "reasonable" course. I simply felt that everyone *should* get out of my way and I worked that expectation into my voice, increased the volume, and added what I considered a dash of menace. But no one got out of my way. Simon suggested I broaden my stance, retract my pelvis, relax my neck and throat, make eye contact, and bring the sound up from my belly. I listened to these unfamiliar ideas, tried to coordinate them all, and failed. Feeling embarrassed and useless, I reacted out of frustration and self-contempt, and taking a deep breath I tried again. Quite unexpectedly, I roared, "Get out of my way!" from the depths of my being, and the person in front of me fled. Encouraged by the effect of my new power, I drove through the queue and arrived at the other end panting and sweating. A magnificent new feeling of vibrancy and power flowed deep within me.

In that moment the course of my life changed.

I returned the following week, confident and prepared. In the circle, when Simon asked what we wanted from the group, I answered boldly that I wanted to do the Bus Stop exercise. Everyone lined up as before and I repeated my experience of the previous week. As I had expected, I felt euphoric. Simon was beside me and I beamed at him.

"Do it again," he said, "but this time say, *See me.*"

The other participants were told to get out of the way only when they felt they could really see me. Clearly this involved some personal revelation by connecting with something genuine inside me. As I met the eyes of the person at the head of the line, I knew this was going to be more challenging. Instead of directing my energy out, I had to invite the other person *in*. One of my difficulties was maintaining eye contact with this degree of intimacy. I simply wasn't used to it. I felt a strange mixture of repulsion and longing—wanting to be seen and wanting to hide at the same time. Soon I was shedding copious tears. I felt uncomprehending and emotionally overwhelmed whenever any-one got out of my way, and each time it happened something inside me was deeply touched by the acknowledgment that I was doing it right, that I was being seen, that I was acceptable—the layers of sig-nificance and meaning deepened, apparently endlessly. By the end I felt more vulnerable than ever before; my heart was pumping wildly; and I was filled with a roaring torrent of powerful energy.

The two variations of Bus Stop introduced me to the male and female sides of my psyche. As I persisted in inner work, veils began to lift off me. I had always known these veils were there. They had come between me and my experience of the world when I had shut down through the years of growing up. Each time I had shut down I could remember looking out at the world through an ever-thickening fog. I had felt increasingly deadened, grayer, more numb. But when I released my emotions in the groups, the veils lifted and the world became vibrant again.

Over the next few years I was driven to carry on my self-explo-ration. It was like waking out of a sleep and returning to life. I dis-covered inner treasures I had lost. The world of the spirit began to seep back into my life. I made the journey of psychological growth and spiritual discovery that returned me to myself. I re-experienced being carried in my mother's womb, my birth, and the solitude of my childhood. I confronted my fear, anger, need, sadness, and despair. I worked with my hopes and dreams. I explored my façade and dis-covered a "victim" inside me who wanted to sabotage my life and take revenge on those who I refused to forgive. I acted out the rites of passage that I discovered in my unconscious world, grew through initiatory experiences, discovered the wisdom of dreams, harmonized the energies in my body, grew more comfortable with powerful and intense emotions in myself and others, learned the vocabulary of feeling and touch, developed my sensitivity, and profoundly deepened my capacity for awareness. Over time, I connected with other inner seekers and discovered a community of souls who were intent on healing themselves, who recognized and honored the spiritual and the deep peace and understanding beyond the world of changing appearances.

In Summary

In this introduction we have considered how we come to self-exploration and inner work. Please pause now and consider how you started your own inner journey. It has been said that it is the work of fifty million to pioneer change in the world consciousness.[4] We have been living through a dark time, an era of materialism, conflict, and delusion. To be seriously engaged in the invisible realms puts you in the vanguard of individual and collective awakening. Before we go on to the first level of awakening, take some time to review this section using these questions:

1. How did I begin inner work and how far am I in my inner process? Was my entry through crisis or disappointment, or a mixture of the two? What can I learn from this, and have I fully appreciated the events that led to my starting this process of self-discovery?

2. What does my persona or mask look like? How do I present myself? And how am I—*who* am I—beneath the mask?

3. How has this mask of personality now cracked?

4. What do I have to give up to become the real me?

---

4. Paul H. Ray and Sherry Ruth Anderson, *The Cultural Creatives: How 50 Million People Are Changing the World* (Three Rivers Press, 2001).

Stage

ONE

The Process of Self-Discovery

1

The Basis
for an Inner Practice

In this chapter we will examine our response to deep inner longing, inner-work practice, the essential practice of awareness, and the art of listening.

A Response to a Deep Longing

The inner journey is a response to a deep longing ... for the truth, for the Divine, for ourselves. Once, the mystical philosopher P. D. Ouspensky was speaking to a group of pupils. He said "I ..." and fell into a profound meditative silence. It was a long time before he came out of that silence. Inner work is like that. "I" is the subject title of the accumulated experience of a human life. We unpack and explore the unfinished business of our lives until one day, unexpectedly, we arrive *here*—in the moment.

The inner journey returns us to ourselves, to our original sense of being. We lose ourselves in our attachments to actions, achievements, and outer relationships; we "do" so much physically and mentally that the doer gets lost in the doing and we lose touch with our being.

Over the years, many people have shared their inner journeys with me. They have spoken of their most private feelings, thoughts, and experiences; they have unpacked the baggage of their personality and discovered deeper truths beneath their self-image. Some have used this insight to deepen their exploration and seek even more profound levels of awareness, being, and consciousness. Out of a deep longing and intuition that there must be more, they have sought their true nature, their essential self.

The inner journey spirals around our true Self. Each turn of the spiral brings us closer to it. In time we arrive at the border of timeless space and being. Then we need journey no more, because we have become one with ourself; we have awakened. As the ancient Indian *rishis* would say, the river has remembered and returned to the ocean.

The ocean transformed, through the action of clouds, into the form of rivers, ceases to be itself. So indeed have you forgotten yourself through the power of conditions. Oh friend! remember your full Self. You are the Real Self... the ground of existence ... the All. —The Upanishads [5]

But how will we remember? Where will we turn to for guidance? How is it to be done? And how will we navigate through the awesome geography of our inner world and find the ocean?

Inner-Work Practice

It is fine to simply read through this book. But if you want to get the most out of it, establish your inner-work practice *now*. Here are my guidelines to help you.

1. ***Do it your way.*** Inner work may be done on your own, with a friend, or in a group. No precedent has been set to dictate how you should go about it; for everybody it is different, because

---

5. *The Spirit of the Upanishads; or, The Aphorisms of the Wise* (The Yogi Publication Society, 1907), 20.

everybody's personal journey is unique—as unique as finger-prints, as unique as each of the billions of pebbles on the beach. So don't let anyone fool you, you should and must do it your way.

2. ***Methods—explore themes appropriately using a variety of ways and means.*** Your criterion should be which techniques are relevant and inspiring. For example, writing, drawing, con-templation, meditation, dance and movement, active imagina-tion (interacting and dialoguing with inner parts of yourself), fantasy and visualization, free association (spontaneous "first thoughts"), keeping a dream diary, keeping a notebook for insights and recording major life statements,[6] awareness exer-cises, and conscious breathing. The notebook will be of partic-ular use when you feel dejected about inner work and require some evidence that you have made progress, as well as when you need to revise your inner work or recall some event or insight. Some seekers have even published their notebooks to serve as guidance for others. Often I have resorted to my inner-work notes for illustrative purposes in this book.

3. ***Space and equipment—have a space where you can gather what you need for your inner-work practice.*** Often you will choose a method intuitively, so it is essential that you have everything you may need ready so you are not distracted by having to find things. These may include: paper, a notebook, a drawing pad, pencils and pen, wax crayons (preferably not felt tips because they are nowhere near as expressive). Please write by hand with pencils and pen rather than use a keyboard, because the hand and the body, and particularly the heart, is linked through handwriting in a way that is virtually impos-sible to preserve through writing with a keyboard. You may also require: musical instruments, a sound system, an altar evoking

---

6. Life statements are family beliefs either tacitly or explicitly expressed that we come to adhere to in early life and that serve as unconscious guidance in later life—until we start to examine them in inner work.

higher energy concerns, and aesthetic or devotional objects that give you pleasure. The room or space should be private, comfortable, warm, and safe. Disconnect telephones, turn off mobile devices and the doorbell if you can, and be sure that all your chores are done or scheduled ahead, so they don't worry you during your inner-work time.

4. *Time—inner work should be scheduled and made as regular as possible*, preferably at the same time each day. An alarm clock or visible timepiece may be desirable. Setting the time— say, half an hour—ahead encourages you to persevere, even when you don't feel like it, and to stop, even when you feel like going on. Giving yourself a time boundary allows you to contain your inner work and helps to ensure that you keep to your discipline, but it also gives your ego the chance to play up and become visible, which in turn gives you material to work on. Either way, you win.

5. *Help from others—when the time is right, be willing to ask*. There are unparalleled advantages to working with others. A trusted friend or a group of like-minded seekers are indispensable to your journey at some point. When the time is right, try it, persist in it when it feels right, and use the reflection, mirroring, witnessing, and understanding of the other to highlight and bring to awareness your projections and transferences and provide insights into your emotional, behavioral, and relational patterns in ways that you could never do on your own.

   At some point, you too will need a guide to support, encourage, and conduct you over significant thresholds. When the time comes, remember two things that are of the utmost importance. One, the most vital aspect of the healing process with your guide is the *relationship*. Two, take responsibility for choosing the right (not the easiest, not the most obvious, not always even the most difficult) material to work on and don't waste any time. While you are practicing inner work on your own, these two points still apply.

6. *Finally, attitude—the way you approach inner-work practice is crucial*, because your success or failure depends on it. At the outset of an inner-work session, ritualize your approach to your work. This ritual should be self-directed and it can be as simple or elaborate as you wish, but it should bring you to your inner work in a relaxed, alert, vibrant, and open state of heart and mind. So, conscious relaxation, breathing, physical centering, lighting incense or a candle, preparing the room mindfully, bowing, stretching, humming, chanting, or bringing hands together in the prayer position are all appropriate examples. The important point is that the ritual has inner significance for you.

The questions at the end of each chapter of *Your Essential Self* are designed to stimulate and inspire you in your self-exploration. Usually I have left it up to you to choose how to approach each inquiry. In some cases, a plural approach—for example, quiet contemplation followed by writing, and ending with a gentle ritual—may be the required response. Another time, dance or movement—for example, when working on setting boundaries and experiencing energetic freedom—may be appropriate. As I have said, there is no set way to approach this; allow yourself the freedom, both inner and outer, to work in as inspired and pleasurable a way as you can. Finally, always respect and honor your intention to explore, grow, and awaken. Inner work is essentially a solo flight, and it can sometimes be lonely. You are the one who must congratulate yourself when you do good work, and you are the one who must be mindful when you are practicing avoidance or denial. Above all, make your inner-work practice a pleasurable and rewarding experience that you will want to develop with enthusiasm and return to with passion.

Two practices underpin inner-work practice. The first, awareness, is by far the most important principle to grasp. The second, listening, applies to interpersonal dialogue as much as listening to yourself.

The Essential Practice of Awareness

Awareness is the vital practice and beating heart of inner work. Awareness brings our alertness and attention to everything, connects us to our real nature, and in time provides the vehicle through which we witness the process of transforming reality. In the beginning it is expressed in our ability to be present and observe.

Awareness stems from a sense of presence. When we are aware, we are present, awake; we are *in* ourselves and "turned *on*." But many of us have learned to "turn off." We have fallen asleep, and lost our vibrancy, our sense of wonder, and our thirst for life. We have become fully automatic, jerking along in our stilted conditioning. Nothing short of a great shock, a tremendous effort, or a peak experience will dislodge us from our state of comfortable numbness.

There are many obstacles to awareness. We develop marvelous ploys for "turning *off*," avoiding, refusing, and getting *out* of ourselves. Anyone who has been in counseling will be familiar with the *window of fascination*. When we are nearing the limits of our tolerance, because what is being spoken about feels too threatening, we gaze out of the window intensely as if it is the most absorbing thing in the world. Usually our gaze is defocused or hypnotically trained on an object—either way we are glazed over, transfixed and absent, while inside we are busy denying the reality of what is happening.

Then there is the *floor of shifting patterns*. Many times I can remember swimming in an undulating tide of nauseous, hypnotic lines and patterns in the carpet or wooden floor in a desperate attempt to escape some dawning inner revelation. Another defense is the *fingers of refusal*. At a crucial point in self-exploration the seeker lifts a hand in front of his eyes, examines it in great detail, and becomes totally engrossed in one or more fingers.

Less demonstrative, but equally effective, is *mental absence*. As we get closer to suppressed emotions, we progressively blank off in a hypnotic trance of unawareness. We find ourselves unable to focus or respond to the question we are exploring, and sometimes we are completely unaware of what we have set out to explore. This technique for avoidance uses fantasy, imagination, and distraction to repel some inner threat to our small sense of self.

We drive the traumas and the suffering of our lives down into the unconscious in our efforts to "survive." Denial, repression, emotional numbness, unresponsiveness, inhibition, and over-intellectualizing feelings are all ways in which our wounded selves attempt to control and suppress uncomfortable or painful emotions.

The window of fascination, the floor of shifting patterns, the fingers of refusal, and mental absence all echo the distractedness of the TV generation. Most of us have been raised on television to a greater or lesser degree. We have sat passively and inattentively in front of a flickering screen, gazing at images for excessive lengths of time. The result is a kind of chronic state of hypnosis that we carry over into our everyday life. Many of us are unable to participate fully in natural life, and gazing into space has become a "normal" pastime. Today, the cost of screen-gazing rendering the eye passive and the mind numb is high in very small children, as well as in adults. Prolonged exposure to computer monitors, mobile devices, and in-car and in-flight movies, along with the standard TV and DVD screens in every home and office, dominate our work and leisure time. The technological barrage of entertainment and information continually batters our senses into submission and unconsciousness. Our attention becomes numbed, deadened, and conditioned to engage partially for only minimal lengths of time. Our ability to focus has weakened; our capacity for sustained reflection has withered. Most of us are not even able to think for ourselves. The cost of being incapable of practicing awareness is enormous.

So, how do we retrieve our awareness and stop distracting ourselves? First, we ask ourselves where our awareness is focused now habitually, routinely. Notice that mentally, emotionally, and physically we express our concerns and manifest our values in what we do and how we are. We can see what is important to us and what we value simply by observing how we spend our time and what we do with it. What we do, think, and feel reveals our present practice of attention. Second, we become conscious of how we are using our awareness. We can do this by withdrawing into a neutral inner place and gathering our awareness back into ourself. When it is within us, we feel an inner vibrancy, centeredness, and energy. Sit with this energy for a little. Finally, before you reapply it to an object of focus outside yourself, be sure that it is what you want to do.

We can discover a great deal about others by simply practicing awareness openly, without criticizing or judging. By watching how someone enters a room, starts the car, eats food, or handles objects, we get a glimpse into their inner world.

One of my clients[7] habitually "wiped" the money off her hands when she paid me at the end of her sessions. She handled the paper bills with deep disgust and agitation, like they were excrement on her hands. When I pointed this out to her, we focused on this matter until the reason became clear. Her husband was a successful businessman who frequently traveled abroad earning large sums of money. At home, he handled all the financial transactions and when he went on a business trip, he left her a modest allowance. She associated this with being given pocket money as a child, so she felt patronized, devalued, and treated like a child in her marriage. She was angry and disgusted with herself for accepting her husband's treatment so passively. When she paid for her therapy sessions with her "pocket money," it was this disgust that came across.

Following her exploration in therapy, she decided to take a part-time job, although she had no financial reason to do so. Nevertheless, it was crucially important to her that she readdress her relationship to money and personal empowerment. In time she replaced her entire wardrobe with clothes she had paid for herself and, at the end of her sessions, she proudly presented her payment out of her own earnings.

Being aware of others is usually easier than being aware of ourselves. Our activities and thoughts are pervaded by an inner atmosphere. We carry unconscious attitudes that preside over our interactions with the

---

7. To preserve anonymity and confidentiality, all references to clients and case histories in this book have been made unrecognizable by changing details and identities, and altering events, so that no one should be able to recognize themselves or anybody else.

outside world and are revealed in expectations and assumptions. In inner work we may uncover these background assumptions through exploring our unconscious preconceptions.

These preconceptions belong to the inner bias or position we take toward life—a fixed self-image. We may be sufferers, martyrs, or wounded souls; helpers, healers, or saviors; survivors, victims, or depressives; happy, zestful, and confident; sad, angry, fearful, defended, or alienated. Whatever image we adhere to, it is simply a mask we have worn for so long that we have forgotten that it's there. When we bring awareness to ourselves, we see these masks clearly.

Sometimes we are confused about our inner states or our outer behavior, and we feel helpless to do anything about them. Practicing awareness is usually all we need do to penetrate the confusion and reach clarity. For inner clarity all that is required is the attention of the heart.

Attention of the heart underpins the practice of inner awareness because the heart embraces everything as a unity, while the mind divides and separates, criticizes and judges. Therefore, the heart is consonant with awareness, whereas the mind is dissonant with awareness. Awareness requires our willingness to be with what is happening in the present moment, openly and without judging. It is harder than we may think. We become easily distracted, lose ourselves and our focus, and then return to ourselves, time and time again. But with practice and good intent, we can become more skillful at it.

When, through practicing awareness, we can truly "see," we experience ourselves as "object" and begin to witness our lives. This leads us to ask the crucial question, "Who is it that is aware of my self?" As we practice, the witness grows stronger until it becomes as strong as, or stronger than, our habitual way of seeing things. The individual self begins to lose its exclusive hold as the witness sees through our defensive and aggressive games and the fear that underlies them.

Awareness may be thought of as a threefold process of opening, experiencing, and learning. First, we *open* to everything, without being selective and with a deepening willingness to be present with an inner emptiness. To do this, we have to overcome our resistance and the mind chattering that constantly distracts us. Second, we *experience* by feeling an increasing sense of presence, releasing our judgments and being in the moment, and not trying to change things. Third, through being with things as they are, we *learn* from what arises in the present moment. Truth and wisdom are constantly manifesting, ever-present and inviting us to learn.

In his classic film *Seven Samurai*, Akira Kurosawa illustrates the three stages of awareness and their consequences. A samurai chief is recruiting warriors to defend a poor village against a band of marauding bandits. He needs the best warriors he can find, so he devises a way of testing them. One by one he invites them to a meeting. Behind the entrance door he hides a young samurai who has instructions to assault the prospective warrior as he enters.

The first samurai isn't fooled. He parries the blow and throws the young samurai to the ground. But in spite of passing the test, he is proud and takes offense. He refuses the invitation to join the samurai group. He shows us attention in the middle stages of practice. As we develop awareness, our egos tend to take credit for our practice and revel in our accomplishment. Proud of the new powers awareness gives us, we indulge in self-aggrandizement. We are aware, but we are not yet wise, and we maintain a distance from others because we are not yet secure in our position. The first samurai opens, experiences, but fails to learn because he is caught in his attachment to the ego.

The second samurai stops within a few strides of the doorway, glances at the ground, cries, "Jokers!" and chuckles. He senses the young samurai's presence behind the door before he has even entered. He accepts the invitation to join and fight the bandits, not because of the suffering of the poor villagers, but because of the qualities of the samurai chief. The second samurai demonstrates awareness at its most effortless. His is a true accomplishment. He carries his achievement lightly, because he has attained true awareness, so he is not self-important and insecure like the first samurai. He accepts the invitation to fight because he is wise enough to know that to truly help others, we must first help ourselves. He joins the samurai group because he is humble enough to know that he has more to learn. The second samurai opens, experiences, and learns with a light attachment to the ego.

The third samurai is proclaimed a tough and ferocious warrior, but when he arrives he is hopelessly drunk and oblivious to everything around him. Lurching through the doorway, he is easily struck and overcome. Following a struggle, he collapses in an unconscious stupor. He is carrying false papers and it is doubtful whether he is a genuine samurai. However, he asks to join the group, and through his persistence he is accepted and turns out to be truly heroic. The third samurai embodies the ego-driven person who has no awareness whatsoever and merely sleepwalks through life. He gives no attention to the world; things simply happen to him, and he is effectively unconscious. Many people are like this. The third samurai is the ordinary person. He may not even be a true warrior, but the samurai test awakens vital forces in him that he cannot resist—it is an opportunity for his spirit to be released. He pursues the group of samurai and becomes a member of the group, which aids his awakening. The third samurai starts at the bottom, a true beginner, and embarks on the process of awareness, developing ability and compassion.

If you get the chance, study these scenes for the comic and serious aspects of practicing awareness they portray so vividly. Kurosawa was a highly accomplished student of human nature; he never shied away from the minutest detail through his masterful practice of awareness.

Awareness practice is at the very heart of inner work, and it is the foundation of true wisdom. Closely related is the profound practice of listening.

The Art of Listening

When we really listen to someone, they reveal themselves to us. But we must be open, receptive, and attentive with our whole being. When we listen to tone, pitch, pace, rhythm and—only afterward—content (which is never as revealing as the other things), we can sense whether a person feels anxious, peaceful, discontented, happy, worthless, proud, angry, or loving. If we continue to listen, we discover who that person thinks they are. Then we can begin to create the conditions for deepening that lead to self-discovery. Eventually we can invite them to uncover layers of truth within themselves and be who they never dared to be: their authentic self.

In my childhood home we had terminal difficulties communicating. We didn't expect to be listened to or heard. We seldom paused to give and receive in conversation. We often all spoke at the same time. My parents were usually too busy to stop and listen to each other and too tired or self-absorbed to take each other in.

This quality of "taking the other in" distinguishes listening as the single most important healing tool. The ability to listen is one of the most precious human treasures, because it enables us to connect with each other. Listening validates, acknowledges, recognizes, and assures us that there are others in the world who care enough to be interested in what we have to say, what is important to us, and who we truly are. In deep friendship, group healing, and creating community, listening is one of the most important gifts that we can receive and give.

Of the five senses, listening is particularly receptive. The experience of opening and receiving through listening can open our hearts. For many of us, the sound of beautiful, transcendent music changes our lives forever. In childhood or adolescence we are particularly susceptible to sound because we are strongly connected to our souls through the senses. Music, spoken words, or the sounds of nature all communicate to our hearts.

Although it sounds simple, the "listening relationship" is hard to master. In conventional conversation we are usually engaged in a non-relationship of action and reaction. We react to what we hear with sympathy, shock, fear, surprise, antipathy, or reassurance, depending on our point of view. Commonly, we identify with the speaker and take what she is talking about as a cue to recount a similar event from our own experience. Sometimes we don't hear the other at all, because we are so caught up with ourselves.

We need to be listened to and heard with openness; not criticized or judged. The hardest aspect of listening to another person is to listen and really hear, to receive and experience, to be aware and accept the complexities of tone, feeling, and content ... and not "do" anything, not problem-solve, not act in any way.

If we grew up with people who couldn't listen, then it is likely that they couldn't express themselves either and that genuine communication was limited. When people cannot listen to others, they cannot listen truly to themselves either, and their speech may hide their emotions.

Speech that is unnatural and colorless hides emotions beneath the words. When we don't feel, connect, or resonate with ourselves or others, we become insensitive and subhuman, and this is reflected in our speech.

Dick was an example of this. He was a young man who had adopted an alternative lifestyle. He lived in a van and spent a lot of his time at music festivals. He was frustrated at not being able to sustain an intimate relationship. Whenever he met a woman he was attracted to, his throat would tighten and he couldn't talk. Relationships usually ended with him being rejected. On the few occasions when he had experienced a relationship of any intimacy, he had abandoned his partner when *she* had fallen in love with *him*.

His early childhood was characterized by material plenty and emotional poverty. In conversation with me, he repeatedly pointed out that in his family home there had been good meals, warmth, cleanliness, and a glut of birthday and Christmas presents. But other than practical contact he couldn't remember any emotional expression, any hugging or physical contact, or any verbalizing of emotions. His early home life was practical and emotionally barren—not even cold. Dick spoke of his emotions without feeling them. Whatever words he used for feelings like love, anger, hate, frustration, sadness—his intonation was always the same: flat and expressionless. Between his throat and his heart was an energetic shield. He felt it as a painful band over his chest. This band choked his vulnerable feelings, throttled expressions of love or tenderness, and made him sound depressed and robotic.

The negation of self, the ignoring of our emotional life through not connecting and listening to each other, often arouses an angry response. Underneath Dick's depression was an angry little boy who was frustrated at not being heard. He discovered that his adult stance of "rebel" had been fueled by this frustration in his early life. He wanted to be noticed, to be seen and appreciated by others, and the way he chose was to rebel against any authority figures who resembled his parents.

Dick's inner work took him into the realms of the heart *energetically*, through deep breathing and awareness of his emotions. He practiced speaking about his emotions with congruence and relevance, experienced how his physical body expressed his emotions, and developed his emotional capacity. Gradually, he was able to fully recognize and honor his emotional life, transcend his repressive conditioning, and sustain a loving relationship.

In group or couples inner work, when we practice being open and available to listening and hearing the other, the acceptance and healing that takes place can be spectacular. One summer, I joined a group of therapists and teachers to facilitate a personal growth holiday on a Greek island. Over a hundred participants came to live communally and experience the workshops and classes. Previous participants had dropped out when they became overwhelmed by the emotional intensity of living together with such sustained exploration. So the organizers had decided to introduce small groups that met at the end of each day to share feelings and experiences as a safety net for the expression of feelings.

I was asked to facilitate a process with the whole community, in which the participants arranged themselves into groups of about half a dozen, and instruct them in listening. Listening was a subject close to my heart. I had written an article on therapeutic listening and considered it central to my approach. So I instructed the community in the kind of holistic method that I had found most effective: First, you breathe and clear yourself of tensions and thoughts and emotional states. You return to "neutral." You need not seek perfection here; usually the intention is enough. Second, you center yourself in your ears and heart and cultivate being receptive. Your listening is not going to be confined to the ear and mind only; you will be listening with your whole being, simply taking in the other. Third, as you listen in this way you should not react externally. Your body posture should be one of openness and availability toward the sharer. If you find yourself thinking, criticizing, or judging, you should allow it to be light, to simply flow through; don't hold on to it or add to it with fear or react in any way; be aware that a look, a sigh, or a fidget can communicate a value judgment. Finally, listen without criticism or approval so that no assessment or opinion—other than the sharer's own—is expressed.

At the end of the group session, a senior leader told me that the way I had taught listening was incorrect. He told me that they usually instructed people to comment and react to each other freely. However, he did admit that very few small groups made it through to the end of the holiday.

At the end of the holiday we all met again to give feedback about the experience of listening. Unusually, almost all of the small groups had met daily throughout the entire two weeks. Furthermore, it was generally agreed that this particular community had a strong feeling of mutual caring, respect, harmony, and closeness.

In inner work we listen to our hearts, to our minds, to our souls, and to each other by creating inner emptiness and developing the inner receptivity that provides the space to take the other in. As our inner turmoil lessens, we are able to listen with our whole being. Our inner critic—the one who comments with judgment or approval—recedes. By being openly available to another, we truly connect and practice the art of listening.

In Summary

We have discussed the basis for an inner practice and the two fundamental practices of inner work—awareness and listening. Before we go on, take some time to ask yourself these questions as a way of reviewing the first chapter and giving it a personal flavor and understanding for *you*:

1. How aware am I of myself? What are my blind spots? How do people and events in my world mirror me back to myself? How

can I grow and develop emotionally, mentally, and spiritually out of my self-awareness?

2. How am I distracted habitually from my natural state of awareness? How aware am I? How aware are the people I am in relationship with: my primary relationship, friends, relatives, work colleagues, acquaintances, and other life companions?

3. Explore your self-image and become familiar with your expectations and assumptions. For example, are you a sufferer, a martyr, a helper, a survivor, a victim? What are your characteristic emotional traits? For example, sad, angry, fearful, defensive, alienated?

4. What are your childhood memories of listening—being heard, paying attention, and listening to others? And of judgment and criticism?

2

Identity, Separation, and Division

In this chapter we will examine going back to childhood; our personality, character, and personal stories; and, finally, how we give to ourselves as a way of working with ego.

Going Back to Childhood: Deepening in the Present

Ideally, childhood is characterized by openness, excitement, spontaneity, unforgettable discovery, and newness. If we were fortunate, we may remember something of these feelings from our memories of our own childhood. But as we "grow up," we lose the depth, absorption, emotionality, and profundity we experience in our early years. The secrets of the childhood experience—joy, spontaneity, and trust—are lost.

Our seminal experiences flow in our memory like waves on the sea, forming and reforming, defining the ocean as the ocean defines them, interdependent and interconnected, momentary and ephemeral. But many of us cannot even recall our childhoods. We have obscured our memories of the painful and the intolerable, as well as of the times when we were totally immersed in experience, with layers of forgetfulness. Inevitably we experienced the end of joyful living, and the beginning of survival.

When I was very young, spirit was in everything; God was everywhere; and everything was bright and alive. I was a part of everything and everything was a part of me: we were in relationship. My inner thoughts and outer reality—neither one was more real than the other. I experienced, imagined, felt, and saw, and yet I was not "other" than I experienced, imagined, felt, or saw. When I was four years old I was digging in the back garden. Accidentally I cut an earthworm in half, and I instinctively "died" along with it ... and then was reborn as it separated and became two little worms going in opposite directions. I flew in the sky and was subsumed by the earth—there was no "I" to interfere with the relationship. Later on I underwent the need of others to be a "somebody": the defining process that led to "me." I was like my father, like my mother, I was this, I was that, I would fulfill the dreams of one person and confirm the insecurities or failures of another. Slowly I responded out of my childish need to please. Like a mirror, I reflected the image of the needs of others and became *someone other than myself.*

It is this process of becoming something other than ourselves that we uncover through inner work. When we ask to know ourselves, we have to find out how we have become other than who we really are. What mental and emotional constrictions do we perform to limit ourselves to "me"? What has made us give up so much for so little? How do we do it and how do we sustain it? Who or what do we do it for?

The sense of "me" is the creation of our child's mind. We become a subject of our own creation by spinning a web of personal stories. In adult life we continue to spin this tale of self and, like gossip, the more we repeat it, the more it sticks. The defining collection of our individual characteristics and foibles, accruing personal anecdotes, habitual behavior, and emotional patterns are bundled together to create an illusion of substance. We posture as "a somebody." The origins of our façade are to be found in our childhoods. We think of childhood as being in the past, and we imagine that we "go back" to locate early memories. We navigate through our lives by the twin stars of progressive time and shifting space, and within these matrices we conceptualize and interpret our life's events. But conceptualizing is always at odds with direct experience: concepts are the map, and we imagine that we must take a journey to reach our destination. When we look carefully at how we "go back" to childhood, we see that it is really *deepening in the present*.

Everything we talk about is in the past. By keeping our present issues in the past we avoid insecurity, our fear of life, and the uncertainty of change. Life is reflected in the mirror of our projected childhood with all of its unresolved issues.

Locating our unresolved personal issues in an imagined past is a way of distancing ourselves from them. We tuck them away safely in the past, so we don't have to own them or feel them in the present. But the issues are as present as we are.

"Being with" an issue means to reveal and explore it, to own and accept it without judging. The past is simply a projection of the present. We may find useful reference points for the personality through memory, but the solutions to our problems are not in the past, but in the only place where healing can occur—the present. The present is where we live life responsively and vibrantly, without reference to memory or anticipation, beyond the defenses of our character.

Our attachment to our defensive character is reminiscent of the plight of Hiroo Onoda, a young Japanese soldier in World War II. He was one of the so-called "holdouts": men who fought on in isolated regions long after the Japanese military surrendered, either unaware or refusing to believe that the war had ended.

In 1944, Onoda was sent to a small island in the Philippines to lead a group of guerrilla soldiers and ordered to fight until he was relieved. Two months later the Allies attacked and took the island. Onoda and his men continued to fight, surviving in the jungle on rice, coconuts, and bananas. When a local resident sent a note saying that the war had ended, Onoda thought it was a trick to flush him out of hiding. Later, fliers were dropped from planes and newspapers were left, along with letters and photos from relatives, to let him know that peace had been declared. Friends and relatives speaking to him over loudspeakers failed to convince him. He successfully evaded search parties that were sent out to find him. In Onoda's mind the war had not ended, so he thought that each attempt to flush him out of hiding was a clever hoax constructed by the Allies. Onoda lived in the jungle, carrying out acts of sabotage as part of his guerrilla activities, and attacking local villagers who he believed were enemy spies.

When he was eventually found, in *1974*, Onoda refused to surrender unless he was officially ordered to do so. His commander, Major Taniguchi, who had long since retired from the army, was brought to convince Onoda that the war was over and that he was to cease fighting. Following a moment of quiet anger, Onoda pulled back the bolt on his rifle and unloaded the bullets, took off his pack, laid down his rifle, and wept. Onoda had spent twenty-nine years in the jungle fighting a war that had ended long ago.

This is what it's like for us when we are faced with surrendering our personal defense systems and meeting life openly, with feeling. We cannot believe the enemy has been defeated, the conflict is over, and that we have nothing to defend ourselves against anymore.

Mandy's early life had been "de-humanizing." She had developed an "Ice Queen" persona as a defense against her feelings of sadness, pain, and self-disgust. Her father had found her intimidating, and she felt that he was afraid of her power. So she grew up believing that she had to protect others from her power, rage, and need. At age nine, she remembered him taking her off his lap and telling her that she was "too big to cuddle." Her inner work with me was stormy—soon after she began she wasn't sure if she would continue. She resented that she only got attention when she was in trouble. She felt that she was only "seen" when she did something wrong (and got hit and pushed around in her early life). The men she had relationships with were all, in her own words, "slimy men," which confirmed her belief that good men didn't want her, and in turn confirmed her father's rejection. When she met a new man, she felt she would put him off with her sexuality, her eating habits, and her appearance—in fact, she felt everything about her was potentially a "put-off." In one session she stumbled upon a play on words: "I'm left over and over … I'm a left over."

Working through her defenses, she discovered the "poor me" part of her that was sulky and angry. She found out how deeply she wanted her father to respect and admire her and how she unconsciously made men reject her. "I am never held long enough," she said, echoing her father's rebuffs, "so I don't want to be held at all." She worked with her strong sense that something was missing in her (or outside that she was pushing away?). Eventually she hit rock bottom, declaring, "I am so wrong, I shouldn't be alive."

At some point in childhood we hide our essence and make an internal pact with ourselves to ensure our survival. We learn to please those whom we depend on for the basic necessities of life. We know instinctively that it is vital that our essence remains intact, even if we never show it again.

This internal pact is the "promise" we make to ourselves that we will never again reveal our true selves, because it would be too great a threat. So we hide our authenticity behind complex bands of psychological defenses. Next, we forget what we have done, because it's safer to deny what has happened, and we can convince others better when we have convinced ourselves. So we forget who we really are or how we concealed our true Self. The key to unlocking these defenses may be lost, even to ourselves, in our effort to protect our essential self. In later life these defenses become barriers to contact, relationship, and intimacy.

In one breakthrough session, Mandy spoke to her father. "I won't be dead for you," she cried. She finally realized that the compromise (or the "promise") she had made in her childhood was simply too great. She worked through her life statements, unpeeling the childhood experiences and the promise from the present reality. Over time, she began to feel that it was safe to come out from behind her self-imposed barricade of suspicion and mistrust.

As children we may have to put up with a lot, from insensitivity to brutality. But we are amazingly resilient, and we possess a profound spiritual understanding and a deep connection beyond the limits of our individuality.

For most of us, the experiences of being a child are more potent than we can remember or imagine. On the one hand, we might recall the endless days of childhood summers, the experience of magical play and oneness with Nature, and the fascination of simple pleasures. On the other hand, the pain, the abandonment, the endless hours of neglect when each moment is an eternity; being ignored, misunderstood, not being given enough time; and living in a world that puzzles us with its bullish insensitivity can be overwhelming. The resulting hurt may be incalculable, and the legacy can feel unbearable. The dark things may only be the result of the inability of the adult world to understand the life of children, and the adults in our world may have been too caught up in the outside world to give us what we needed.

In childhood, we may retain a connection to our essence through externalizing intimacy in a relationship with a toy, a pet, an imaginary stranger, or an understanding relative or family friend who understands us better than our immediate family. This special relationship preserves our connection to our essential self and maintains our relationship to our intrinsic wholeness.

For many of us, our preservation is won at the expense of a sense of reality. As we grow up, the person we become is detached from any authentic sense of self. When we look into the eyes of children who have learned to protect themselves by closing down, we see a vacant stare, a robotic disconnected quality.

One of the goals in inner work is to get gently beneath these defenses and liberate the essence of a person from behind the protective layers of "the promise." In his poem "Oxbow," Federico García Lorca describes childhood as a journey from the shadow to the flower—from the disowned defensive self to the essential self. The promise casts the shadow that conceals the flower. The darkness of early experience conceals our greatest riches and the flower of our authentic being. To regain our whole self, we have to possess a strong desire to return to that darkness and liberate ourselves by searching deeply beneath our character and personality.

Attachment to Personality and Character

Character is an inner defense system we create in response to our earliest life experiences. Although it exists primarily in the psyche, it is articulated in our physical structure, facial expressions, and body movements. These demonstrations of character are the nexus of our persona or mask—known collectively as the personality. We create personality by organizing inner objects. It is a process of selection rather like the biblical separating of the sheep from the goats. What we like about ourselves is retained in consciousness; what we don't like about ourselves is relegated to the unconscious. Our choice is based on lovability and approval, as demonstrated by our parents, teachers, and society. The Jungian analyst Robert A. Johnson calls it "the great leveling process that is culture." The art of personality is not being yourself; it is showing what you want people to believe is you.

We become attached to our personalities. But personality is the creation of thought and experience—the way we make sense of events, our response to conditions, a defense between us and life. In the same way as we sense something constant beneath our changing roles, we recognize the reality of being behind our character and personality. Our small sense of self is expressed through character and personality. For the small self is not the intrinsic creation we believe it to be, but a delusion, merely a costume we wear.

"I want to feel more real!" It is the cry of a middle-aged man sitting in a personal growth group feeling the despair and discomfort of fifty years living inside an envelope, his authentic self hidden beneath layers of a false self he has fed and nurtured out of his instinct to protect himself and survive. But now he sees that the compromise has been too great. He feels his life has been a sham, a living death. As the enormity of this insight grows in him, emotions flow thick and fast. Angry cries of despair alternate with dark waves of shame, complemented by occasional bright flashes of clarity, eruptions of terror, and expressions of his determination to change.

Another scene: a woman is sitting opposite me, her eyes glazed and her face taut. She reveals how a friend's angry reaction has put her in touch with the hidden, underlying tone of anger that was perpetually present in her own family. Her tears begin to well up and overcome her defenses. Her chin trembles as she bursts into tears. Afterward she describes how, as she broke down, she felt her physical form start to dissolve and how she felt the edges of her form becoming increasingly blurred; and the less solid she was, the more she could allow the expression of her overwhelming emotions.

We are resistant to being ourselves. But when we refuse to be who we are, we are compelled to identify only with our personality and we become hopelessly superficial. As we explore our personal issues, digging away at the layers of self that protect us, we discover the buried issues underneath. Deeper down, we touch on the core issues; and deeper down still, we reach the central kernel of ourselves where we feel our actual existence is under threat, where we feel that we do not exist. In summary—highly condensed—it works like this:

> I hurt because . . .
>
> I don't want to feel the pain of not being loved . . . because . . .
>
> I feel totally alone . . . because . . .
>
> I feel disconnected from others . . . because . . .
>
> I feel fear, terror, grief . . . because . . .
>
> I should not exist . . . because . . .
>
> I don't exist

Our feelings, subterfuges, emotional and mental dynamics, manipulations, fears, and desires all fall away to reveal a deep truth: we would rather function in habitual patterns of behavior, perpetuating misery and suffering, constantly reinventing ourselves, and cultivating resentment, than face the existential horror of nonexistence.

This is the core issue in inner work. The real problem is not how we feel about others and ourselves, whether we are happy or not, whether we are fulfilled or not; it is that *we have made a compromise to exist at any cost*. When we discover this, everything is turned on its head. No longer do we need to develop, heal, grow, or make ourselves better. We see the layers of our small self as so many coverings over the true problem, which is the terror of not existing. Our neuroses become the pathway to the profound truth that we are not who we appear to be.

We invest an enormous amount of energy in maintaining our emotional defenses. The energy it takes to stay mentally fixed, physically held, and emotionally centered reflects our determination to hold a position with our ideas and opinions, patterns and character defenses.

We define ourselves in constant mental chatter. This inner dialogue maintains us in illusory experiences and constant background anxiety. When we quiet the mind, we experience the great vividness, simplicity, and beauty of life. Our inner chatter confirms us in our roles and character by stating and restating familiar themes. We become obsessed with unworthiness, anxiety, insecurity, regret, or inner conflict. The chatter invents and supports our fixed beliefs about ourselves and is reflected in our physical and emotional contraction.

For some of us this chatter is so overwhelming and our hold on the self is so slight that we express it outwardly. "I am a happy-go-lucky type of person," "I am a simple man," "Everyone is so judgmental," "People are so uncaring"—all are examples of externalized mental chatter that defines us through denying and suppressing our real feelings. After all, people with a happy-go-lucky character defense are resisting anxiety, and people with a character defense of simplicity are protecting themselves against handling complexity.

We share a common source, but no two of us are ever the same. Clothed in our uniqueness, we see the world from our personal viewpoint, which is only one angle of perception. We take a position on an issue and our opinion gives us credibility and confidence. Through it we are a viable person and we can be compared, contrasted, and competitive with other viable people. Usually, it is more important to us that we stand alone, distinct, and separate than that we meet in confluence with others. It seems that we prefer to argue rather than agree.

The Sufi teacher Rumi illustrates this in the story of the blind men and the elephant. Once some blind men came upon an animal they had never met before and they were told it was an elephant. They reached out and began to touch it. One of them touched its leg and said the elephant was like a pillar. Another felt its ear and said it was like a fan. Another touched its tail and said it was like a rope. As each man offered his individual experience of the animal, disagreements began and a fight developed.

Like the blind men, we are afraid to reach beyond our personal limits, touch the edges of the known, and cross over the borderline of our personality. We cling to personality, perspective, and the certainty they provide, even in our understanding of the divine. The great Hindu mystic Ramakrishna said: "A man who has seen only one aspect of Truth limits Truth to that alone."

The theme of personality extends beyond the individual expression of inner characteristics and perspective. Groups demonstrate collective, plural identities bound together by common characteristics that create a homogenous connectedness. A small group community I knew exhibited this. Everything about them was chaotic and disorganized. My introduction to them was typical. They appeared one day outside my house in the north of England in two battered Ford Transit vans with children's arms and faces flailing out of the windows, hooting and demanding directions to their destination. They set up their community and became near neighbors. As I got to know them, I found their life was severely disordered; their home was untidy and messy, their thinking muddled and confused. They dressed messily and lived in a constant state of frenzy. Making arrangements with them was impossibly complicated. When the work that supported them fell through, they had to relocate and the last picture I have of them is similar to the first as they drove off in their habitual pandemonium.

Habit and identity tend to make our personalities and perspectives rigid and fixed. Everything is in a process of change, yet we perceive ourselves as unchanging creations. Our fixedness leads to familiarity, and familiarity can be stultifying. We are never so aware of our bodies than when taking our first steps after being bed-ridden through illness, never so aware of the sunshine than when the sun shines through the clouds on a chilly day in midwinter. When we visit new continents, the culture is "foreign" and unfamiliar. We are fascinated by the landscape, the streets, and the architecture. The air carries unfamiliar aromas and sharpens our sense of smell. The sound of people talking, the tastes of the food, make our senses acutely receptive. We are intensely observant, alert, and aware. But if we remain there, within a few months it no longer seems "foreign," and as we grow more familiar, we no longer give so much attention.

Familiarity dulls new experience through the filter of memory and illusion. We struggle to familiarize ourselves with the unknown and the unfamiliar, and we render our experience bland. For fear of losing ourselves we fix ourselves to consistency and become blinded by expectations and assumptions. As comforting and attractive as it can be, familiarity anesthetizes us into hypnotic numbness, unless we are strong and wise enough to remain alert. Keeping our relationships to people, events, places, and activities fresh and alive, not familiarizing ourselves, presuming, or predicting what will happen next, is the result of practicing being aware in the present.

Try this simple exercise: walk slowly and mindfully. Mindful means being aware, full of the living present, undistracted by thought, and taking nothing for granted. So do not even assume that the earth is beneath your feet. Rather, unfold your toes, instep, and heels onto the ground and experience the newness of connecting with the earth with each footstep, in each moment. As you walk, feel and experience the sacredness of life and the miracle of existence. Become sensitive to the enchantment of life, and practice deep acceptance in a state of total awareness, seeing life as-it-is.

"Seeing life as-it-is" is rather like asking a fish to be aware of water. But when we practice awareness of ourselves, we gradually refine our seeing so that we witness ourselves and others objectively and clearly. In time, we cultivate respect over assumptions, so everything is fresh and new, and in a process of becoming. Like a beginner practicing, like a traveler arriving, we witness the magic of the manifestation in all its vivid beauty.

As our inner work leads us on toward change and transformation, beyond the confines of character and personality, we can prepare ourselves by practicing this simple walking exercise with simple self-awareness, so we can experience without assumptions and revivify the freshness and the brightness of our experience.

Personal Stories

On the inner journey we are the adventurer, the explorer, the voyager to inner realms, the traveler who finds joy and fulfillment in discovering the new, moving on, never staying still—a spirit in movement, in search of the spontaneous, and open to whatever comes. But inevitably, experience calcifies into the record of memory, legend, and personal mythology that creates a personal story.

We constantly revive our personal history by recounting it to relatives, friends, and new acquaintances. Explanations followed by resentments, frustrated accounts, and tales of modesty and glory, boasting and self-aggrandizement, disillusionment and injustice project our self-image, so the person receiving the desired impression can behave as we want them to, think about us as we want them to, and assume and expect what we want them to.

The story of our life seems to have accrued in layers of experience, a series of events and periods of development, an unfolding narrative. As we retell our personal story, both inwardly and outwardly, we compound our narrative and invent a sequence of personal stories. We are, as the Buddhists would say, perpetually "creating beings." Spinning our individual narrative, we create the life of a "somebody" defined by relationships and conditions. We may be someone who is beaten or thwarted by the world—a failure or a victim. We may be someone who is successful, fortunate, fulfilled. We may be someone who is burdened with duty and responsibility or someone who doesn't really fit in or feel a part of anything. The permutations are endless and unique to each person. We all have a story that defines who we are; we all have a story to tell.

But how fixed are our stories? Our personal narratives depend not only on circumstances and events, but also on the perspective from which we view them. *How* we look at an experience dictates the experience itself. And how we remember creates the stories we tell, and believe, about ourselves. If we think we are separate from what happens to us, we see life as a duality because there is always a subject (me) and an object (what happens to me). Alternatively, if we think of ourselves as part of life, then we see unity and connectedness between "me" and events.

Negative experiences can have positive outcomes. A near-death experience can lead to a spiritual awakening; the loss of a highly paid job can enable someone to do what they always wanted to do. Positive experiences can have negative outcomes. A whirlwind romance leads to an early marriage, but ends in an acrimonious divorce; a financial windfall leads to a life of excess, ill health, and an early death. The nature of our perception is changeable; the experiences defined by our perceptions are never truly fixed, but merely how we see them at the time.

Mostly we see things from the driving seat of our ego. In Greek mythology, Sisyphus cheated death but was condemned to roll a huge stone up a hill for eternity. When the stone reached the top, it was driven back and rolled down to the bottom of the hill where Sisyphus's task began all over again. The hell of Sisyphus resembles how we are bound to our personal stories. Sisyphus needs only to stop and make the decision never to roll the stone up the hill again, but he is condemned to keep it rolling. Like Sisyphus, we seem doomed to re-enact our stories, producing the same series of emotional, physical, and mental reactions unless we refuse to be enslaved to our character any longer.

When we are unaware, our behavior is automatic and habitual. Instead of stopping and reflecting, we become fixed, consistent, and imprisoned by the character we have created. We are attached to a mass of personal habits that support our creation. We imprison ourselves in these limitations and call it suffering.

Our small sense of self thrives on limitation, and even when we attempt to shed our old habits it counters our efforts by imposing its will in order to avoid change. We want to change, but change is beyond our personal will. We cannot force change, but we can create the conditions for change to enter our lives, through openness, surrender, and grace. Change is all around us, always happening; we are in a sea of it. All we need do is create the right conditions and wait.

Some life events challenge the limitations of our character and make us look deeper into how we see ourselves and others. Such life events may even take us to the very edge of our resistance to change. They reveal the power of habit and fixedness and directly challenge our ego control and personal narrative.

This is the story of my Indian friend Abhisar. These events took place in the mid-1970s. I was in my early twenties and had just begun inner work. I was reassessing my life, letting go of old friendships, and feeling a lack of connection to those around me. For me, as for many others of my generation, my journey to India was a voyage of personal discovery.

I met Abhisar on a bus traveling from Bombay to Goa. The bus was crammed to the bursting point with people, luggage, and livestock. We rattled along the mountain roads, stopping at every roadside shrine for the driver to make offerings to the gods for our safe passage. It was mid-July—the monsoon season—so the temperature was humid and unbearably hot. Perspiring heavily, I was sitting shoulder to shoulder with a young Indian dressed in a white nylon shirt. He smelled powerfully of cheap aftershave. As the bus made its erratic progress along the uneven roads and we jogged together on the red plastic seats, his head rolled over onto my chest and he began to snore. After a while he awoke, straightened himself and, turning to me, asked if I smoked *bidis*—a cheap handmade cigarette that is common in India. I told him that I smoked one occasionally. The bus continued to jog along for a half hour or more.

Turning to me again, he asked, "Should I offer you one?"

"If you'd like to," I replied, perplexed and charmed by the slow pace of the conversation.

We smoked bidis together silently for a while, then he asked me where I came from. "London," I replied. He asked innocently whether I knew his relations who also lived there. I explained the size of England's capital, and he told me that his name was Abhisar and that he worked as an estate agent in Bombay. We chatted and, after a while, the bus stopped for a meal break in a tiny rural village that served as a pit stop for the journey. I made my way to an empty table in the café and ate a plate of spicy vegetables, raita, and chapatis. Just as I finished, a lurid pink and green dessert, the kind you only find in Indian cuisine, arrived at my table unordered. Looking around, I found Abhisar beaming and hailing me from across the room. I raised my spoon in thanks and ate the sugary pudding. When we reentered the bus, he declared, "Now you are my friend!"

I stayed in a remote spot, a little jungle enclave behind the beach away from the town. I had no transport and received many visits from my new friend. He always brought me a useful gift and showed concern for my welfare. I, however, was unable to take the friendship seriously. I was young and suspicious. I wanted to know what he wanted from me. Unaffected, he continued to treat me as his lifelong friend.

Just before I was due to return to England, rumors began to circulate that Bombay airport had burnt down in an accidental fire, and anxious speculation spread among the foreign visitors in my area. We didn't know whether to believe the reports or not. As usual my friend turned up with just what I needed—a copy of the daily newspaper. The news confirmed the rumors, but the news had been somewhat exaggerated. The airport control tower had been destroyed in the fire, but the rest of the airport was intact. However, all international flights were cancelled, thousands of people were stranded, and many of them were camped out in the airport lounges. The length of time it would take to repair the damage and reschedule the flights was uncertain— this was, after all, India.

Abhisar continued to be attentive. I received his gifts and concern unbelievingly and mistrustfully until I left Goa. I was unable to make sense of his singular devotion to me until some years later, when I read Robert A. Johnson's story of an Indian friendship. In its genesis it startlingly resembled my own. Johnson explains that if you want to make friends with someone in India, you edge up beside them and wait. After a long period of time a token invitation is made (the bidi offer and the pudding), and your acceptance denotes a potentially lifelong friendship. You become, as Johnson says, "blood brothers."

Johnson's Indian friendship developed further than mine. When he became ill and was hospitalized, his friend, Amba Shankar, slept under his bed. When Johnson's temperature rose to 104 and he was beginning to lose consciousness, Amba offered to die in his place. Johnson was speechless.

Reading Johnson's story, I felt strangely bereft even though my brief friendship with Abhisar had taken place two decades before. But the inability of my youthful character to recognize and trust the genuineness of my Indian friend's open declarations of friendship revealed my own limitations. I would have dearly loved a true friend, but when one presented himself so transparently I looked straight through him because my thoughts and fears were in the way.

As we reveal our stories to ourselves and others, a new clarity dawns inside us and with it comes a new freedom. As we become familiar with our personal narrative, we see how we cling to it out of fear. We notice things we hadn't seen before and understand more. We have to work backward to make a new sense of the world. We see how we have masked our feelings of futility through compulsive "doing" and avoided life in all its spontaneous, uncertain creations; how we have preferred to talk, conceptualize, and "do" rather than simply "be"; how we have fallen into habitual and numbing familiarity; how we have felt desire and lack and made survival our modest aim and compulsive focus. When we become separate from existence, life becomes our enemy. Our fixed selves abhor the natural flow of change until we truly see ourselves.

We have discussed at some length personality, perspective, and biography. Let's now look at what underpins them all: the small sense of self, the "I," me, mine—the ego.

Giving to Ourselves: Working with Ego

When the Zen roshi Shunryu Suzuki was asked, "How much ego do you need?" he replied, "Just enough so that you don't step out in front of a bus."

Ego is an *activity* of our small self that enables us to be in the world. Ego negotiates between desire and conscience and enables us to be introspective and self-aware. Consequently, ego occupies an ambiguous place in our inner world. The difficulty lies not so much in having an ego, but in attaching ourselves so strongly to the ego and its pursuits that we cannot see the difference between what the ego is doing and who we are.

Ego is a human function, a mental creation to which we are attached. When the automatic functioning of the ego becomes fixed, it creates a psychic prison and we turn into our means of survival. This is how the ego oppresses and confines us. It selects certain aspects of ourselves and maintains that is all we are through identification, while confining the rest of us to the shadows of our unconscious. Ego is a great preserver: conforming and resistant to change. Ego expresses itself in the mask of character that conceals our genuine thoughts and feelings. While we need an ego as a vehicle for our individual life, we must shed our attachment to it in order to become who we really are. The ego is to our inner world as our body is to the outer—merely a vehicle. The price of identifying with ego is high: conceit, pretense, false pride, and self-importance are all ego tendencies that cause suffering. Ego plays the superior/inferior game of "I am better than you" or "You are better than me." Ego uses thought to dissect experience and juggles with our center so that we remain separate and alone.

Our first experience of separation is separating from our mothers who nourish and sustain us from conception to infancy. As we move toward autonomy, we move from dependency to independence, from "being given to" to "giving to ourselves." What, and how, we give to ourselves reflects back on our ego. Ego survives through separation, but when we give to ourselves we are faced with an exchange between self and other that challenges our separateness. So, becoming aware of how we give to ourselves is a most effective way to expose the ego.

We find it hard to accept being given to. Receiving can feel threatening to the ego and our sense of separation. The way we receive depends on how strongly we are attached to our ego. The looser the hold, the easier it is for us to receive; the tighter the hold, the harder it is for us to receive. It is a kind of immediate karma that reveals the nature of desire. Desire maintains a deceitful dynamic. It is like a train on an endless track that refuels without losing momentum or stopping and never reaches its destination. Our lives lurch between two poles of insecurity: the fear of not getting what we want and the fear of getting what we want.

Many years ago I explored this two-faced fear in the form of the question, "What do I want now?" Working with this question resulted in some strange and profound insights. At first I had fantasies of spectacular scenarios of desire—sexual, gastronomic, financial, prestigious, and ambitious. I imagined intense scenarios of fulfillment. But as I carefully watched myself, I saw that the feeling of desire triggered a distancing mechanism in me. The object of my desire had to be remote, out of reach, and spiraling away from me. But when I stayed with the question "What do I want now?" something curious happened. The spiral went into reverse and turned toward me with equal force, causing desire to wind back and come to rest inside me. In this way my fantasized extremes of desire transformed into simple needs like "I want a cup of tea" or "I want to go for a walk."

The question "What do I want now?" taught me a lot about myself: how much I distanced myself from fulfilling any desires, how desperate I was to have what I wanted … and how scared I was; how spiraling out "protected" me from the feelings of fulfillment and frustration; how I placed myself between fear and hope, and prolonged and strengthened desire by being fully in neither place.

Having what we want dispels the fantasy and the magic in which the wished for thing is bathed. Having what we want would be dangerous. We would become complacent, succumb to our fears, and be consumed by our lack. We would grow miserable at our satisfaction.

Desire is as complex as the human being who feels it. We fear getting what we want, because satiating our desire would mean the cessation of desire, which in turn would mean the end of our identity with the ego, because *without desire there is no ego.* It is a deep contradiction that ego encourages us to fulfill our desires, while forbidding us to quell desire entirely. One desire leads to another, apparently endlessly. Ego depends on frustration: we get a little of what we want, but never all that we want.

Often what we want is far from what we need, while what we need is simple and easily within our grasp. A client recounts this experience of an inner-work session with me, which has become my own reference point for such simplicity:

> Richard lived about an hour's drive away. Each week I would make the long drive to see him. At the beginning of one particular session I closed my eyes to consider how I was feeling and what issues were most on top for me. Before I knew it I fell soundly asleep! Almost an hour later, Richard woke me to tell me that there was five minutes to the end of my session. My instant reaction was to think, "What a waste of time and money! I have driven over fifty miles to pay to fall asleep!" But on further reflection I thought, "What a gift I have given myself! I gave myself exactly what I needed!"

We don't always want what we need. And when we get what we need, we don't always receive it so gracefully.

A middle-aged man named Geoffrey, a chief executive in the civil service, came to see me because he was having "a hard time with his inner child." His historical models of adulthood were his mother, a lifelong martyr, and his father, a retired high-ranking policeman. His parents, ambitious for his future, had pressured him to achieve, to be ambitious at school and in his career, and to value work over play. The result was a little boy who resented missing the opportunities to be creative and have fun. Somewhat predictably he had become a workaholic with a fiercely crammed personal schedule that allowed no time for pleasure. Fun was almost a dirty word to him.

I encouraged him to ask the child within him what he wanted and what his idea of fun was. Geoffrey listened quietly to himself for a minute and then turned to me shamefacedly. "Well, what did he say?" I asked expectantly. "Alton Towers," he replied. Alton Towers is the largest theme park in the United Kingdom, with roller coasters, water rides, candy floss, and spectacle for family days out. Working against tremendous resistance from the hardworking "adult" part of him, Geoffrey took a day off to go to Alton Towers. When he returned to see me again, he was a different man. Smiling, happy, and full of joy, he enthusiastically related details of the fun he had. He had to find a new definition for "adult" in his life, which included fun, relaxation, and excitement, and balancing pleasure with duty and responsibility.

Like many of us, Geoffrey had to work with deceptive life statements that demeaned his self-worth, invalidated pleasure, and curtailed desire: statements like, "I don't deserve to have what I want," "If I get what I want, it will be taken away," "Only good children get what they want." We can only give to others when we have learned to give to ourselves. When we know ourselves well enough to ask and receive what we need, generosity wells up within us and we are able to give as we have allowed ourselves to be given to.

In time the distinction breaks down, and giving and receiving begin to merge. We become aware of what we receive in the act of giving and what we give in the act of receiving. For giving and receiving are only possible where separation exists. When separation no longer exists there is no giving or receiving, only connecting in true relationship. Without giving and receiving to reinforce it, the power of the ego is weakened. As our ego lightens its hold on us, our sense of limitation and confinement lessens. We see the door of our psychic prison, walk out through it, and release ourselves into a life of great potential where pleasure and work are not separate, where we can have what we really want, where ego is no longer a tyrant, and where we can respond to life.

In Summary

In this chapter we discussed the origins of identity, separation, and division. All of these begin in the seminal experiences of early life and are compounded in the formation of personality and defensive character. They create the perspective of our worldview, the foundation where we stand and from where we conceptualize the inner and outer worlds. Before we go on to the dynamics of our inner world, take some time to make this material come alive for you by personalizing it, using these questions:

1. Do you remember your childhood? What do you remember? Write down some early memories. Why do you remember these particularly? What do they mean to you? How did your childhood experience shape you into the person you are today?

2. Define your character. Your character is what you are like, or more accurately what you *appear* to be like. Even more deeply, it is how you defend yourself from the world and experience. Now what's underneath?

3. Write down some statements that people who know you would think characterize you. Remember: this is not who you are or what you're like from your perspective, but how you think others see you.

4. What personal stories and memories are most precious to you because they define you and express your most beloved characteristics? Compile your top ten favorites and experience your attachment—positive or negative—toward them.

3

The Dynamics
of the Inner World

The Lessons of the Father and the Mother

The primary paradigm for how we relate to others, and to life, is drawn from our experience of the family we were born into, particularly our first models—our parents.

In our personal relationships we re-create the unresolved emotional dynamics that are left over from our early experience of family. Virtually everyone who comes to inner work is motivated, consciously or unconsciously, by their historical family dynamic. So the present conditions that reflect our unresolved family issues are priceless opportunities for release, change, and freedom.

Some people who come to see me go to great lengths to reassure me that their childhoods were happy and that their parents were caring and loving—before I have asked them anything at all. Their confessions have an air of self-soothing and delusion, and I can only feel bewildered and inquisitive. It is like the friend who announces without prompting or warning that he is *not angry*. This person is angry, and the people who attempt to persuade me of the virtues of their parents and the positive attributes of their upbringing are hiding something!

The family is a ferment of need and desire, longing and frustration, love and hate, beauty and challenge, confrontation and nurture. Our passions, fears, and desires are manifested and magnified in the melting pot of the family, and they are intensified beneath the hothouse layers of protection and concealment.

The inner seeker who is obsessed with the virtues of his parents has confused the ideal with the actual. Our notion of the ideal is associated with the term *archetype*. Archetypal comes from two words—*archaic* and *typical*—and it means the original model or the perfect example. The word expresses something all of us understand. For example, when we think "child," we think of certain qualities like innocence, openness, and purity. This is because we share a collectively inherited unconscious idea, thought pattern, or image. So it is with "mother" and "father."

The Mother and Father Archetypes

Some people comment on the archetypes, as others do on dreams, that they are not "real." But this is to make the mistake that waking life as we experience it is the *only* reality. The archetypes, like dreams or imagination, are real in their own milieu. Archetypes are real stencils or prototypes on which specific examples, such as our biological parents, are based.

The father archetype is evoked by images of worldly power and control. He is the elder, lawmaker, king, heavenly father. Heaven is the physical location of thought and wisdom, and the conscious realm of the father archetype. The archetypal "father" is associated with power and awe, activity and focus, differentiation and judgment, fecundity and destruction. Of course these words don't necessarily describe our actual fathers, but they do describe a religious, engendering, superhuman force of creative energy. As children we may well experience our father as superhuman and powerful. As we grow up we may see him differently. He may be good and caring, but equally he may be destructive and preoccupied with power.

The mother archetype is expressive and caring. She is associated with home and family. She may be creative and destructive, life-giving and nurturing, terrifying and tender, and life-preserving. These words express the qualities of mother in an idealized way. They may or may not describe our actual mothers, but these qualities are associated with mother through our inner image. She may offer support, mercy, compassion, patience, and inner joy. In contrast to the skyward realms of the archetypal father, her domain is the earthy unconscious. We may experience our mother as warm, loving, and comforting in childhood, although as we grow up we may see her differently.

It is the dissonance between the archetypal parents and our actual parents that causes us confusion and inner conflict in early life. No given set of parents can ever live up to the expectations of the ideal all the time. But as children with little or no experience or understanding of the limitations of the world, the ideal is our unconscious yardstick, and how we deal with our parents' shortcomings affects us deeply in early life and beyond.

When he was ten years old, my eldest son wrote, "When I was young I thought that parents were always there and that children couldn't grow into parents but just reach a certain age and then die. The parents would come to the funeral and then have more kids and the parents would never die. I thought that my parents were the healthiest and the cleverest people who knew the best way to do everything."

Male and Female Qualities

Our parents are the two pillars that support our childhood reality. Their attitudes and actions provide us with models of how to live in life's two essential aspects: doing and being. As children we intuit our father's innate, male quality of outgoingness and our mother's innate, female quality of inwardness. So usually our father provides us with our model of doing and our mother provides us with our model of being. How our parents relate to security, self-worth, and personal empowerment creates a blueprint for how we feel about ourselves. How we relate doing and being creates the relationship between our inner and outer worlds and gives us a sense of meaning, self-worth, and purpose.

The expression of outward forces that our father represents embraces achievement, ambition, creating an impact on the world, either negatively or positively, effectively or ineffectively. His thoughts and beliefs affect us particularly in our "doing" and provide a springboard for how we live in the outer world. In childhood, we absorb his evaluations, judgments, and prejudices consciously and unconsciously. Some are buried deep inside us. In later life, we may see how similar we are to him in our behavioral and emotional patterns. His hopes become our own, as well as his disappointments, and his overall attitude to life provides the backdrop over which we lay our own life experience.

But our need to please our father results in the compromise of our integrity. We feel that we have to be someone other than ourselves to please him and make him accept and love us. We try to become how we think he would like us to be.

When children become antagonistic to either parent, they may be acting out the unrealized unconscious shadow—the disowned instincts and emotions—of the parent's psyche. So, for example, our rebellion against our father may reflect our father's suppressed rebellion against his own father. In one sense this is the opposite—what he doesn't want us to be—but his repressed emotions create an inner shadow that has an unrelenting need to be realized. So becoming what our fathers don't want us to be is also a kind of fulfillment for him and sometimes a deeper one. The father who is unconsciously stuck in an antagonistic position may secretly look at his rebellious child with envy and pleasure. As children we may have to choose between our father's conscious demands and the deeper requirements of his unconscious. Either way, we are doing what our father, either consciously or unconsciously, needs us to do. Wishing to please and also afraid, we conform to our father's desires. In an effort to heal him we try to gain love by being what he wants us to be. A child's unselfconscious compassion extends to offering his very life to heal his parents of even their unconscious wounds.

Some women function principally from a male orientation, because of their childhood devotion to their father and his values. They may be daughters who follow in their father's footsteps by pursuing a career similar to his or by making decisions that are designed to win his approval. Their judgments and assessments of life are patriarchal, and they tend to side with men against women. A woman may imagine that she is close to her father when following a similar profession or pursuit to compensate for the lack of tenderness and intimacy in their relationship. Of course, she is never successful in closing the emotional gap. The distance that the father set on the relationship with his daughter will always remain, because it is a thing of the past, a memory that can never change. Whatever she does to please her father, even if she dedicates her life to trying to change the relationship, the dynamics between father and daughter remain static.

The Lesson of the Father

Each parent offers a profound lesson that provides a foundation for living. The lesson of the father is *nothing we do will ever make us feel loved*. Our fathers learn this from their own fathers and, although it may instill a wound in the psyche, it can lead us to invaluable insights.

Working with the lesson of the father teaches us to distinguish doing from being and allows us to bring the two into the right relationship. When being precedes doing, our actions are rooted in an inner sense of self. Nothing we do will ever make us feel loved because we yearn to be loved for ourselves, not for what we do. Doing as a means to love sends us on a frustrating cycle of trying harder to be better, to deserve love. Even if we receive praise for what we do, we have to try harder to be loved simply for being. But all our efforts are futile. The father's lesson reveals the deep truth that love can have no object other than itself. Just as love simply is, we want to be loved for simply being. Nothing else will satisfy us. The reassuring and—if we are open to it—deeply healing words "I love you just as you are" affirm our worthiness and lovableness. When our parents fail to give us the love we need, we have to find it in ourselves.

Spiritually, as well as biologically, the father principle is the creative, engendering force. He provides the active impulse through which we come into existence. Men characteristically spend their time in external acts of creation: devising, planning, and realizing projects—like commerce, architecture, transportation systems, and war—in an unconscious, often irresponsible need to control and dominate Mother Nature, the great embodiment of the mother principle.

The Lesson of the Mother

In contrast, the mother embodies a sense of being that generates inner creation. Our bodies, emotions, and senses are all associated with and inherited directly from our mothers, as is our attitude to them. The feeling world relates to our mothers as the thinking world relates to our fathers. Mother's closeness to the cycles and currents of nature within (and outside) her own body affects us directly even before birth. We absorb her emotions, sensations, and experiences in the womb and are later permeated by them in infancy.

Our individual mothers stand before the mother archetype. The mother archetype is nourishing and healing. She stands for nature and abundance in all its life-giving aspects. She is the embodiment of all-embracing love, and the lesson of the mother is *love is more than any individual expression of itself.* The mother's love is unconditional. She teaches us about love through her expression of it, through her loving essence, whether that is hidden or expressed. She teaches us the lesson that the universal is to be found in the particular; that divine love can be reflected and expressed in human love.

The lesson of the mother shows us that love is real and not just an ideal. Whatever trials and disappointments we go through on the path to love, we may always return to the certainty that individual expressions of love are reflections of our deeper state, the essence of our being. As our experience of love deepens, we become more intimate with it and with the partner we share it with. But even as love becomes more personal, we become aware of its impersonal aspect. It is as if we are drawing on a vast reservoir to nourish our worldly life. Love can be all-consuming and personally transporting and it can make us behave in irrational ways. Love has the power to lessen the hold of our small sense of self and hurl us into an experience of ecstasy by opening our heart. The elation of love gives us a taste of freedom beyond our individual self.

The mother's lesson can be compromised in various ways and may also leave a psychological scar. If the mother is possessive and jealous, it can degenerate into competition, as in "Your mother is the only one who loves you" or "No other woman is as good as me." It can assume the threat of retribution or implied punishment, as in "I am unhappy, and if you leave me and become happy, you will be disloyal to me" or "When you grow into a man, you will mistreat me like your father did." Or it can be expressed in a reverse symbiotic relationship in which the mother takes what she needs in the guise of "giving" love and affection to her child. Later on this may manifest in the mother masquerading as a peer, for example, or by creating a sisterly relationship with her daughter, thinly masking the hidden dynamic: "I live through you," with the justification that her daughter gives her back the young life that she lost when she gave birth to her.

Families: The New Reality

Sociologically, patterns of family life have changed radically. The old ideals of family life have largely become fantasy. Mothers and fathers with mutual sons and daughters sitting down to meals together and behaving in ways that were modeled to us in our childhoods have become anachronistic. The new reality is broken families, single-parent families, and multiple families.

Today the division between fathering and mothering roles cannot be taken too rigidly. Through a process of psychological adaptation, it may be that in the future we will find father modeling "being" and mother modeling "doing" for their children. Each particular set of parents consists of two individuals, who themselves comprise both male and female characteristics. Their relationship has a reciprocal dynamic in which each may act out the projections of the other. Certain male attributes may be dominant in a mother, while certain female attributes may be dominant in a father. This reversal can be so extreme today as to cast the mother in the role of the male, "fathering" parent and the father in the role of the female, "mothering" parent. When this is the case, either in part or in whole, then the characteristics of the mother are exchanged for those of the father, or vice versa, with the added dynamic of the suppression of the female or male characteristics in the father and the mother to add to the confusion.

However they manifest outwardly, a principal task of the human personality is to reconcile and harmonize the male and female energies within. Male and female characteristics are less differentiated in children and old people. Between childhood and old age we realize ourselves as either man or woman, and biologically, physically, emotionally, and mentally we develop our sense of ourselves as one or the other. But at each end of our lives, the harmonization of male and female takes precedence over defining ourselves by gender. For example, boys display more female characteristics when they are younger and women display more male characteristics as they grow older; old men may develop their female side and become more gentle and sensitive, and young girls may be tomboys.

Becoming an Adult

As we explore the legacy of our fathers and mothers, we can see that we must go past them to become ourselves. Understanding and supporting this may be the greatest gift that a parent can give to a child. Self-development challenges us to become indifferent to the demands of our inner parents, to ignore the restrictions they impose, and to be prepared to disappoint them when necessary. We have to pass beyond the confining boundary they represent in us, which may be expressed by their inner voices and internal influence, and free ourselves from their dictates and limitations.

The perceived value system of our parents provides us with our personal limitations. Their beliefs and constrictions give us a line to cross, a way to test our power in the world. Behind the line we are in relation to our parents and psychologically centered in our conditioned child. Over the line we are in relation to ourselves and psychologically centered in our true adult and able to relate to others and to the world in a responsible and giving way. Parents provide the resistance we need to create an identity for ourselves. Their challenges and lessons provide the opportunity for us to discover and shape who we are.

To reject our parents is a massive act of disloyalty, but without it we can never become ourselves. We remain psychologically childish, dominated by internal parental standards and commands, until we can overcome their restrictions. While our commitment, like a child's, is to our parents, rather than to ourselves, we live in conditions that mirror our early childhood struggle to survive. Many people remain undeveloped and unfulfilled until the end of their lives. While we remain psychologically dependent children inside, we can never become truly adult. Life is devoid of excitement, spontaneity, and authenticity as we merely repeat habitual behavior entangled in a web of confusion and predictability.

At some point in our inner work it is wise to have minimum contact with our parents to enable us to distinguish the outer parents from our inner parental images. The parent and the parent image are distinct and different. The parent image is internal and based on our early experience and perception of our parents. We are attached to the parent image through our unresolved issues and needs, in the form of hopes, fears, and resentment. We are unable to let go of the image, however accurate or flawed our perception of our outer parent was. The parent image is internal and subjective, while the person who is our father or mother is external and objective. So, not only do we have outer parents; we have inner parents too. The outer parents may not change, but it is within our power to transform the inner ones, because we created them from our experience of our parents during early childhood.

My personal inner work started and finished with my parents, as I will recount later, in chapter 7. My inner journey took me through love, longing, disappointment, hate, frustration, revenge, and anguish to the borders of "me"—a vision of who I might be if I released myself from them. Now I am at peace, and deep within me my resolved child's heart is grateful for my father and mother as the ancestors who gave me life, who did their best, who were real people with their own personal difficulties and virtues. Without attachment and in clarity, I love them now as fellow human beings.

The Baggage of Inner Characters

Inner exploration shows us that *an individual is not one self, but several*. Although you and I have come to see ourselves as homogenous entities with a central core or self, in fact each of us is a collection of satellites revolving around a space, an inner core, or essence. This means that our decisions are subject to inner responses and varying views that we experience as indecision, deliberation, and conflict. Our individual character is the sum of many different parts. While we may never feel more alone than when we are in a crowd, we may never be more in a crowd than when we are alone.

Within us are all the people—parents, teachers, and friends—whose opinions, judgments, and criticisms have affected us, and all the influences—conditioning, life events, and character strategies—that have shaped us and given form to our personalities. Our inner world is filled with the images and voices of characters who express the many diverse aspects of our personality. But to discover our authentic self we need to see behind the opaque screen of inner characters that prevents us seeing ourselves as we truly are.

Our attachment to people and circumstances is dependent and emotional. We want something from them. This restless dynamic means that we can never be at peace with the inner characters that populate our inner world. We need to open our inner eye and work with *how* we are attached, because we can never become self-referring while we look outward for direction and guidance. The expectations of people from our past, particularly our parents, can be so influential on our psyches that they may dominate our entire life with their inner clamor.

Mary's mother was dominating and overbearing. Nothing Mary did would satisfy her. In an attempt to defend herself from her feelings of powerlessness, Mary fought back by rebelling. She dressed in ways her mother disapproved of, dated boys her mother disliked, and chose a career her mother despised. She had started this behavior pattern when she was sixteen; now she was forty-two. As her inner work deepened, she made a surprising discovery. Underneath what she believed about herself, and her rebellious self-image, she craved her mother's approval. Even deeper, she desperately wanted her mother's apology. Everything she did to destroy her own life was motivated by her desire for that apology.

Through inner work we discover how we have projected different parts of ourselves onto others. Projection is a usually unconscious defense mechanism of the psyche, by which we attribute unwanted or unacceptable thoughts or emotions to others. For example, by blaming someone else for our own failures, we can avoid taking responsibility for our own shortcomings. We look inside and identify the different selves that make up our personality. A throng of interior characters are clustered around our inner essence. These inner characters and their influence wither and diminish when we take responsibility for them and wind our projections back in. Self-exploration begins inside, where outer and inner processes meet. Until we have dealt with our unfinished business, the outer world is merely the reflection of our inner world, so we see the world *as we are*. Through recognizing and owning the baggage of inner characters that mask our true center, we dispel the confusion.

We have created dramas out of our hardened memories of past experiences, and our lives have been formulas of familiarity and habit. As the creators of our own unhappiness, we have bought identity dearly at the expense of freedom, gambled for survival, bargained for our security, and our lives are forfeit. This is the compromise of the self.

Initially, facing up to this is humbling and disorienting. The task feels daunting. Yet this intensely human work can lead us to the highest form of human understanding. When the spiritual teacher Sri Nisargadatta Maharaj was asked how he came to reside in the supreme reality, he answered simply that he no longer created and populated a world (a false world of his own making), because he had become undeceived.

Owning the deception is humbling when we see that we ourselves have been the deceiver. We deceive ourselves (and others) by offloading parts of ourselves through projection. The outer world is populated with our inner projections. When self-exploration reflects us back to ourselves, we can start to work with our projections and judgments through our outward relationships. Our inner work becomes the mirror in which we see our projections, so we can own them and return them to ourselves.

For example, a young man named Bob came to one of my workshops, and on the first day, during a group sharing session, he looked at me and announced, "I don't think I like you." Over the next couple of days he quietly participated, watching and taking everything in. I felt no antagonism from him and suspected that some form of quiet healing was taking place. On the third day, during the group sharing, Bob addressed me directly again. "I *do* like you," he said.

Perfunctory statements though these are, they belied the deep inner change that had taken place. I fitted the projection of some set of internal characteristics that Bob was ready to let go of. In his quiet way, he had processed his attachment to the part of him that was hidden within his inner crowd through his dislike of me and gently processed and released his projection.

Most of us populate our world to the point of overcrowding; memories haunt us and people from the past appear before us. Yet we travel through life essentially alone. We can share the innermost thoughts and feelings that reside in our aloneness in intimacy with another. We can press through the inner clamor of inner characters and inhabit the core, or essence, at the center of ourselves where we are grounded and genuine, and experience our being. Our ability to be with ourselves provides us with a strong foundation for forming real relationships of worth, caring, and mutual understanding. But relationships require boundaries.

Boundaries Enable Relationship

Boundaries are where "I" ends and the other begins. Boundaries are about where and how we meet and affect each other and the world we are in. Working with boundaries is working with relationship, because without a sense of boundaries we cannot truly know where we are or where another is, so we cannot truly relate.

We seek people who have boundaries that are compatible with our own. Yet some people have very different senses of where their boundaries are, and others have little or no sense of boundaries at all. There are many kinds of boundaries: time boundaries, space boundaries, physical boundaries, and emotional boundaries. We speak of establishing boundaries, respecting boundaries, breaking boundaries, and invading boundaries. They are invisible and energetic, often unconscious and highly emotional. For some, boundaries are all-important; for others, boundaries are simply rules to be followed blindly or broken unconsciously; and for still others, boundaries have little or no real meaning at all.

So, since they are so important, why are we so confused about boundaries?

We acquire our early sense of boundaries from our parents and families, and then later on at school, both from our peers and from the way we are treated by those in positions of authority. Boundaries give us our sense of personal space and identity. They allow us to know who we are. Someone who doesn't know who they are almost certainly has a problem with boundaries. Most likely their sense of place, personal freedom, and independence was not respected or nurtured in their early life, so they have no substantial sense of themselves. A healthy, strong sense of boundaries is vital to us in childhood. But it may be impossible for parents to teach healthy boundaries if they have not been taught them by their own parents.

Once I was invited to facilitate a workshop for the members of a "free" community. Within the community was a free school that practiced children's rights and self-regulation. When I arrived, a young woman with a small boy met me and offered to show me the room where I would be leading the workshop. While she was showing me around, the boy ran to the door, spread his body over it with his arms outstretched, and when we tried to leave he refused to let us out. His mother negotiated with him for several minutes while the boy became increasingly determined to prevent us from leaving. Softly spoken and patient, she bargained with him to let us pass. She spoke to him as if he were a grown-up, but what I saw in his eyes and bearing was a little boy who was scared and crying out for boundaries and containment.

How frightening it is to be given that much power as a child. As a backlash to rigid Victorian rules and discipline, some parents today give children total license. They feel uneasy about discipline and authority. Their "instincts" tell them not to interfere and to allow children to express their individuality. In contrast, their grandparents' generation believed in and often practiced unfeeling, rigid discipline and punishment. Guidance for today's parents when they were children was more straightforward, but although the old certainties have now gone, parents today can feel as certain about libertarian principles as previous generations of parents were convinced about authoritarian ones. Hard, heartless authority directly contrasts with gentle, heartfelt guidance. But authority and discipline can be applied with love and integrity.

A blind person needs to know where the walls and structures are to feel safe and navigate the space, as we do as children. In childhood we experience boundaries as powerful holding and secure structure. They make us feel safe and cared for, like being embraced by loving arms. An essential aspect of loving children is responding to their need to be contained. A child cannot ask for these boundaries directly; the wise parent needs to able to understand and respect that their child needs them. The wise parent provides safe boundaries through being firm and loving. Without boundaries a child is in a state of chronic fear and uncertainty, which manifests in challenging behavior, temper tantrums, moroseness, or non-cooperation. Today children are so desperate to feel "held," to experience the security of being contained within firm, loving boundaries, that they challenge adult authority in an attempt to get what they need.

Adults who grew up with inadequate or over-rigid boundaries have a weak sense of who they are. Their external reference points may be strong and they may identify with their roles in the family, in relationships, at work, and with their achievements in the outer world. But their internal reference points are weak, because they have little sense of their inner being. When we have a sense of ourselves, we have a sense of who the other is.

By setting limits and working within clear boundaries, we empower ourselves to relate to others and invite others to relate to us. In relationships, boundaries occupy a continuum between the two poles of merging and distancing.

Distancing is expressed in coldness, detachment, hostility, or isolation. People who distance themselves in relationships are masters at abandoning and rejecting others. This kind of boundary is like a steel wall. Boundaries get confused with limitation or being emotionally closed. They become associated with withholding, separation, and loneliness.

Merging is expressed in intrusiveness, overinvolvement, dependency, or inappropriate behavior. People with no real sense of who they are cannot live independently. In relationships based on dependency and need, people meet their desires mistakenly through merging with others in an infantile attempt to fulfill their needs.

But healthy boundaries fill the space between these two misguided extremes. Boundaries make relationships possible through sharing, giving, and receiving. When boundaries are just right for two people, they respect each other as individuals. When we set boundaries for our personal space and our likes and dislikes, we are able to relate truly to another, and express our needs without intimidating or threatening our partner. Knowing our boundaries, we are self-aware; and knowing our limitations, we can live growthful lives.

How do we learn to practice healthy boundaries? First, know and respect what you feel, what you need, and what you have a right to. If you have issues with low self-esteem, passive behavior, and disempowerment, explore them and make it your aim to heal them. Here's an exercise that may help. Write on a piece of paper "I want ..." Now write endings to this sentence without thinking too much. Now do the same with the words "I need ..." How do you feel about these lists? How much of what you want or need do you actually get?

Second, learn to be assertive and skillful at caring for yourself in personal relationships. Ask for what you want, do not be fearful of rejection or rejecting, and be prepared for the possibility of getting what you want! If you have a loving partner, ask them to give you some leeway as you experiment with the spectrum of demanding to sensitively negotiate for what you want.

Third, take responsibility for your needs and allow others to do the same for themselves. Do not confuse your needs with theirs; this is the quintessential boundary issue—where I end and you begin— so find a balance in reciprocity, between giving and receiving. For example, what happens in your primary relationship when a choice needs to be made? Do you habitually defer to your partner or does your partner defer to you? Try it a different way: both say exactly what you would like to do. If it is really hard to express your preference in speech, write it down and compare the two answers.

Finally, learn to ask, learn to say no, do not be a people-pleaser, and discard "friends" who do not respect healthy boundaries. Practice the first three of these by considering self-loyalty and its consequences. It is a rule of life that if you are dissatisfied, not only do you become an increasingly unhappy person but so will those who are in relationship with you. Happiness brings happiness; misery brings misery, so take self-responsibility for your happiness *now* and practice asking for what you want, saying no, and primarily pleasing yourself. Friends, partners, and loved ones who are unable to respect healthy boundaries must not necessarily be abandoned right away, but they should be firmly encouraged into raising awareness of how they relate to others and seeking help when necessary.

Central to healthy boundaries is that you know yourself, know who you are, know your truth, and remain consistently loyal toward it. Boundaries should be strong but not permanently fixed; firm, gentle, but flexible. By remaining fluid and yet relating through healthy boundaries, we open, learn to change, and develop in our relationship to others. We have the freedom to behave appropriately and change as our needs and desires of our relationships grow and change. Our sense of boundaries enables us to act appropriately and sensitively.

Personal Empowerment

Each of us is a unique being with an amazing potential for self-knowledge and deep wisdom. Yet out of attachment to the conditions of our early life, many of us develop a self-image that is inconsequential or damaged, and we become disempowered.

Disempowerment has become a disease of epidemic proportions. We have become little people who are scared of our own light. We are afraid to know or ask for what we really want or to be who we truly are. Priests, educators, politicians, parents, and other authority figures defined our ancestors. Today, we have replaced the old authority figures with the faceless and impersonal forces of commerce, advertising, and global communications. We are defined through indoctrination, manipulation, and fear. We have become acutely aware of people's flaws and particularly delight in bringing down people who are in the public eye or in positions of authority. The hidden collusion and insistent assumption is that we are small and powerless. The world has become big and we have become small. We are helpless in the face of ecological disaster, conspiracy theories, and abuses of power. As our consciousness of global matters grows, our conscience is stimulated and manipulated into accepting merely superficial consolation.

In the outer world, we have come to accept that we are disempowered and ineffective. But in the inner world, disempowerment involves our reluctance—even our refusal—to be all that we are. We project our inner strengths and personal power onto others and fear their reactions and their power. We disown our beauty and our talents and search for them outside ourselves. We project our humiliation and despair and perceive it in the neediness, helplessness, and disadvantage we see all around us.

In our work on ourselves, we take back all that we have disowned and projected. Re-owning these aspects of ourselves is how we discover who we are and eventually become whole. Usually we disown the aspects of ourselves that were unacceptable to others, and that is how they become unacceptable to us. Working on inner disempowerment lessens the projection of our fears, so we become more empowered and effective in both inner and outer worlds.

Power emanates from two sources: inner and outer. Outer power is competitive, insinuating, intimidating, known by its actions and results. Outer power dominates; it is power "over" something. We have power over others, power over nature, power over events. Exerting outer power gives us control and choice in getting what we want in the material world. In its negative form, outer power may be bullying or acting out our prejudices, exploiting others, and acting cruelly or inconsiderately, which often stem from a lack of inner power.

Inner power emanates from a strong sense of being. Power that is based in the inner world is the core power at the center of each individual. This kind of power does not seek power over anything; it is simply the courage and awareness to be ourselves.

All of us have a natural urge to be ourselves, because we carry within us a kernel of selfhood, a unique being with an innate drive to be realized in the world. How we respond to this urge to *be* defines our relationship to power, both inner and outer. When we compensate for our lack of inner power with outward shows of power, we act out of fear or anger, and we demean ourselves.

Acting from our conditioning always involves compromise. Most of us feel that, in early life, we were not fully accepted for ourselves. So we learn to adapt and please, but this brings about a compromise to our inner integrity that becomes increasingly hard to tolerate as we grow older. Nevertheless, most of us continue to compromise by rejecting ourselves as we felt our parents did us. Our inner power diminishes and our orientation toward the outer world increases, with acts of outward power manifesting in achievement or success and concealing the inner conflict.

Manipulation is a complex expression of disempowerment. Manipulative behavior involves compliance on the part of the one who is being manipulated. This compliance is collusive—the "manipulator" gives the cues, which the "victim" reacts to with self-manipulation to bring about the expected result. But it is really all an act. We might feel like we are being manipulated, but really we are manipulating ourselves. All manipulation is self-manipulation. And we disempower ourselves similarly through weakening our energy and assaulting our integrity.

When we practice skill, diplomacy, or tact out of good intentions, it doesn't cost us energetically because we are aware of what we're doing. We are not trying to hurt anyone, or assault their integrity or our own. A conscious strategy with good intentions is not manipulative or disempowering. But when we are servile or ingratiating, we plug into our worthlessness with negative consequences. Only we ourselves know whether we have sold out or acted wisely. Disempowering ourselves and consciously using our strategies are a different quality of act. Disempowerment leaves us with unfinished business to work on; conscious and considerate use of strategies does not.

Disempowerment becomes the hidden contract in our outer relationships. We enter into a collective collusion to be small. This stunting of individual growth and self-acceptance hinders the full flowering of our personalities. In colluding to disempower ourselves (and others), we maintain our individual survival. We are fighting for our lives, and it seems that the best thing to do is to conceal ourselves. We believe that if we keep our heads in the sand for long enough, the danger will pass. But it won't, because we are caught in a prison of our own conditioning.

Disempowerment thrives on unawareness. The raising of awareness is fundamental to inner work and essential for individual choice, change, and personal empowerment.

Gisela came to me with severe anorexia. She had been an actor and a dancer in a touring theater company until she became too weak to continue. To convalesce she had moved in with her father, a film director who possessed a powerful, controlling personality. Gisela was so weak that, in spite of living within a short walking distance, she came by taxi.

We explored her childhood issues with personal power, how she felt unacceptable, unloved, and unable to be herself. In her teenage years she refused to eat as a desperate way to feel that she had some choice and decision over her life. Now at age twenty-eight, she was able to gain insights into the reasons for her decision to refuse to eat and to re-experience the strong, childhood feelings that kept her in a state of dependency on her father. Fortunately she was ready for inner work, and her commitment to her process resulted in rapid insights and understanding. As we talked together, she relived her early experiences and entered into a deep process of inner healing.

On the day she broke out of her disempowerment, she danced around the room expressing strong feelings and reveling in her new-found freedom. As she swung her arms and legs through the air, I looked on in amazement. Exerting tremendous control and body awareness, she missed ornaments, potted plants, and furniture by mere millimeters. Now she was in total control. Her instincts refined her movements to a tremendous degree. Her dance was an exuberant celebration of her life force, of energies she had long suppressed. She left to spend a day at the beach, swimming and anticipating the beginning of her new life.

Several months later, she wrote to me to say she was performing again in a new, more prestigious theater company. She had started a relationship, and her happiness radiated from the pages of her letter.

Inner work shows us that we are more powerful and more wonderful than we ever imagined. Almost everyone's self-image is flawed in this respect. We are not little people: we are infinitely more than we hope or fear we can be. When we are able to embrace all we are, our dreams turn out to be closer than we had realized.

In Summary

In this chapter I have introduced you to the dynamics of the inner world. Next we turn to relationships and how we project and transfer inner aspects of character that we deny or repress onto others. Before going on, spend a little time reflecting on the subject matter we have covered so far. Here are some useful questions to ask. Feel free to add your own questions and pursue individual lines of personal inquiry:

1. Who are the inner characters that constitute my inner world? What are the relationships between them, individually and collectively? Which one(s) have the most power?

2. What have I to learn, or what have I learned, from my parents?

3. What is my awareness of boundaries? Personal boundaries, professional boundaries, familial boundaries? What are my strengths and weaknesses boundary-wise? Assess your sense of proportion in life: how are you sometimes too much or not enough?

4. Personal empowerment is an inner sense that is expressed into the outside world. Consider your friends, colleagues, relations—how empowered are they? How interdependent are the members of your social group? What is your own honest assessment of your personal empowerment?

4

Relationships

Relationships and Projection

An intimate relationship—partnership or marriage—is one of the most potent catalysts for wholeness and authenticity there is. Relationships can also be the most deathly and least life-enhancing environment for the human spirit. It all depends on honest and open communication, deepening and growing in intimacy, and the courage and willingness to venture into unknown territory together.

Love relationships have the power to re-stimulate the unresolved issues of our early childhoods, because when we are in love we are at our most open and vulnerable. Since most of us didn't get all we needed or wanted in our early lives, these same needs and desires arise in our relationships and are often expressed inappropriately. We may have the unrealistic expectation that our partner can fulfill all our needs. We may idealize our partner, who can then only fall from grace and disappoint us. We will never find a partner who meets all our historical desires, because these desires belong to the past: they are part of our frozen history. Relationships compel us to face ourselves and offer us the chance to resolve the unfinished business of childhood, because they reopen our issues around dependence, nurture, and care.

For those of us without a loving relationship, the promise of finding someone can unleash idealistic fantasies. We can dream about how lovely it will be when we find that special person who will cherish and care for us. From a distance, a loving relationship is all soft-focus—comfortable and idealized. But relationships have the potential to take us to the very edges of our personalities and uncover the hidden aspects of ourselves that we hoped no one would ever see. Relationships insist that we grow, open our hearts, and become authentic.

A relationship that measures its success on pleasure and fulfillment is hard enough. But when a relationship is considered primarily as a vehicle for growth, we open ourselves up to profound psychological and spiritual challenges. The journey of human love may be the most profound activity for a human life. Depending as it does on our ability not only to know ourselves but also to know our partner, a growthful relationship must be firmly founded on awareness, clarity, acceptance, and trust.

Difficulties arise when one partner wants a growthful relationship, while the other is content with comfort and warm familiarity. The partner who wants more is most likely to become the agent of the breakup. The prospect of breaking up is what most often causes a couple to look more deeply at their relationship.

Usually one half of the couple is for and one is against the relationship continuing. This polarization is the outcome of the interdependent, projective aspect of the relationship, which began at the couple's first meeting. When we meet someone whom we are to develop a relationship with, a highly complex exchange happens. Unconsciously we offer denied aspects of ourselves to each other and the dynamics of the relationship are created. These dynamics give the relationship its fundamental form and dictate its unfolding. Through the psychic exchange, each partner now "possesses" a part of the other. Over time the two partners become polarized and resentful, because the other has a part of them that prevents them from being their whole self.

The buried negativity arising from persistent compromise rises to the surface as the years go by and finally spills out in burgeoning resentment that poisons the relationship. Couples in difficulty must inevitably *separate to join*. The separation must take place whether the two partners stay together or break up. Only by separating and finding a sense of themselves as individuals are they enabled to relate to each another anew, perhaps for the first time. Strong, healthy boundaries enable relationship, as we saw in chapter 3. But how do loving relationships turn sour? How is it that the future partner we see across a crowded room and are immediately attracted to turns out, after the "honeymoon period" is over, to be just like the previous partner whom we learned to despise? To answer this, we must look in more detail at the psychic exchange that takes place at the first meeting of the two individuals who become a couple.

In the laws of physics, opposites attract, but in interpersonal relationships, the reverse is true: *similars attract*. The way in which this works is unconscious and mysterious. We meet someone and experience a strong attraction. During that first meeting, we establish a contract—a binding agreement in which inner aspects of ourselves are exchanged through the process of projection. We may give the other our beauty, our confidence, or our ability. Our future partner unconsciously invites and accepts these inner qualities to compensate for an imbalance or lack that she or he feels inside. This exchange of qualities goes on quite invisibly and unbelievably rapidly when we meet a prospective partner. The success of this invisible process is so crucial to the emerging relationship that its failure is more common than we imagine. We are usually only aware of this mating ritual as a charged social interaction.

The remainder of the relationship may well consist of attempts at taking back and re-owning the projected qualities that we gave each other and that were ours all along. This is often painful. We have, after all, projected the qualities onto the other because we had a reason to deny them. We are resistant to taking them back because the defenses of our character depend on our projecting certain qualities successfully to substantiate our character and justify our defense. Suppose, for example, that a key element of our character defense is unlovableness. Then we need to wear our partner down, however much he or she may love us, until they give in to negativity toward us and confirm that we are unlovable.

Most often, even amid the difficulties, the partner we are with is the right one for us. The two people in a love relationship are merged and somewhat mixed up as a result of exchanging projections. Consequently when a couple is divided over the inner journey, one is most likely acting out the inner search for the relationship as a whole—one expressing resistance, the other expressing willingness. Since projection is unconscious, the desire of the resistant one is hidden, even from themselves. It is perhaps unsurprising, then, that when a couple breaks up because one of them is practicing inner work and the other is against it, the resistant one finds himself on his own inner journey after a few months, doing what he had been so opposed to in his partner when they were in the relationship. The end of the relationship has meant that he can retrieve the part of him that wants to find out who he is and, without the partner carrying that projected part, he is now able to do it for himself and face his resistance, balanced with his enthusiasm to explore.

Ritualizing the End of a Relationship

Intimate relationships are an expression of archetypal energies or gods—the same kind of energies we encountered earlier when we looked at the lessons our parents teach us. Archetypal forces are impersonal, though they dwell within us. Our life gives them form and expression, and our personality embodies them. When we treat archetypal energies with contempt and dishonor, they become a personal threat. When a relationship breaks down, the god becomes a devil and, as the mythologist Joseph Campbell pointed out, the devil acts like a god in reverse, exerting negative, threatening power.

In relationship we evoke the gods—the personifications of powerful energies of life that act in both inner and outer worlds—and this is why the end of a relationship can be so devastating. It is a deeply responsible act to work on ending a relationship in a way that leaves the least residue or unfinished business. Resentments should be released and appreciations expressed to create clarity, understanding, and forgiveness, to allow each partner to go on in their lives with space in their hearts.

The dark side of relationship reveals its potency. A relationship that is not open, that stores up resentment daily, that leaves things unsaid and feelings unexpressed, eventually ends. Either it withers and dies, or it explodes. When it withers, the partners maintain a façade of relationship, but within there is no life or love anymore. When it explodes, the partners physically break up and any further contact is based on anger and hatred fueled by built-up resentment.

Sadly, many couples who break up never resolve their differences or achieve a satisfactory ending. Though some try, there is no real willingness to let go of the resentments or clear up the emotional litter of the relationship. A mere mention of one partner's name and the other partner's face distorts and spouts vitriol. Each is concerned with what was done to them and how they were mistreated, betrayed, rejected, and abandoned. They will never truly forgive each other as long as they live.

Deep beneath this layer of blame and hatred lies the true motivation for maintaining the resentment: *without resentment the small self cannot survive.* The small self is our identification with our conditioned life view, the character we have formed out of past experience that limits present experience and inhibits personal development. It is only by creating situations in which resentment can flourish that we nourish and sustain this small self. Love relationships are not only one of the most potent ways to grow, but they are also one of the best ways of providing us with material for resentment, bitterness, and hatred.

While resentment sustains our illusion of separateness, relationship and intimacy move us steadily toward wholeness and integration. Self-exploration makes a profound impact on relationships. When one partner in a relationship practices inner work, the other is challenged to look at himself. If the partner who is on the inner journey outgrows the one who is not, she is likely to become estranged and the stability of the relationship is threatened.

The partner exploring inner work is usually charged by the other with "navel-gazing," too much self-absorption, and not caring about others. Often the partner who is against the inner journey adopts a political, ecological, or charitable position. They express concern about the state of the world and what can be done about it. These lofty concerns then become a way of avoiding and projecting their own needs of the relationship.

To love a flesh-and-blood person who is close to us seems to be a harder challenge than to love the whole world. The whole world is faceless and does not require personal intimacy for us to love it. We can feel some kind of love and compassion for people who are distant from us. They can be imagined or idealized, so we can project our thoughts and emotions indiscriminately. This kind of love is one-way traffic, without the difficult dimension of relationship dynamics, differences, and negotiation. Most of us have the potential to open our hearts and share ourselves intimately with another, but we may lack the emotional capacity to let the other in to our inner world, when there is so much filling us up already.

When a relationship ends irreconcilably, the two partners are usually left with unfinished business in the form of unexpressed resentments, built-up anger, blame, and hatred. These feelings seem to have no healing outlet and no apparent possibility of resolution. I have seen many couples who are trying to revive, dissolve, or reinvent their relationships. Very often by the time they get to the stage of coming to see me, their relationship is floundering and sometimes in its death throes. When a couple acknowledges that the relationship is at an end, even when they wish it wasn't, great honesty and emotional transparency are called for to enable the two people to go on in their lives in an empowered way.

The end of a relationship should match its beginning. Where there has been a long courtship or journey into intimacy, a similar depth of process is needed to release the relationship. Where the couple has passed through a marriage ceremony, a similar ritual is required to break the ties. But couples may be reluctant to release each other, break the ties, or recognize the need for ritualizing an ending. Instead, couples who have separated and consider themselves "out" of relationship with their exes remain very much attached—in some cases for the rest of their lives.

This is a human tragedy that can be avoided. With honesty and commitment, the issues that still bind the two people together can be healed. Inner work for couples breaking up requires an open space for expressing appreciations and resentments, which is empowered by a third person (or persons) who acts as a witness and should be neutral in regard to the two partners' grievances. The witness facilitates the healing that leads to mutual acceptance. The process of inner exploration should be concluded with a ritual: a ceremony devised by the two individuals themselves, in consultation with the witness.

This is a very powerful form of release for both partners. The couple must be willing to be transparent, and partners often experience a strong impulse to be more honest with each other than they have ever been before. With nothing to lose and no investment in preserving the relationship, intimacy may deepen and, ironically, the couple's communication can reach depths they never achieved while they were together.

The liberation that results from the ending ritual is beneficial for both because it infuses subsequent relationships with new clarity and deeper understanding. When we can clearly acknowledge what we have gone through and what we needed to do with our partner; recognize what we were given; state our resentments; wish our ex-partner well; and offer our regrets, our forgiveness, and our appreciation of all that we have shared together, we can truly let go.

A young couple, Pamela and Bill, came to see me. They were resigned to the fact that their relationship had ended and they wanted to finish as thoroughly as they could. Together we devised a ceremony. In a ritual attended by their two closest friends, Pamela and Bill spoke of their disappointments and their failures, their shame and their grief, as well as their joys, their fulfillment, and the love they had shared. Pamela spoke of her frustration with Bill. She felt that he didn't really "see" her and acknowledge that she had grown into a strong woman. She resented Bill's lack of openness and his unwillingness to grow with her in new ways. Bill expressed his disappointment that their relationship had failed. He was still attracted to Pamela and was nostalgic for the early period of their relationship. He resented the arguments,

Pamela's fiery tempers that he could not understand, and that their child would now have two homes and two separated parents. When all these things and more had been said, they expressed their desire to forgive each other, appreciate what they had shared together, and create the space in their lives to move on.

When the mirror our partner provides is taken away, a flood of raw projections returns to us. Now we may be able to see ourselves as never before and, if we are able to accept ourselves, lessen our need for someone to act as a screen on which we project our disowned parts. If we can stay with it to its closure, the end of a relationship can be an intense period of growth. If we don't shrink from the challenge, we may begin to see ourselves more clearly and with more awareness.

Paradoxically, withdrawing projections and the self-acceptance that arises from reclaiming them is precisely the dynamic that enables us to relate truly to another. Therefore this time can bring about a change of heart. Couples may decide, after all, to stay together.

The Path of Love

If we can make it through the romance and enchantment of the "honeymoon period," relationships have the potential to develop through three essential stages.

The first stage is *loving enchantment*. We love the other as we would like to be loved ourselves. We cannot do enough and we put our own needs on hold while we bask in the warmth of the first flushes of intimacy. The accumulated pain of our past relationships and childhood conditioning is washed away in the joy and elation of love. Fascinated by everything our partner is and does, we are devoted to expressing our love and pleasing them. This is a truly magical time dominated by feelings of self-expansion and being *in love*.

The second stage is *projecting past hurts*. In time our resentments surface, as our idealized partner and our relationship begin to show flaws. We feel justified in revealing more of ourselves—what we need and what we want—and our deep urge is to express a darker side of ourselves and still be loved. If we become more open and honest, we may be willing to show our darker side. As we become more familiar with each other, we may even break the boundaries of honoring and simple respect. Alternatively, we may experience the darkness in our partner as a further opportunity to love them, ever more deeply. This is a time to choose, either consciously or unconsciously, to deepen together or to abandon love and the relationship.

The third stage is *spontaneous love*. It represents a quantum leap and is the stage that most of us avoid because there is no going back from the insights and the heart-opening it offers. We start to love in a wholly different way, understanding that the lover is more blessed than the beloved, and we begin to love our partner more deeply than ever. We value the precious opportunity to love more highly than our fragile, human need to be loved. At times we transcend the usual restrictions of human love, which are so inevitably bound up with fear, need, and desire. Our relationship is characterized by abundance, generosity, and real love. We may explore the deeper questions like "What brought us together?" "What do we need to fulfill in this relationship?" "How can we be true to ourselves and honor our relationship?" knowing that the pairing of two human beings is bigger than the sum of the two halves.

Love between two people is always indefinable. We can say what it is *now*—in this moment. But our definition never holds true for very long, because love manifests spontaneously and sometimes unpredictably. As we surrender to deepening forms of love, it may not live up to our personal expectations, so we may become disillusioned. When we do, it is because we have confused need and desire with love. If we can distinguish clearly between these three human experiences, then we can open to a real deepening in relationship. When we truly love someone, we are centered in our hearts. Out of our love of ourselves we are able to extend love to another, and we tend to be less confused about our needs and desires. Need and desire are innate human experiences. So it is best to own them and respond to them honestly and treat them as a valid part of us. Sometimes simply sharing our needs and desires openly with our partner will take some of the urgency out of our demands. Making need and desire transparent lessens the darkness in which they are repressed.

Many of us feel ashamed of our needs and desires. Needs persist whether love is present or not. If we can't answer the question "What do I want and what do I need?" and be open and clear about what we really want, we cannot grow and flourish in a truly successful relationship.

To grow in our relationships we must address the issue of *time* seriously, because of the complex demands on us. Too much time spent in outward pursuits can lead to neglecting the relationship, which needs our time and care to grow. Relationships do not just happen, and they do not survive neglect. Making time for intimacy, sharing, and deepening enables our relationships to grow and thrive. Considering how we balance our time is essential for the health of a growing relationship. How do we find time for ourselves, time to be together, and time to fulfill our responsibilities in the world?

We must work at achieving a balance. Structuring our time in a disciplined way between these three basic needs (and being aware when we get out of balance) is enough. A third of our time fulfilling duties and responsibilities, a third of our time in relationship and service to others, and a third of our time in relationship with ourselves and meeting our personal needs is a good model to aspire to.

When two people enter into a relationship in middle or later years, there is a tendency to want to relive the past through a sham of adolescent romance. If this is done with awareness, knowing that the relationship is fulfilling some missing experience, it can be successful and rewarding. But often, the sham of romance in the middle years kills the relationship, because it is not appropriate for the age of the partners involved. Older people, who have not replaced their youthful desire for a purely romantic relationship with a deeper longing, sadly miss out on a more profound fulfillment. From the fifties on, if a new relationship is to work, it must be based on mutual growth and spiritual values, a more searching connection of inquiry, reciprocal concern, consideration, and caring. Small things, which directly contrast with the more spectacular emotional bonds of our earlier years, like fondness, living together harmoniously, and cups of tea in bed, are valued, vital, and more important than they used to be. While our partner may still be a sensuous and sexual partner, he or she is also now, more than ever, a companion in love, a fellow traveler to that far horizon that is closer than ever before.

Today, relationships are subject to a floating paradigm that is in such a restless process that it offers no solid guidelines. There is a lot of space for creativity and experimentation, as well as a lot of potential for insecurity and misunderstanding. The variety is extensive: heterosexual, gay, lesbian, interracial, diverse age, mentally impaired, physically impaired relationships—all pose particular challenges and offer unique rewards.

Furthermore, we face the choice of relating to one person or having a variety of relationships—a monogamous or polygamous love life. What is the value of monogamy today? Unfortunately, many examples of monogamy are based on the fear of ending the relationship that stems from cultural expectations and morals dating back hundreds of years. It is questionable whether such values and morals apply to us today. But despite the negative associations, a committed monogamous relationship yields some of the most profound and growthful treasures we could ever receive, both psychologically and spiritually. In a sustained monogamous relationship, we cultivate the qualities of loyalty and commitment in the challenges of constancy and the tests of time. A truly committed relationship challenges us to deep acceptance, to the healing of everything about us that we consider unlovable, to grow and develop through hardships, pain, and joy. As the relationship goes through the inevitable and often tough changes of a shared lifetime, we face the prospect of being truly known by another and sustaining something enriching and unique.

Ultimately, we can meet the test of deepening in love to such a degree that we are no longer separate, no longer on our own. We cannot do without the relationship, and we cannot do without each other. But this is not the unhealthy dependence born of the regressive merging of two individuals, the infantile dependence we discussed in the previous chapter when we looked at boundaries. Rather it is our heart surrendering to the liberating path of deep intimacy. Our happiness is bittersweet, because we know that we will have to leave each other someday. With profound wise foolishness, we love rather than refuse to love. We can no more deny the stirrings of our hearts than we can renege on our humanity or our spirit.

In real love the specific merges with the universal. The boundaried individual leads us to unboundaried freedom. In a delicate play of the heart, we at once respect and love the individual we are with and at the same time we honor existence through our love of them. Our love is both personal and impersonal, both individual and transcendent. We see all men or all women in our partner, and we honor the sacredness of life through our relationship. If we are blessed with the path of relationship, the riches we receive can be immeasurable.

One of the benefits of relationship and intimacy is support, encouragement, and companionship on life's path. No one stands alone; we all need one another.

Acknowledgment and Support

Acknowledgment and support are needed in inner work to cultivate inner strength, give us the will to endure, and deepen our trust. When the results of inner work are intangible, invisible, undefined, or slow-going, genuine acknowledgment and support may sustain us through periods of uncertainty or despair.

Support entails encouragement, listening, understanding, sometimes not interfering, and "being there," uninhibited by inner blindness, denial, prejudice, judgment, or projection.

Acknowledgment is trickier. Sometimes it is quietly noticing, valuing the changes and the growing process; sometimes it is a quiet understanding, a knowing of experience. It is life-affirming and unafraid, uninhibited by the ignorance of inner processes, a lack of depth, or awkwardness about silence or unawareness. Instinctively we may look for these things in the people we are closest to. But often they are unable to meet our needs, because they feel threatened.

Our self-exploration suffers when it conflicts with our loyalty to our loved ones. When husbands, wives, relatives, or friends are antagonistic to our personal growth and withdraw their support, we may have to choose between loyalty to others and loyalty to ourselves. If we choose the former, we become alienated from ourselves; but if we choose the latter, we become alienated from our loved ones.

If the people close to us have never engaged in inner work, they may find it difficult to give us the support we need. They may be unable to understand what we are going through, and it is unlikely that they will respond positively to our growthful changes. They tend to have an investment in our remaining as we are, or, when they see some "fault" in us, in correcting it in a way they would prefer. Either way, they cannot provide the kind of openness and acceptance we need.

With relations and friends we play roles, and when we step out of these roles things become uncomfortable, for us and them. Like performing a well-rehearsed dance routine and suddenly changing your steps, everyone is thrown off. Finding someone who is reliable and trustworthy enough to confide in can prove hazardous; openly sharing our self-discovery can arouse denial and defensiveness in others.

In his book *The Alchemist*, Paulo Coelho shows us that blatant honesty may even invite ridicule. Sometimes stating the bare truth sounds so preposterous to the prejudiced listener that it is certain to be treated as a joke.

Following a series of adventures, the boy and the alchemist are riding through the desert with the legendary Philosopher's Stone and the miraculous Elixir of Life in their saddle bags when they come across a group of Arab bandits. The leader demands to know what they are carrying, and the alchemist replies that they have an elixir that dispels illness and a stone that turns metal into gold. The bandits burst out laughing and allow the two of them to ride on with their belongings. The boy, thinking that the alchemist has gone crazy, asks why he openly revealed their precious cargo. The alchemist replies that when you possess great inner treasures and try to tell others about them, seldom are you believed.

Our inner discoveries may not be believed by others too. Either through cynicism or fear, the negative response of others can be enough to plant in us seeds of doubt.

The effects of inner work become outwardly visible over time, but the last people to notice any difference are often the ones closest to us. Unless they are also working on themselves, their image of us may be so strong that they resist even obvious outward signs of our inner changes and doubt us.

In her unpublished autobiography, Helen Schucman, the unlikely channel of *A Course in Miracles*, describes the response of her husband, Louis, to one of her transcendent experiences. Riding on the subway one day, Schucman perceives the human race in all its physical, emotional, and sensory sordidness: coughing and sneezing, nauseating odors, and dirt, vomit, and perspiration. She feels overwhelming revulsion, disgust, and sickness and becomes convinced that she herself is fatally ill. Then a blinding light fills her, and in a vision she falls to the ground and kneels in profound reverence. Embraced by a loving arm, she disappears and with the light growing ever brighter she experiences a love so intense that it makes her gasp and open her eyes. This love pours from her to everyone on the train. Then the light fades, and as it does the scenario of human degradation returns. Greatly disoriented, she reaches for her husband's hand and tries to tell him about her extraordinary experience. He responds by patting her, declaring her experience common, and encouraging her not to think about it. Many people similarly have their deep inner experiences dismissed by people close to them.

We ask a lot of someone when we expect them to understand our deep inner processes. We not only require them to be open and willing to really hear us, but we also ask for their intuitive empathy and understanding. We may ask their understanding for what we do not yet understand ourselves. Until we are very solid in our truth, we need to be acknowledged by someone who can really be with us and hear what we have to say, without criticizing or judging. Often we will not be able to justify ourselves or our behavior toward them and others. We need to be allowed a great deal of space, without always being able to make sense of what is developing inside us.

Judy was the epitome of the "good little girl." Now a woman in her mid-thirties, she was a devoted wife and a shining example of domestic efficiency. She came to see me, partly at her husband's request, when their marriage became stifled and lifeless. Through her self-exploration she uncovered deep historical resentment toward her father, who had made her his favorite and manipulated her to meet his expectations to win his affection. As her emotional blocks began to thaw, she had uncharacteristic outbursts of raw anger. Anxious to preserve her relationship, she asked me how to deal with this in her marriage. I suggested that she tell her husband that she was likely to express her emotions unpredictably just now and prepare him for what might happen. This way she could anticipate his reaction and not turn her outbursts into arguments. He also needed to understand that this was how she would achieve emotional health, rather than suppressing her feelings, and that the relationship could grow in time out of a new healthier basis of aliveness and openness.

This type of strategy demands genuine understanding and real caring. If we don't feel understood, we may become self-conscious or embarrassed when we need to take ourselves seriously. We can become the saboteurs of our own process if we feel that our inner processes are threatening our relationships. We may not be ready to put our close relationships at risk when our partner's image of us collides with our new emerging self.

Our partners, friends, and relatives may be tested and challenged as they witness the changes in us. Naturally, we feel we want to share our new experiences with those we love. But as we change, what we need from our friends and partners changes, too. As we recognize the different aspects of our character and shed life-stifling patterns, we expand and grow. If our relationships feel too confining or our roles with our partner and friends are not suited to our deeper self, we may outgrow those close to us.

Friends or partners who are not supportive of our personal growth may feel excluded, confused, and threatened. They may sense some distance growing in the relationship. We may be unwilling to adapt, compromise, or limit ourselves in the ways we did before. So, however much we reassure them, their concerns are justified because as we grow we change. When we engage seriously in inner work, we are bound to emerge a different person. The relationship or friendship will then have to accommodate or embrace new dynamics. Our partners may be hurt and behave reactively. We may feel that we are forced to choose between compromising ourselves for the sake of our partners and remaining loyal to ourselves. Sometimes the connection is not strong enough to accommodate such far-reaching changes.

At times we may ask ourselves whether our personal exploration justifies the hurt we cause our partner and friends. We may ask whether our love for them doesn't warrant the sacrifice of our personal journey. It may not be all right to hurt them, but what right do we have to hurt ourselves by stunting our growth? Caring for them and caring for ourselves may seem equally important. We may decide to follow our own process in spite of the pain it causes others. The man or woman who blazes a trail uncompromisingly, lives life fully, takes risks frequently, and is sincerely committed to personal transformation may be forgiven much.

The acknowledgment of our family may be hard or even impossible to obtain. One woman went to her father for support and encouragement for the insights that were coming up in her inner work. He was clearly threatened and scared by what she was discovering. His aggression startled and repelled her, as it was no doubt designed to do. But this didn't dissuade her from trying to gain his support several times. Some sort of innocence motivates us to try to include our family and loved ones in our inner exploration. We feel that since we have found the courage to open up to our inner world, those close to us can somehow share in it. Coupled with our need to be acknowledged, recognized, and supported by those who played a part in our historical dramas, we can be seized by an irresistible need to have them involved and on our side. We may also need them to admit their part in what has happened to us. Sometimes it seems that their acknowledgment or confession is *all* we need for our healing to be complete. But we are unlikely to get it. Usually we will have to live in the knowledge that the other members of our family are in denial, or don't see it the same way we do, or feel so guilty that they will never admit to any responsibility.

Inner work represents a radical act of disloyalty to the past. By sharing private confidences with another or in a group, and sometimes even simply by admitting them to ourselves, we may feel that we are betraying our parents, siblings, spouses, and friends. Our personal shame reflects the collective shame we feel toward our family. But with acknowledgment and support from people we respect, we can succeed in a correspondingly strong act of loyalty to ourselves.

Acknowledgment and support are crucial for the success of inner work. Receiving them as gifts from others gives our inner work substance and validity. But the most important source of acknowledgment and support is ourselves. Self-acknowledgment and support strengthen our commitment, refuel our inner resolve, and encourage us to strive, to go further on our inner journey.

In Summary

We have explored relationships in this chapter. It is hard not to draw the conclusion now that relationships fill in the gaps in our self-awareness. Relationships are so powerful at revealing our blind spots. But their potential goes beyond that. The healing fulfillment and richness of a powerfully loving relationship in our lives is one of the most precious blessings in life, and the man or woman who is surrounded by loving presence is indeed fortunate. Before we go on to look at stages of transition in a human lifetime, take a little time to review this important chapter using these questions for your inner-work practice:

1. Look at the differences between men and women and be aware of how these gender differences affect your relationships. What have you noticed already? What could be your blind spots about the opposite sex? About the same sex?

2. If you are in one (and if not looking back to past relationships or forward to future ones), what is your primary love relationship based on? What are its strengths and weaknesses? What is its potential, and where is your relationship headed?

3. If you have a wounded heart from a failed or broken past relationship, take steps to work through and go beyond it now, or as soon as you can, using the guidelines in "Ritualizing the End of a Relationship." Don't wait or hesitate!

4. Assess the support—the acknowledgment and encouragement —you have for your inner work, for your striving to fulfill yourself and to live your potential. Particularly identify relationships that confront, conflict, or do not recognize and acknowledge the values and pursuits that are important to you, and which may drain your energy.

5

Stages of Transition

Everything is in a process of change. The aesthetic, the pleasurable, the adorable, and the attractive will dissolve and vanish, leaving us only with impressions of their deliciousness, our memories of enjoyment, as well as the pain of their ineluctable absence. Clinging to impermanence leads to sorrow. Old age and death are the mantles over the manifest and changeable events in a human life. Seeking fulfillment in outward phenomena is futile, since our desire for fullness ultimately leads to an ending. Our lives move incessantly onward without respite, regardless of what we churn up in our wake or leave behind. We change and adapt in biological, physiological, mental, emotional, and psychological cycles through childhood, adolescence, adulthood, middle years, and old age—the unfolding of a human lifetime.

Thresholds of Maturity

An individual life passes through a series of stages that are marked by psychological thresholds, which seek expression in initiatory rituals. At each stage we enter a creative conflict that results in the choice to deepen in wisdom—fully incarnating at age seven or eight, the arrival of puberty around the age of 14, bridging adolescence and the twenties at 21, owning our life path at 28, meeting the challenge of selfhood at

35, attaining true adulthood at 42, resolution at the spiritual threshold at 49, the crucial point of choice at 56, giving back to the world at 63, and the complete turn of the wheel of life at 70. Each of these stages presents us with a specific challenge and, depending on how we meet the challenge, we enter the next stage with either renewed wisdom or unfinished business. Our choice dictates the backdrop and the circumstances of our lives over the ensuing years.

Most of us need to experience a certain level of disenchantment and frustration with life before we are motivated to turn inward. So we are unlikely to begin inner work seriously before our late twenties. Even that is unusually young. The usual catalysts for the inner journey are some form of disappointment, disillusionment, or dissatisfaction. When we have suffered the hardships of life long enough, pricked the bubble of fascination deeply enough, we have probably reached our thirties or forties. So that is usually when the inner journey begins.

But there seems to be no upper age limit to self-inquiry. People in their seventies or eighties have a different sense of time than younger people do. Each moment is precious to them. Whether it is a gift of biology or the tendency of the older personality, people who turn to self-discovery in senior years tend to be deeply inquiring and open. They bring a quality of mature respect to the process of healing and inner work.

Since most people engaged in the inner journey are in the thirties to fifties age range, we will focus in more detail on the thresholds that we meet then. The influence of the different thresholds can be felt before and after each specific age. But the age points of the thresholds are specific. The urges and impulses of biological and psychological development are stronger than the ego's preferences. Some people are offended by this; it seems to challenge their notion of being a free agent, and they feel they want to do what they want to do when they want to do it. When the stages do not seem to describe your life experience, consider what you might have missed before you dismiss it.

On the other hand, models are never beyond challenge. While most of us conform to these thresholds, some exceptions are inevitable. Certain people defy the rules of age, but they are the rare ones, and few of us fall into this category.

As we age we may feel that our body is betraying us. We dye our hair, buy anti-aging creams and serums, get Botox injections or face-lifts. All of this is a deep affront to the older person who is emerging from inside us and it disrespects the profound wisdom that comes from embracing senior years. Modern insults reflect this: behaving like a child is synonymous with behaving like an old woman. Even the pains of aging and illness teach us about our bodies and yield new wisdom about our physical form. When old people criticize young people, they project and reject their youthful self, which lives on inside them and embodies the youthful qualities of taking risks, dreaming, and fantasizing.

We tend to have strong feelings about our age. We want to be younger, or older, or to pass through certain ages more quickly or more slowly. We become defensive, so some of us are reluctant to reveal our age, our awareness of time passing, and our embarrassment, which hides the shame of leaving so many things unfinished in the past. But if we can surrender to the process of maturing, each threshold offers us specific gifts.

The 28-Year Threshold: A Radical Re-evaluation

At age 28 we face a complete re-evaluation of our lives. We rethink the suitability of our life circumstances and assess how satisfied we are with our lives and the choices we have made. If we are practicing inner work, then the examination will be conscious. If not, the process may be semi-conscious or even unconscious. This re-evaluation leads us to make a decisive choice. Either we recommit to the values and circumstances of our life and go on as we are, or we reject them and make radical changes. At this time many people marry, divorce, decide to have children, change careers, move into a new house, or make other far-reaching changes that create a new framework for their lives in the years to come.

The transition is generally turbulent, because our decision involves a conflict of impulses or desires. We feel pulled in two directions: one conforming and resisting change, the other rebelling and welcoming it, usually amid confusion and feelings of loss, fear, and frustration. The experience of the late twenties shows us that we do not yet know who we are, and the form our lives now take leads us nearer to, or further away from, our authentic self. The threshold of 28 offers a choice between courage and complacency, security or risk, rising to new challenges or staying put. For a time, we don't know which to choose. The solution lies in surrendering to a power greater than ourselves, whether we call it intuition, inner guidance, or destiny. Although it feels like a conflict of will, it is really the surrender of will—our personal will surrendered to a greater one. We are subject to archetypal forces at this time; a god holds us in the palm of his hand.

Inner work at the 28 threshold requires waiting and careful listening to ourselves and being aware of the force and variety of changes that are available to us. Our patience and tolerance can be sorely tested, as we wait in hope and see hope dwindle only to be replaced by fresh hope. Like fruit ripening on a tree, the form our life takes as we emerge from the 28 threshold should be allowed to define itself in its own time—rushing it only hinders the process. Waiting, deepening, tolerating the indecision and confusion, attending to what is happening inwardly, and sometimes "riding the storm" are the wisest responses.

The payoff is that we develop courage and inner strength. The outcome is invariably to choose between a deeper commitment to our old life or an entirely new direction. If we respond to the 28 threshold by learning openly and deeply, we enter our thirties with awareness and clarity.

The 35-Year Threshold: Worldly Challenge

At age 35 we face the challenge of becoming who we are *in the world*, achieving what we really want, and fulfilling our potential. This is the challenge of worldly accomplishment and ambition. Some of us meet this challenge head-on; others may reject the challenge out of a negative judgment or lack of self-confidence. Either way, the challenge offers us a choice. But unless we know who we are, we cannot know what we want. This inexorable logic escapes many of us, as we drive ourselves toward unhappiness nailed to the cross of compulsive achievement—martyrs to unawareness. What we do never satisfies us when we don't know who we are. So by age 36 or 37, many of us experience the inner murmurings of existential dissatisfaction and personal disillusionment. The world we find ourselves in may not be the world we imagined for ourselves. A robust sense of self, inner and outer harmony, and personal fulfillment may be lacking in our lives.

By our late thirties, we may experience an inner restlessness, which heralds a deep impulse to look at our inner self and accelerate our personal development. It is a process of preparation, but with new enthusiasm and impatience urging us to resolve historical issues. We feel the need to make decisions and deal with issues that we have procrastinated over or denied. We want to feel that we have made an impression on the world and achieved something lasting. We need to know or decide exactly what it is that we want in our lives—indecisiveness will no longer do. The preparation is in anticipation of our forties, in which the unresolved issues of childhood that we have carried over the preceding stages of our lives can only be sustained with great inner cost.

Inevitably we try to please our inner parents (really our inner parental images, see chapter 3), if not our outer ones, or by substitution our spouses or partners in our late thirties. Unconsciously or consciously we feel the need for transparent self-honesty, because our actions may be connected to duty and responsibility toward our dependants: our partners, wives, husbands, and children. Without self-honesty we cannot know how we truly affect them. We need to be honest enough to examine our conscious motives to discern how different they are to our core motives—what is true and real for us alone. Only then can we sense the presence of the disempowering voices inside us. We may feel compelled to process and heal ourselves of being less than authentic, less than whole.

No longer projecting hidden aspects of ourselves onto others, we live now from our wholeness. When we see that no one stands above us or has responsibility for us, we become our own primary authority. No longer can we blame others for our shortcomings or our failures,

and likewise no one else may take the credit for our virtues and suc-
cesses. Our challenge is to find the courage to stand alone, as we truly
are, and face life. This is the psychological condition of true adulthood. Without the qualities of self-referral, self-responsibility, and
inner authority, the term *adult* has only superficial meaning. To be
in touch with our inner wisdom and make decisions from our center
replaces our need for outer approval, prepares the way for personal
authenticity, and leads us to adulthood.

The 42-Year Threshold: True Adulthood

True adulthood is available to us around the age of 42, although most
of us are entirely unprepared for it. In a world where the invisible
qualities of the psyche and spirit are undervalued, few of us recognize,
let alone prepare for, this crucial threshold. The childhood patterns
that have survived in us unconsciously and have not been resolved are
ripe for working on at this stage, but there are many distractions for
us in the outer world. Our emotional conflicts become more prob-
lematic in our forties, but we possess the inner resources to resolve
them. We feel a strong compulsion to clear the unfinished business of
our earlier lives in order to meet the exacting challenges of the forties
with a minimum of psychological and emotional baggage.

We feel an immense lack in ourselves at this time if we have not
found a real sense of self, and out of that, a true sense of our meaning
and purpose. We sense the passing of time acutely and fear missing
the opportunities for growth that are available now because this could
mean missing them entirely, as we move on toward the challenges of
our middle years.

The biggest mistake we can make at this threshold is to seek the
solution to difficult challenges in the past. The past must be shed, not
re-enacted. Beginning new enterprises without a deep understanding
of what is required of us simply creates further obstacles. The inner
call is to move forward, but our dilemma is that we cannot move on
without resolving our historical patterns. They must be put behind us
because the future requires our mature involvement, not our childish
repetition.

This stage of life is misunderstood and mismanaged so often that it is popularly known as the "midlife crisis": the usually ill-advised attempt at deferring the challenge of adult maturation by regressing to a more youthful life orientation. Instead of deepening in his relationship, a man abandons his partner and family to embark on an affair with a younger woman in an attempt to repeat adolescent pleasures. Instead of withdrawing her projections onto the male world in a hard-won career, a woman perpetuates her dependence on men and patriarchal structures by staying in a soulless job and ignoring her inner urge to change. She sacrifices the development of her maturity and the ability to be self-referring, which is asked of her at this stage of life.

At least part of the reason for the midlife crisis is that there are gaps in development through earlier stages of life. Some challenges are deferred and some experiences are not entered into fully, which cause us to be "called back" to fulfill the demands of these stages before we can truly go on.

Inner work can bring us insight and clarity into a childhood of unfulfilled needs, teenage years that suffered from a lack of guidance and support, or how we avoided our twenties out of anxiety and the fear of failure. When some essential stages of life have not been lived adequately, we may have to reappraise our life. If our attachment is too strong, we must move toward the object of our desire. For example, the middle-aged woman who didn't experience life in her twenties, because she left her childhood home when she was young and immediately married, needs to ask herself what the unlived 20-year-old part of her needs to do to be fulfilled. Or the 40-year-old woman who missed out on her adolescence, because as the oldest child of the family she had to look after the younger children, needs to ask the same question of her adolescent self. Or the overintellectual man who has climbed the professional ladder, only to find he is middle-aged and in deep despair over his unhappiness and lack of an emotional life, needs to ask himself what he needs to do to develop emotionally, physically, or spiritually. Each of these circumstances offers a choice. Either we can shed our feelings, unfulfilled desires, and needs and release them, or, if we cannot do that, we have to find a way to fill in the gaps in our development with new experience and seek fulfillment for our needs and desires.

Great courage, surrender, and openness are required to meet this crucial threshold. The impetus toward change is overwhelming, if we can only harness it. Conversely, the strength of our resistance can be overwhelming. We may seek to avoid the challenges by capitalizing on our new confidence in our abilities. At this time of life we may have become accomplished in our chosen field, senior to others, and wiser in the eyes of our juniors. We may have crossed many outer thresholds in our career, in acquiring material possessions, in making money, in our marriage or partnership, and in raising children—all of which may have appeared daunting to us when we were younger. But if we look for further increase in our capabilities and acquisitions, if we seek individual fulfillment in our accomplishments and actions, we fail ourselves now.

Ambition and achievement, psychological self-esteem, and material security may be necessary to build our outward life on strong foundations. But the challenge now is *inner* maturation. It is comparable to our biological birth, but this is the birth of our psyche, our psychological birth following a gestation of 42 years in the world. We need to take full responsibility for our lives and rid ourselves of the old resentments that feed on themselves inside us. In particular, we must re-vision all that we consider negative in our lives and see how we have grown through our suffering. For many of us this is a hard challenge, but through this process of inner cleansing we reaffirm or discover our life's direction and purpose, and create a strong and lasting inner foundation for our life.

Many people begin the inner journey in their late thirties or early forties sensing this opportunity for impending change, but without necessarily knowing why. The inner impulse to meet the threshold of true adulthood can be stronger than any aspect of their outer lives. Outward conditions are far less important than the need to become adult and fulfill the psychological demands of their biological clock.

When we are aware of and responsive to these inner processes, the forties can be a liberating time. We are no longer caught by the obsessions of our early conditioning, no longer dominated by ambition (or our rejection of it) or compelled to walk the knife-edge of success and failure, as we did in our thirties. Even more distant are the insecurities, aspirations, and pretenses of our twenties. If we successfully cross the threshold of our early forties, we become a true adult—a psychologically developed individual with a solid sense of self. Through the forties we strengthen the self, seasoning the inner personality, as we draw closer to the spiritual threshold of the fifties.

The Fifties Threshold: Spiritual Gateway

At age 49 we cross a threshold into the spiritual realms. We may experience a renewed impetus to heal the unresolved past issues we still carry; if we deferred the challenge of the forties, we get a second chance. The strain of carrying the unresolved past is now too burdensome when fresh concerns clamor for our attention. If we missed the opportunity before, there may be a fresh urgency to clear up the past, once and for all, because we are now rapidly approaching the immaterial or spiritual period of our fifties.

For many of us, this may be the first time the spiritual has appeared in our lives. Having lived through five decades, we begin to anticipate our final years. We could live another fifty years, but it is more likely to be twenty or thirty more years. Life is clearly finite now that the seemingly endless possibilities of our earlier life have narrowed and dwindled. Now the choices are more limited, the gap is closing, and the distant horizon is closer than ever. Our perspective too is more limited. We will not be able to do everything that we thought we would do. Furthermore, we may feel we have spent too much of our time in activities and ventures we never imagined ourselves doing, or wasted our time on tasks that now seem pointless. We may have got stuck or lost our way in life. The fifties present us with the question "Is my life fulfilled?" and we cannot answer it satisfactorily in purely material terms. Whatever the extent of our achievements, we now face the immaterial, the invisible, the unknown. We know we will die one day, and that day is not as far off as it once was.

We feel the need to prioritize. We ask, "What is truly important to me?" and prune away those pursuits that we don't really have our hearts in and the many activities we have postponed that we may never now get around to doing.

When I turned fifty, I looked around at the paraphernalia I had collected over the years. I saw that a lot of me was "on hold." I was waiting for some imaginary day when I would have the spare time or the enthusiasm to take up the activities for which I had collected and hoarded the equipment, in some cases for years, without ever getting around to using it. I finally grasped that before I would do any one of these deferred activities, I would prefer to meditate, read, and spend time with my wife and children. Though it was a wrench, because I still felt my attachment to these other pursuits, I found the strength to let the paraphernalia go, along with the expectation that, one distant day, I would get around to doing these things. This process of letting go freed me and created valuable space, both inner and outer. I had more energy and heart for what I really wanted to do, as my life became more clear and simple.

In our early fifties we enter, if we are willing, an awe-inspiring stage of life. We realize, as the Sufis say, that we are in this world, but not of this world. In moments of silent communion we deepen in consciousness, experiencing ourselves as "other" than the body, the mind, and the personality. It becomes easier for us to fly beyond our individuality and experience the unity in all things. If we have practiced a spiritual discipline, our lives may now be blessed with less attachment, less clinging, less striving, and deepening acceptance.

The fifties are a time of great potential for spiritual realization; they contain a persistent invitation to spiritual experiences and initiation. Little wonder then that many feel great resistance to the challenges. The inner urge toward spiritual development may be ignored in favor of increased material ambitions, doing even more of what we can do very well already, leaving one's family and starting again raising another one (similar to the regression in the forties midlife crisis), or rejecting the call of the immaterial with more materialism—more money, more children, more relationships. But this is not the time for strengthening our attachment to increase. If *more* does come to us, we need to cultivate a looser relationship to it and become less attached. This is the time for simplification and lessening ourselves. Our lives may grow gloriously simple and direct in our fifties, as we set our hearts on spiritual goals.

In Hinduism a human life is considered in four stages. First is the *student stage*, which entails learning and training for professional, family, social, and religious life. Second is the *householder stage*, where the focus is on marriage, responsibility, earning a living, and supporting a family. Third is the *forest-dweller stage* of renunciation and spiritual practice. Finally, the *sannyasi stage* of total devotion to the spiritual and divine arises when non-attachment leads to the breaking of worldly ties.

At the fifties threshold, the person who has fulfilled the duties of a householder withdraws into the forest and "turns his face to God." The forest dweller focuses on spiritual development and grows in wisdom, drawing on life experience, relationship, love, and duty to develop spiritually. In the final stages of life, he adopts the robes of a monk and becomes a *sannyasi* and, renouncing all worldly things, enters into a life of total devotion to the realization of the true Self.

For the West, the essence of the Hindu stages of life is profoundly useful, because we have no equivalent model of our own. To make use of this model, we need to find our own way, a way to give it an expression that resonates with our culture. What is most important is that the spiritual search becomes our principal focus. When we do not give attention to our spirituality, we may be thrown into confusion. When we fail to address the demands of the fifties threshold, we suffer from an inner emptiness.

Gary was typical of the man in his mid-fifties who had missed the fifties threshold. He was a successful marketing consultant, happily married with two grown-up children. He enjoyed status, wealth, and job satisfaction in his profession and family life. He had a rich social network and had been successful in his various hobbies, including competitive yachting, in which he had won several prestigious trophies. Before he came to see me, his needs were mainly material. Acquisition and ambition dominated his life, and his success was undeniable. But old, suppressed material had begun to rise up into his consciousness. He had begun to feel again his early feelings of inferiority, inadequacy, and insecurity and the need for guidance, which had been lacking in his childhood. He felt guilty about a past, secret love affair that he had never revealed to his wife, and he had started to worry about his "difficult" relationship with his eldest son. But it was at work that he faced his most difficult challenge. For some time he had felt "hollow" in his professional role. While giving presentations, which he had always excelled at, he now experienced the irrational fear that he would be "seen through" or "found out" by his audience.

Gary explored his complex relationship with his father. Seemingly unable to be encouraging or supportive, Gary's father had been dominating and harsh. At times Gary had suffered from his father's physical assaults. One poignant memory seemed to epitomize this father-son relationship. Bent over his bike with a wrench in his hands, the nine-year-old Gary struggled to loosen a nut. Curtly his father snatched the tool out of his hands and performed the task silently and efficiently. The message was in the silence and the manner of the taking over—and in the only way in which the child Gary was able to make sense of the experience: "You can't do it; I am better than you; you are no good."

For nearly half a century Gary had carried the hurt of this experience and others like it in his unconscious. He had buried a sense of his own worthlessness deep inside and covered it over by developing his creative and practical abilities to a very high level in his professional life and leisure pursuits. Now an inner voice was urging him to move on. This urging was expressed in his irrational fears. Gary realized that these fears belonged to a nine-year-old part of him that felt invisible, unacknowledged, and unappreciated by his father, whom he desperately needed to "see" him. For the first time he began to listen to his inner self. Gary expressed and communicated what he needed from his father and could never get, how he felt about being treated like a nuisance and an idiot by his father through often unspoken but nonetheless potent criticism, and how angry he felt and how scared he was of expressing this anger to his father. Finally, how he had adopted a compliant and obsequious disguise to hide this powerful constellation of suppressed emotions. He felt his need and his fear, his shame and his sadness, his pain and his rage, and bit by bit he regained himself. By the end of his therapy he had become a 56-year-old man who was ready to meet the challenges of his senior years from a solid inner foundation.

Lena was typical of the woman in her early fifties who had missed the fifties threshold. She had a series of unfulfilling relationships behind her, including a broken marriage. She was uncertain about her personal boundaries because of psychological abuse in her early life, where she was made to carry the collective guilt and anxiety of her family. She had maintained a steady over-focus on finding the "right" man, but he had never appeared and she had begun to think that she might be happier and more fulfilled on her own.

She suffered from the cultural expectation that middle-aged women should have children and grandchildren and that their identity is to be found in the family they have provided. She remarked, "People think you are not a real woman until you have had children." As an older woman without children or grandchildren, she felt weak and undefined. She believed others considered her inferior and lacking. She felt socially excluded, even when her sense of personal empowerment and independence was strong. She reacted to this lack of acceptance with a growing inner sense of cynicism, jadedness, and judgment, which conflicted with her feelings of openness and compassion. While her inner issues remained unrecognized and unresolved, the inner conflict manifested in the outer world. Lena experienced the paling of her idealization of life and sunk into depression and withdrawal.

Her inner exploration showed her that this idealization was a reflection of the spiritual vision that lay ahead of her if she chose to embrace it. It is this vision of purity toward which we strive and which may inform us and guide us through later life. The dawning independence and deepening wisdom born of a lifetime of experience and awareness can enrich and strengthen us and make this time fulfilling and precious.

A Brief Summary of Further Thresholds

At age 56 we face an opportunity to choose and deepen that echoes the 28 threshold. We are offered the opportunity to redefine ourselves and establish who we are beneath any remnants of the "I" that we are still attached to. The saturnine gravity of this choice is less acute and painful than it was when we were 28, unless we have held on to too much and refused to cross the psychological and spiritual thresholds along our life's path.

In our early sixties, so long as we have avoided becoming embittered or cynical through the calcification of unresolved emotional patterns, we may experience the urge to "give back" to life, either through our creativity, in service to our wider community, or by finding a new role in our families. The sixties represent a natural balance and an outflowing of wisdom and life experience.

At age 72 we start again, refreshed with new innocence and genuine openness. It is the second age of the child, but with the wisdom and insight born from the life we have lived.

Responding to these stages in a human life with conscious awareness is a wonderful gift to ourselves and others. Appreciating the miraculous ability we have to witness and reflect, we can live fully, openly, and authentically. We can learn, as Confucius says, to "follow the dictates of our heart." With guidance from our center, our lives may become a journey of purification in order that natural wisdom flowers in our hearts. The trials and tests of our younger selves, immersed in the challenges of the thresholds of maturity, assume the deep significance of the journey of a soul returning to its eternal state. We may look back with fondness and compassion at our struggles, recalling our younger self grappling with what were at times overwhelming and all-absorbing challenges. As we pass through the dramas of our life, a new perspective, a new freedom and tranquility dawns in us, along with the deep knowledge that our true Nature is beyond all worldly transitions.

The person who lives through these changes from a spiritual perspective is enriched in a numinous dimension that the person who is merely outwardly oriented can only guess at. The problems we encounter with resistance, denial, and aversion are made easier when we live from this spiritual dimension. We learn to flow, deepen, and nourish ourselves through the changes, and participate fully in the growth and fulfillment of our humanness. The outer world is filled with significance and power. Through symbols, insights, ritual, and initiation, life is always teaching us.

Learning from Everything

As we deepen in awareness and acceptance, something extraordinary happens. Our inner acceptance reflects into the outer world and leads to a deepening surrender to *how things are*. We begin to learn profound lessons from life when things go well or when things go badly. Happy or sad, well or sick, succeeding or failing, we find our experience contains a nugget of illumination. Everything helps us to learn. But not all of us choose the way of awareness; inner work is not for everyone.

The *Tao Te Ching* tells us that a third of us are *life-seekers*; a third of us are *death-seekers*; and the other third of us are sleeping and content to remain asleep. This Taoist insight provides a sobering perspective and provides a basis for our tolerance, acceptance, and understanding of others just as they are.

Life-seekers are people who choose life and follow where it leads. They are the adventurers, the ones for whom a closed door simply waits to be opened. Since you are reading this book, it's likely that you are a life-seeker. Whether this is your first step in personal growth or you are a long way up the mountain, you have felt at some time in your life that, behind the appearances, there must be *more* to life. Life-seekers do not gloss over experience, because they know intuitively that there is a deeper truth. Life-seekers recognize life experience as opportunities for growth, and by embracing those opportunities they accept and revere life. Each experience is a gift that invites our open relationship to what is real and deepens our understanding. Whatever happens to us, whether fortunate or unfortunate, we can learn and grow, accepting the lesson with gratitude and grace.

Death-seekers are people who choose death, not necessarily literal death but self-destruction, negativity and nihilism, life-negating thoughts and activities. They are the destroyers of themselves and others, of feeling and experience. Death-seekers negate life's lessons and the search for deeper understanding. They moan and complain about life or appear superficially positive. They may say that everything is "fine," whether it is or not, and in so doing they "kill" the opportunity to feel, experience, and learn.

Some people are "sleepers," ignorant and unaware of life's myriad depths and meanings. They are satisfied because they know nothing else and they are not affected by, or open to, deepening experiences or insights.

We all know the sleepers. They are content with a very low level of awareness and consciousness. Satisfied with superficial pleasures, they do not search or strive. Their needs are simple, revolving exclusively around lower-energy concerns like food, shelter, and material possessions.

Death-seekers may be more difficult to distinguish. They are not necessarily Satanists or devil worshippers! Sometimes their negative behavior is concealed beneath a positive exterior. Those people—often personable, smiley, and talkative—who drain us and leave us feeling unexpectedly tired, angry, or critical, may well be death-seekers. And we need to trust our feelings about negative people and death-seeking behavior. Trusting our energy may be the only way to distinguish who they are.

Life-seekers are bright, positive presences in our lives. We learn and feel invigorated whenever we are with them. We know them intuitively and identify their bright life-affirming, enriching presence in our life. One old Japanese story tells a tale of love and equanimity, and affirms the spirit of the life-seeker. Zen master Hakuin lived in a little hermitage on a hill outside a village. He was renowned for his moral purity. A girl from the village became pregnant. She was reluctant to name the father of her child, but after much persuasion she admitted that it was Hakuin. After the child was born, the girl's parents, accompanied by a great procession of local dignitaries, carried the child up the hill to Hakuin's hermitage. They knocked loudly on the wooden gate, and Hakuin's face appeared at a little hatch. Declaring that the child was now the monk's responsibility, the girl's parents passed the baby through. Hakuin simply bowed and said, "Ah, so."

Hakuin took good care of the child, having milk, cloth, and everything that was needed brought up from the village. Some years later, while still young, the mother of the child became fatally ill. On her deathbed, she confessed that the real father was a young man who worked at the fish market. Once again the procession of dignitaries and the girl's parents climbed the hill to the monk's little hermitage. They explained the situation at length with plentiful apologies and appeals for forgiveness. Hakuin simply bowed, said, "Ah, so," and passed the child through the wooden hatch.

This story symbolically illustrates the open attitude of the life-seeker. Through changing perceptions and shifting circumstances we, like Hakuin, can remain constant and adapt to what life offers us. Regardless of whether we are giving or receiving, we can remain responsive and open. The movements through the wooden hatch are like a pulsating heart, opening and closing, expanding and contracting, reflecting the natural rhythm of changing life. Hakuin epitomizes the life-seeker. He shows us that we can learn from whatever comes our way.

A friend wrote to me recently with the sad news that a dear friend of hers had died tragically in a plane crash. In the depths of her grief, she perfectly expressed the choice of the life-seeker with these words: "I am learning in the experience of being in the depth of faith or the depth of despair."

Learning from faith or despair, practicing the "ah, so" of acceptance, and seeking life are positive responses to opportunities for growth. We learn from whatever life offers. When we learn from everything openly and willingly, we discover precious opportunities for understanding through grace and stepping stones to enlightened action.

℘

There is no precedent for our next subject. It is universal in its application, one of the aspects of inner work that cannot be avoided. Not only is it the core message of Christianity, but also it has been the subject of a flood of psychological and spiritual teachings, books, and methods in the modern era, because of its great central importance. The process that leads us to it must be welcomed with a full embrace while practicing rigorous discernment regarding its complete genuineness. Quite simply, everyone needs to relinquish resentment, abandon the desire to punish, renounce anger, and be inclined to forgive. Because the penultimate step into the second level of awakening is forgiveness.

The Seven Stages of Forgiveness

A single act of genuine forgiveness carries tremendous power. Holding on to injustices enslaves us to the past; forgiveness frees us from the past. We conceal feelings of anger and vengeance beneath the virtuous covering of justification to protect us from losing these feelings. Anger can be used as a defense against our deeper feelings of pain and despair. Deep resentment and anger reinforce our feelings of separateness.

Everyone has something and someone to forgive. Guilt and blame are endemic today. Negative states like bitterness, frustration, agitation, anguish, vengeance, and resentment are all expressions of our refusal to forgive. But they are hardly noticed, because everyone shares them. In spite of our pressing need for forgiveness, we are reluctant to truly forgive, because forgiveness erodes the foundation of our personality. Shedding blame, revenge, and a victim mentality threatens our small sense of self, so the wily ego invents ploys, intricate maneuvers, and pretenses.

Pretending to Forgive

When we don't really want to face up to the complexities and surrender of genuine forgiveness, we might try to "fake it." Denying our feelings of blame and vengeance, we may indulge in *fantasy forgiveness*. Pretending to forgive is a shallow byproduct of superficial thinking: a virtuously intended but misdirected attempt at healing, or simply the denial of our repression.

Often spiritual seekers want to be further on in their process than they really are. Forgiveness has become one of those benchmarks of personal growth that confer "spiritual rank." Some people practice *quasi-spiritual forgiveness*. We are impatient to forgive before we are ready. But our spiritual journey is an earthly journey that requires firm grounding. As we develop spiritually, we deepen in our humanness. We honor our feelings without judgment, notice our thoughts without always having to follow our desires, and practice awareness of ourselves and others. We should never use spiritual principles like these to hinder our personal process. Our awakening conforms to natural laws. If we try to get ahead of ourselves, the results are usually disastrous. Often we want to be somewhere we are not, someone other than ourselves, or in a life situation other than our own.

We may try *wish-fulfillment forgiveness*, hoping that, if we wish deeply enough, we will be able to forgive our oppressors, wipe the slate clean, and live in a haze of imagined virtue, as if it never happened. Wish-fulfillment forgiveness is an attempt to bypass the process of forgiveness. But however much we wish to forgive, forgiveness is only genuinely attained through certain necessary stages of inner healing.

Alison was a young woman who had a problem with revenge. She had a dominating, super-critical mother. She had grown up in an atmosphere charged with hate. As a child she had fought against her mother in passionate arguments and open bitterness, mirroring her mother's hate for her. Now, as a young woman, she had so deeply repressed this hatred that the inner voice of her mother had taken almost total control of her life. Nothing she ever did was good enough, and she nursed an almost total sense of her own worthlessness. When she discovered this, it came as a great shock to her. She had read in a self-help book that we should forgive our parents, so she immediately decided to take the easy way out that the book offered. When it didn't work, Alison asked me for help. I explained that *there is no shortcut or easy way to forgiveness*, because genuine forgiveness is a matter of heart-searching, deepening, allowing, and grace. Alison's work became my reference point for the crucial stages of forgiveness on the inner journey. For me, she epitomized the predicament of the modern-day seeker who has too many "easy ways out," and who is burdened by too much knowledge and too little wisdom. Forgiveness is a powerful inner process that consists of a number of stages.

The First Six Stages

The first stage is admitting that we are attached to vengeance. This means owning our feelings of anger and resentment, which often have their origins in the distant past. We must admit that we feel angry and then find out what it is that we are angry about before we can work on our attachment to revenge.

The second stage is exploring the complex emotions that prevent us from letting go of blame and anger and keep us feeling vengeful. Denying or concealing our deeper feelings binds us to the acts and the people we are unwilling to forgive. Our sense of offense, indignation, and outrage may be so powerful that we are unwilling to let them go, even when they cause us great suffering. Our sense of self and our self-importance conceal our victim stance, and hopelessness and self-pity are the adverse byproducts.

The third stage is becoming aware of our reaction: how we dealt with what happened to us and working with our desire for vengeance. We may fantasize about a series of acts that those who have hurt us would have to perform or ordeals they would have to endure to deserve our forgiveness. But in reality we do not really intend to forgive them, whatever their attempts to make amends.

The fourth stage is discovering our investment in blaming, and letting go of it. We may feel self-important and be unable to see our part or take responsibility for what we did to the other. Or we may feel justified in our vengeance. Or we may not want to take responsibility for our life and seek justification for revenge in our suffering. Or we may succumb to feelings of grief and anguish and find our identification and pleasure in these negative states stronger than our tendency toward joy and contentment. The question at the fourth stage is, "What is my investment in blaming the other?" and it is a hard question to answer honestly, unless we take deep responsibility for our negativity.

The fifth stage is finding out *who* is suffering most from our not forgiving, and the answer, of course, is ourselves. We see that we have become our own worst oppressor. The voice inside us, modeled on our mother, father, grandmother, teacher, or whomever it is who rakes over the events of the past, is our own. It is only we who prolong and feed it, so it is within our power to stop it. If we reach this stage of forgiveness, we begin to be empowered to truly forgive.

The sixth stage is the "juggling stage." We must hold all these levels of inquiry together simultaneously—knowing more, feeling more, revealing more, letting go of more, seeing more. Then we see that our sense of ourselves, our feelings of presence, exist only in the present and that this is the one thing that is constant in our lives. One fact becomes startlingly clear: we cannot let go of the past unless we learn how to forgive. Forgiveness is the way to our being who we truly are, the path to our freedom. The insight dawns in us that we have traded our self, the present moment, and our whole life for the dubious rewards of anger and revenge.

As Alison worked through these stages steadily and diligently, the contents of her inner dynamics of revenge became clear. She was already past the first stage, admitting she was angry and vengeful. The second stage, how she was holding on to her feelings, showed her how she justified her anger and hatred through the rational appeal to the unjust and undeserved treatment of what her mother did to her and the horrendousness of that. The third stage revealed how her demonstrations of worthlessness were intended as vengeful retribution toward her mother, who had to deal every day with her daughter's failing life, lack of success, and chronic misery. This was Alison's investment in preserving her vengefulness—payback, to hurt her mother to get her back for what she had done to her, which was the insight of the fourth stage. The realization of the fifth stage, that she, Alison, was the one suffering, not her mother, took a little more time to reach and to feel, but when she reached it the reality of the insight released an emotional catharsis in her that was accelerative and healing. The sixth stage, juggling, comprised an incubation period of deepening understanding, abundant insights, and profound inner growth for Alison. She understood that revenge, and her attachment to it, would forever hold her back from the freedom and happiness she desired, unless she jettisoned it. She persisted and prepared for the act of grace, the event beyond her conscious control that always distinguishes genuine forgiveness.

As we deepen in the "juggling stage," the past gradually peels away and separates from the present. We have been living as if the wrongs that were inflicted on us in the past were happening now. This sense of distance has not previously been there because we have replayed the tape of our past oppression, kept the memories alive, and superimposed the past on the present. Now we know that was then and this is now—and distance grows between us and what is unforgiven.

This gives us one of the most crucial insights of inner work: *No one but ourselves causes our distress or is responsible for our problems.* The present issue is always within our power to do something about. This insight empowers us to change.

It is always in our power to affect an issue that arises in the present. This insight empowers us to change and ultimately facilitates our personal transformation.

Forgiving Ourselves

Sometimes we need to forgive ourselves. I talked with a woman in her mid-fifties who, in spite of many years of inner work, was unable to let go of her feelings about an abortion she had in her early twenties. I asked her if she had ever spoken to the spirit of her unborn child and, looking surprised, she said she hadn't. I asked if she knew a special place where she could go to do that. She said that she sometimes visited a powerful and beautiful spot on a mountain with gurgling streams, huge rocks, and little waterfalls.

"Could you go there," I said, "and talk to your baby, talk to her spirit, ask her why she was conceived and whether or not she forgives you? Look at the lives she has affected. See if you can understand the effects and purpose of her brief life in the womb."

She visited her special place, performed rituals, and spoke to the spirit of her unborn child. Her questions were answered by an inner voice—the voice of her unborn baby's spirit—and it never blamed her for what she had done. She recalled how her pregnancy had deepened her relationship with her mother and her sister, how her friends and family had reached a more real level of being and awareness from the experience with strong emotions and searching questions. After three or four visits and conversations with her unborn child, she was able to forgive herself and feel released. The results were palpable. She was lighter in her spirit and easier in her mind and body. She said that it was as if a stone had been removed from her heart. Through her communions with her child, she had been able to forgive herself.

Guilt and shame, mixed with grief and often self-punishment, represent a formidable challenge, but essentially the stages of forgiveness must be worked through in the same way whether we are forgiving someone else or ourselves.

Forgiving the Dead

Sometimes we feel blame, revenge, or hatred toward someone who has died. We may think that we have missed the opportunity to express our grievances, that death has robbed us of the chance to say what will forever be unsaid, to express what we can never express, and to clear up the issues that will remain inside us with no possibility of resolution. Many of us give up on ever being able to forgive (or be forgiven), and some part of us "dies" along with the deceased person. Anger and blame create a powerful attachment that we cannot shed, without forgiveness.

This identification with the dead person—the fact that both have died in different ways—holds the key. We can speak with the spirit of the dead person, converse with them just as we might talk to an incarnated person, because the one who has died lives on inside us. While we hold on to the unsaid, unexpressed, and unresolved issues that are between us and the person who has died, we keep them alive in a limbo state. Unable to let go of the issues, we are also unable to release the person. Our spirit goes out of us, and a part of us remains suspended between the worlds.

Speaking to the dead person's spirit allows us to release them from the powerful attachment our negativity creates. Following the act of forgiveness, a flood of positive feelings fills us when we have let go of our anger, grief, or revenge toward the dead person. For a while we hold them in this positive way, before releasing them altogether.

The Seventh Stage

In the seventh and final stage of forgiveness, we reach a deep acceptance of what has been done to us by others. Whatever the deed and whoever the perpetrator, forgiveness enables us to take back the power we have lost. We relinquish our right to reject, blame, and hate what happened or who did it. Instead we become aware of how we have grown, not in spite of but through the experience.

Deep acceptance is not condoning what has happened; it is not saying that a wrong is somehow right. Rather it is the recognition that what has happened is now past and we are going to suffer no longer.

Practicing forgiveness leads us to a profound realization: withholding forgiveness maintains the illusion of the small self, our separate, unconnected, opposed identity that fights for survival in a hostile world and defends itself with negativity and concealed aggression. When we do not forgive, we separate ourselves from life. Forgiveness is fiction, because there was never anything or anyone to forgive. The presumption of one person forgiving another for what they did to them is a rational argument riddled with spiritual inaccuracies. At the deepest levels of working with forgiveness, we can see that the idea of a separate entity is transparently false.

Forgiveness provokes the profound acceptance of ourselves. We find that we have been carrying outer forms of madness, blame, anger, and grief that merely mirror the shadow forms of our inner world. Forgiveness permeates our inner world with love and clarity.

A single act of genuine forgiveness carries tremendous power. To forgive once truly is to forgive all. Practicing forgiveness frees us from repeating experiences of pain and outrage, sorrow and grief, and empowers us to live freely, joyfully, and spontaneously in the world.

In Summary

This chapter has been about the thresholds and life transitions we pass through as we mature inwardly, paying attention to the invisible world and exploring our self-contraction (or small sense of self) more deeply, particularly with regard to the momentous process of genuine forgiveness. Consider where you stand in relation to the material discussed (not forgetting that biological age and inner maturity may conflict). Here are some questions to guide you in your inner practice:

1. Review the thresholds of maturity you have already passed through: How did you move on? What are your dominant feelings and emotions about the thresholds? What held you back? Are you stuck in any of the past thresholds?

2. What is the age threshold ahead of you, and what preparation is necessary for you now?

3. Write a series of statements from the point of view of your ego self. Now assess the activities that involve, perpetuate, and strengthen your ego. What can you do about them?

4. Looking back at your life, identify some examples of death-seekers and sleepers. As a life-seeker, what experiences have you learned from? Celebrate the most profound or the most important of these in poetry, drawing, dance, or movement. Express your gratitude and your reverence humbly and privately by creating a beautiful ritual that is known only to yourself.

5. Follow the seven stages of forgiveness through carefully. Now what is left for you to forgive?

6

A New Revolution
in Awareness

The Thinning of the Veils

The final stages of personal work bring our hardest challenges. In the crucible of change that is inner work, we finally break the chains that bind us. Confusion and resistance may rise up stronger than ever, as we suffer the death throes of our attachment to the small self. We meet the tests of faith, engage in healing the original wound, experience unconscious change, and embrace our wholeness. But before any of this can happen, the veils must thin.

These veils form the barrier that separates us from the world and the world from us. They are the mists of lethargy, the numbing to emotion, the hypnosis of habitual behavior, assumptions and expectations, the deadening of suspicion and resistance—all the anti-life aspects of character that have served as our protection since our early years. We have carried so much unresolved material, so much baggage of unsaid, unrecognized, and unrealized words, thoughts, and actions. We have become stooped and frightened. We have concealed ourselves beneath our coverings.

When our veils thin, we encounter the play of opposites—opening to hurt reveals the way to our wholeness; opening to emotional pain reveals the way to pleasure; and opening to confusion reveals the way to clarity. Each of these apparently negative conditions reveals its opposite, positive state.

And we find we have unsuspected allies—fear and resistance.

Fear is a friend who shows us the way to courage. When we stop struggling against it and allow ourselves to experience it directly, fear invigorates and excites us. This vigor stimulates the heart and cultivates the courage and unflinching self-honesty we need to truly confront ourselves. Courage can be gentle—encouraging and sustaining—or ferocious—discerning and uncompromising. Courage leads us to the very edge of fear, where our next challenge lies and our growth takes place.

The small self defends and maintains its dominance by resistance. At this stage, resistance is of two kinds: either intensifying the defensive strategies that worked in the past, or creating entirely new strategies to hinder us. As the mind reacts fearfully to the new revolution in our awareness and creates every possible resistance to growth and change, our attachments grow stronger. But resistance can be positive, shaping us and providing the challenges that lead to personal power. Opposition and struggle lead us to deep inner confidence and peace, strengthening our psychic muscles, developing our skills in being, revealing the limits of our freedom and awareness; all giving us the opportunity to test ourselves by giving us something to push against.

Our old character experiences the release of attachments as a kind of death. Our character reacts to the "threat" by intensifying its dominant traits in an effort to reestablish itself. For example, an intellectual person becomes increasingly analytical or an emotional person becomes more passionate. This may happen in unconscious ways. Latent ambition may come into the foreground of life; our need to fulfill unexplored desires may arise with overwhelming force.

In the last stages of my own personal work, I felt tremendous urgency and responsibility about finding my vocation in life. I was anxious and guilty about not achieving. I felt that I should get back into the marketplace and make something of my life. I almost aban-doned my inner-work practice and relocated to a big city where the opportunities were more plentiful. But I was aware of my primary character defense—*industrious-overfocused*: I valued doing more than feeling, work over pleasure. This was my dominant characteristic and it had been the keynote of my early inner work. It was my workaholic father's legacy to me: *you can always do better; you can always do more.* How could I have forgotten this? Yet this sudden impetus to apply my energy to work in the outer world almost overwhelmed me before my life-transforming breakthrough.

The allure of a new career, a new relationship, or the urge to travel are powerful distractions that commonly arise before the veils thin. As we stay with our self-exploration, the whole smorgasbord of resis-tance—confusion, doubt, cynicism, judgment—intensifies in a des-perate attempt to thwart the healing balm of deep acceptance and clarity. We become increasingly tricky in our inner work, emphasizing the positive qualities of unconscious avoidance in order to manipu-late ourselves and others into colluding with us. If we are courageous, we seize the opportunity to reveal our deep inner conflicts, the resis-tant voices of our inner selves, and the constant turbulent conflict of strong emotions.

Deep inside we are undergoing a purging of fear, anger, and nega-tivity. Life can become unbearable. Sharing life with someone going through the thinning of the veils is a tough challenge. Unpredictable mood swings, pettiness, irrational behavior, egotism, and antisocial behavior are all ways in which the small self communicates through the suffering of its death throes.

For many of us, the thinning of the veils is intensely claustropho-bic. When our excuses and justifications fall way, we see that our life is filled totally by the conditioned past. Psychologically we regress to increasingly earlier states, usually while maintaining the demands of our adult lives. One seeker commented:

Everything became mother. At work and at home, her hands, her feel, her ways … I was overwhelmed by the immense influence of my early life. The past filled my awareness and closed in on me. It visited me every moment, inhabited my waking day in my mannerisms, actions, motivations ... it was all mother.

When the veils thin, at last we see beyond the limits of our conditioned personality. Gradually and gently we arrive at the heart of truth, through confronting our last remaining attachments to our small self.

The Last Grains of Attachment

The final stages of the first level of awakening are intense and concentrated. Like the last grains of sand trickling through the narrow section of an hourglass, time is running out and the end approaches. Our self-image goes through an inner revolution as the last grains of attachment to our small sense of self fall through. Confusingly, we feel waves of elation alongside pangs of loss, as our grief for what is old, past, and dying is matched by our excitement about what is being newly born.

A deep inner conflict emerges now. Our despair is deepened by the profound experience of new discoveries, and we become caught between futility and habit. We know it is no longer fulfilling to carry on as before, though the last remnants of our emotional and behavioral habits urge us to conform to the dictates of the past. But we are not yet quite prepared to enter a new life, because we don't know what it is. The future is as unknown as the past we have shed is known. We feel unsure. Our next step is uncertain. Between the known and the unknown there is only trust ... and faith.

The controversial 1977 movie *Exorcist II: The Heretic* strikingly portrays the testing of faith. One scene in the film left an unforgettable impression on me when I was young. The actor Richard Burton plays Father Philip Lamont, a priest who is struggling with his belief. His search takes him to Africa to a confrontation with a medicine man named Kokumo. Before he can help, Kokumo insists that Lamont cross a moat filled with lethally sharpened wooden stakes, set vertically just under the surface of the water. In dreams, which movies resemble, a moat symbolizes crossing into a new level of consciousness. It represents the risk of death (to the old consciousness) and the promise of new life and awareness. It is not to be entered into lightly. Our anxieties, fears, insecurities, and attachments must all be left behind. We can take nothing with us. Lamont realizes that he must meet this test of faith. Barefoot, he takes the first step, and the stake bores straight through his foot. In tremendous pain he takes the second step, and with blood pouring from both feet now, he falls flat on his face in front of Kokumo. Looking down, he sees that his feet are miraculously whole.

Now in a test of faith we too must put our trust in the unknown and in our innate wholeness. Our tests, like our inner journey, are psychological rather than physical. Developing our awareness and deepening in our commitment help us to resist the temptation to fall into despair or elation. Despair develops from the intense resistance that tries to convince us that inner work is futile, misdirected, and ineffective. The small self takes advantage of this chink in our armor that hesitancy, however slight, creates. Our commitment to ourselves must be total, or despair comes streaming in to prevent us from fulfilling the promise to change. Elation develops from our attachment to the gains we have acquired from our inner work so far. This is one of the hardest challenges to meet. We must let go of *everything*, including our attachment to all that we have achieved so far in inner work. Predictably, our small self rails against this. This has been the downfall of many on the inner journey.

Our faith in the unknown sustains and guides us through the lurching extremes of negativity and positivity, confidence and uncertainty, despair and elation. As we endure this inner revolution we approach the edge of the known, the border where spirituality and psychology meet.

In the process of self-discovery, one challenge remains, but that challenge is absolute and final, and it represents the ending release, a discontinuity with the false character and personality that is based on past events, behavior, and self-image. This release even challenges our sense of reality. Inside us we discover a deep inner division, the wound from where all other wounds have sprung; the theme and source of our conflicts, protection, and basic unhappiness. It is now the final obstacle between us and our wholeness. Now, for the first and only time, we are able to heal it.

Healing the Original Wound

The healing of our original wound is the single most important event in personal work, because it leads directly to personal wholeness. We are deeply divided because there is a fundamental separation, an inner fault line, within us. While this fundamental division exists the original wound remains, and we suffer the pain of internal conflict.

The original wound is the axis of the themes of suffering that have dominated our lives. For the person seriously engaged in inner work who has healed and released emotional-behavioral patterns and persisted in inner exploration, the inner path leads inevitably to this point where all the conflicts, confrontations, dissension, and struggles of the duality of life have their origins.

The symptoms and signs of the healing of the original wound are many and various, and as individual and unique as the individual experiencing them. However, some common themes are deep emotional confusion; intense sadness, pain, or anger; feelings of ambivalence or reluctance to meet the new inner challenge; intangible fear; and edginess, danger, and uncertainty.

We can feel ambivalent about our relationships. Synchronous happenings occur, commonly meetings with people who seem to resemble our mother, sister, father, or other significant person from our lives. We become acutely aware of our character and personality, particularly in its defensive function, in the way in which it represses us and limits our zest, spontaneity, and expression, along with a background feeling of undiscovered life and new potential for experience, intensity, and passionate engagement.

We may have dreams in which we return to school or university, symbolizing our need to learn what is necessary to reach the threshold that now lies ahead. We may have dreams in which we are distant or unfamiliar with friends and relatives (this may also happen in waking life). Dreams of wholeness, featuring the number 4, *mandalas*, squares, rectangles, and circular structures are also common. Symbols presaging wholeness enter our process in waking life, too. A change in our psychological makeup is coming about, a gathering of parts, the meeting of the inner female and male, and the emergence of our personal wholeness.

The healing of the original wound is a process that will take as long as it needs and it is characterized by intensity and turbulence, as is any full-scale life transformation. But let us be very clear: this is *the* life transformation; it will never happen again. It is the psychological equivalent of our biological birth, which is why it is sometimes called the second birth. As the first birth was to the outer world, so this birth is to the inner world.

Everything is thrown at us and we are well advised to desist from action and decision-making, as well as from avoidance or distraction. Our inner healing is most important, and our inner intensity, our feelings of being shaken, the emergence of historical shreds, arises with uncommon strength and presages our realignment with our true center.

In spite of the intensity and discomfort of this time, we should not be tempted by superficial inner work or "doctoring the scar." By not working deeply enough to heal it, such inner work overlays and conceals the original wound in the unconscious, making it even more damaging. This sort of approach is short-sighted; the positive results, such as they are, are fleeting, and we return to reshuffle the same material because it was not worked through thoroughly before. Denial or ignorance preserves the inner schism, and we become numb to its effects.

Stopping inner work at this stage represents a partial journey, not a full awakening from the spell of the personality. However, if we do stop we are substantially more aware than most, so we are unlikely to be challenged on our accomplishments. We can occupy the position of "fake guru" reasonably convincingly. When Fay reached an advanced stage in her personal work, she stopped practicing inner work to concentrate on her career. Her reasoning was that she was taking a break. A "break" at this advanced stage usually means the "end," but she proved to be the exception to the rule:

I made every possible excuse to myself for finishing with inner work just at the moment when I could feel that something momentous was about to happen. Deep down I was scared, terrified of the change it augured. I told myself that I was too young to change, "not ready yet." I needed to concentrate on my career. I took my energy out of inner exploration and applied it to my work and a disastrous love affair. I told myself I was carrying on inner work in a different way. I bought spiritual books, discussed personal psychology, and extolled to friends the benefits of self-exploration. For some I become a "wise friend" who they could turn to for valued guidance, but inside I knew that I was more anxious to talk about inner change than to live it. While I achieved some "cred" amongst my friends for my psychological maturity, I suffered inner torment and confusion for my hypocrisy. Although I was admired and even envied by my peers, I felt empty. I had paralyzed my work toward authenticity, while expounding its benefits and living a lie, because I was afraid. I played my games of falsehood and evasion, and no one knew what I was doing. I had gone further down the inner road than any of them, but not quite the whole way. Eventually I fell into utter despair and self-loathing, and I found my way back to inner work.

Fay acted out her original wound in a dramatic fashion. In the introduction to this book (see "A Crack in the Fabric"), I referred to the wrestling match that goes on between the self that wants to heal and change and the self that wishes to get through inner work healed but unchanged. This is the first presentiment of the original wound. Fay began with it and it remained with her until, after acting it out, she committed herself totally to releasing her attachments and shedding her emotional patterns.

Tales of falling at the final fence, of resistance and failing faith, of huge efforts and bravura strivings that result in psychological defeat make fascinating reading. Some of these tales I will have to save for another time. The questions we must ask now are, "How does lasting change occur? What is the experience of the few (and swelling number) of those who break through their personalities once and for all?" I often say that, while we are distracted in the practice of inner work, we are overtaken from behind by change. It happens when we are least expecting it, indeed when we have forgotten all about it. The walls of our psychic prison are so tight and the adventure of our self-discovery so absorbing that we don't notice that what we have been seeking all along is emerging from "behind the drama," out of the shadows of our unconscious world.

A Gate into New Consciousness

We have been working through a long day's journey into night... and the night too has been an ordeal of the darkest, most challenging kind, a complete heart-searching. Through a process of gradual ripening, we have grown in clarity and understanding. Now we are set toward an inner revolution, a total change. Like watching the sun slowly rising, we are about to witness the dawning of the newest day of our life.

And yet we only notice inner change *after* it has happened: the change itself happens without our knowing. Often change follows powerful discontent with our work: complaining, perhaps, or a painfully slow period of development in which we seem to be getting nowhere. Like ascending a mountain when all we can see is the far-off peak, we climb on until imperceptibly we realize that we have arrived at our destination. Similarly, we perceive change in the inner world as a barely visible movement forward in the growth of our awareness and the flowering of ourselves, in the gentle but undeniable expansion of our awareness and perception, in deepening understanding and increased clarity.

But change doesn't appear when we focus our attention on it. Change may be on the distant horizon for some time before we feel we are anywhere near it. Later we may become obsessed with it, looking for signs that we are getting somewhere, making progress, getting a little closer to our goal. Only when all these signs have gone, along with our concern with them, does anything seem able to happen. After all, life *is* change; it is only our personal contraction, our rigidity, and our resistance that prevents us being carried in its flow.

Many times I have sat with a seeker who looks at me in a new way and declares that *it* has happened … without her noticing, beyond conscious attention … the change is real. Change seems to overtake us when we are least prepared for it, without our knowledge, when our ego defenses are down and our habitual modes of behavior are surpassed, when we are not in the driving seat of our ego.

The powers within us that bring about change are deeply unconscious and housed within dark caverns of the soul. It is as if parallel events have been occurring in another dimension. While we were absorbed in our waking awareness, we have crossed a bridge without knowing it. Like driving on the motorway and realizing that we haven't been aware for the last twenty miles, we awake to find ourselves here, in a new place. We have crossed the shining bridge that lies between the worlds and entered a gate into new consciousness.

We may feel inspired to communicate this experience at the same time as feeling the futility of doing so, because we know that everyone has to do it for themselves in their own way. Everyone's experience is unique. Nevertheless, through poetry, painting, dance, music, or simply telling our story, we may express the elation and liberation of initiation and change. The discovery is always unique; there is never any other when we are awakened beyond our personality; there is never any other moment; there is only now, only peace, only "I." Yet we feel compelled to communicate our experience to others to complete some mysterious circle, to fulfill some inner promise, to discharge some unconscious duty. After all, we are deeply connected to the other souls who have made their own unique journeys.

If we follow this urge, we enter the realms of art in its original sense. The etymological root of the word *art* is "to fit together or join" or "to complete." In the cave paintings of Lascaux and Altamira in Europe we see how human beings first expressed this urge when they attempted to depict Earth mysteries. These caves have been called the cathedrals of the Stone Age, the first temples. Our ancestors felt compelled to express their deep inner discoveries by painting in the darkest reaches of deep caves. Sacred art is an attempt to connect the world of the spirit and the divine with the conscious world. The darkness is an apt metaphor for the deep, buried place inside ourselves from which divine wisdom flows. Art bridges the worlds and expresses the inexpressible. In the act of creation the artist is poised between the inner and outer worlds, connecting both by surrendering unselfconsciously to inspiration.

Now we have dispelled our inner darkness; we are consummate artists in whom life is art and art is life, seamlessly connected. Perfection is the artist disappearing, leaving only his art. The spiritual teacher J. Krishnamurti said that the highest point of intelligence is acting anonymously and spontaneously out of inspiration and intuition. In the relationship between the self and transformation, a certain detachment is crucial as we near the threshold. We must be careful that the ego doesn't snatch away the accomplishment by hijacking transformation for personal pride or self-aggrandizement. If there ever was one, this is the moment for resisting self-admiration.

The momentous event of unconscious change leaves our attachment to the old self behind. We transcend the self that seeks aggrandizement. Art, like inner work, opens us to a spontaneous, inspired depth in which the individual personality is overcome by the impersonal nature of truth. The expression of art, like change through inner work, comes from within us: the secret was only waiting to be discovered.

This unconscious potential is the key for understanding change in inner work. Change is unconscious because *we already are as we are.* It is less an alteration and more a realignment, the shift from a false to a real center of energy and truth. When we discover it, this is one of the "secrets" that we feel reluctant to impart, not wishing to spoil this vital experience for the new seeker.

The process of self-discovery is a complex journey of self-acknowledgment and personal healing. There is no cure-all moment, only the culmination of a series of moments of revelation, acceptance, and understanding. At the end of the process, when the veils of dishonesty and the mists of illusion are removed, we truly see ourselves in our wholeness.

Remembering and Wholeness

As our defensive character diminishes, we begin to *remember*. This remembering is not merely mental, but physical, emotional, and energetic. We begin to yearn for something long forgotten, something that has been lost: our authentic self.

Practicing inner work has taught us to experience the riches of life again, through honoring our breath, treasuring our bodies, and seeing Nature with fresh, innocent eyes. We appreciate our abilities, talents, virtues, relationships, and abundance. But there is a greater challenge even than appreciating the things that we love and admire most about ourselves and others.

The greater challenge is to ask ourselves, "What would I change about me and my life?" When we move to the edge of our aversions, negativity, and inner restlessness, we discover our greatest gift, which has usually remained unrecognized. To accept this gift, we must work with our attitude toward what we don't like—our aversions. This is now our central challenge. It may be physical or emotional pain, lack of money, loneliness, anger, lack of meaning, or feelings of futility. Whatever we like least about ourself conceals our richest gift.

To change our attitude to ourselves and our lives, we must center ourselves in the heart. By shifting our center from the mind to the heart, we stabilize in unconscious change. Instead of focusing on what we would most like to change, we become aware of our attitude toward it. Instead of mentally distancing ourselves from the hated object, we invite the hated thing in and, by getting to know it, we grow to accept and love it. Nothing can withstand the power of the heart. Each of us has a challenge. It may be a speech impediment, a challenging habit, a shameful secret, actions we regret, hidden anger, lack of emotion. For some the impediment is outward and visible; for others it is inward and unseen.

When Natalie started attending my workshops, she presented a singular image of a lonely, needy young woman, seemingly intent on creating rejection. Physically almost everything about her radiated repulsiveness and ugliness. She loped with a depressed air; her hair was lank and dirty; she had a strong body odor; and when she ate, she habitually dropped particles of food on her blouse. She had a particularly repelling habit of removing her grease-stained spectacles and kneading her knuckles deep in her eye sockets, eliciting a loud squelching sound. Her story, as somehow expected, was horrific and heart-rending. She was the only child of two busy, career-minded parents who were regularly absent from home and who gave little or no attention to Natalie when they were there.

Her memories of her father revolved around his sadism. Dangling her over a cliff wall at the beach, he would feign rescuing her from falling. Natalie vividly remembered the panic and her almost unbearable terror. Her memories of her mother were no better—a cold, undemonstrative woman, dedicated to her essentially intellectual relationship with her husband. Natalie recalled her having little maternal sense or instinct.

Natalie had manifested a life in which people treated her as she expected to be treated—without love, hurting her sometimes (a form of attention), distant, and cold. In the workshops I noticed participants recoiling from her, but each was reluctant to be the one who overtly rejected her.

Over the months something curious happened. The group participants grew closer to Natalie until they deeply accepted her. In fact, their acceptance of her seemed to exceed her acceptance of herself. I am sure she continued coming more for the friendship and human contact she felt at the workshops than the inner exploration. I noticed people offering her small tokens of kindness, consideration, and love. She grew under the influence of nourishment and nurturing. Her face became more open and expressive; she smiled more. Even her physical appearance changed, as she became less slovenly and depressed-looking.

Natalie was everyone's rejected self, the one we don't want to acknowledge or recognize; that ugly part of ourself we would rather was *not*.

Our central challenge calls to us like an annoying child pulling at us our clothes, knocking our arm or calling our name repeatedly at the most inconvenient moments. Imagine that you repeatedly turned to this child and said, "I'm fed up with you, just go away." What kind of relationship would you have with this child? How could you restore and heal this relationship? Re-owning the rejected part of ourselves is like taking the child back into our heart, like speaking to that child with love again. It requires forgiving ourselves, being in our own hearts, loving and present.

When we re-own the part of ourselves we have pushed away, we find that what we denied, hated, and tried to separate from—labeling it "myself," "illness," or "nuisance"—is precisely what we need to complete us. Without it we can never be all that we are, but with it we can become whole. The greatest of life's gifts lies hidden in what we most reject and want to change about ourselves. But it doesn't need to be any different; only our attitude toward it needs to change. Now as we remember, we draw closer to our wholeness and we find that this part of us is our greatest gift.

In Summary

This chapter concludes the first stage of human awakening. It signifies a momentous achievement in human development with personal, collective, and global consequences. Each individual who leads a life of authenticity has crucial significance for humankind as a whole. Personal inner work is only a part of inner exploration and the inner journey. Beyond personal change lie the challenges of authentic transformation and spiritual consciousness. Before we move on to the second stage, allow a little time to ponder these questions and exercises:

1. The defensive strategies that separate you from the world act like veils of separation and concealment. Identify your personal anti-life strategies—for example, lethargy, emotional numbing, hypnotic habits, deadening to experience.

2. Separation and wholeness, pain and pleasure, confusion and clarity—how have these opposites been connected in your life experience?

3. Befriend fear and find courage—what does this mean to you, and how can it help you in your inner work?

4. What are some personal examples of inspiring tests of faith in your life?

5. When you find yourself at the thinning of the veils, resist self-aggrandizement by not giving into despair or elation and letting go of your attachment to the fruits of your inner work. How do despair and elation habitually appear in your life? What is your resistance?

6. What is your original wound?

7. Take up sacred art to express, reflect, and deepen in your inner journey—drawing, painting, writing poetry or prose, dance, movement, music. Express ripeness, resistances, and the riches of inner work.

8. The authentic self reflects back to us that we already are as we are. Use this as a focus for meditation and contemplation.

Stage
TWO

The Transformation into Authenticity

7

Becoming Who You Are

Change leads to transformation, which is a radical, permanent shift. During the first stage of inner work, change takes place in often pleasing, sometimes painful ways. But the deeper and most fulfilling kind of change is to become more who we truly are. Following the completion of that part of the inner process where we arrive at inner wholeness, we come to a threshold where we can make the radical choice to be ourselves, to be authentic.

After two years of personal inner work, I approached that threshold of transformation and asked myself the key question, "Why should I choose to go on?" I was faced with the end of my prelude and the dawning of the psycho-spiritual journey I was destined to undertake.

I knew that I had resolved many aspects of my personality, endured a stock-taking and overhaul of my character defenses and habitual patterns, and become increasingly aware of who I really was. Issues that had caused me much suffering and confusion, such as my feelings of being unlovable, my lack of confidence, my sense of unworthiness, and my victim identity were, either wholly or partly, behind me. I had discovered that I was talented, capable, lovable, strong, and well equipped for life and its challenges. The question now was what should further motivate me to follow the path of loss and personal discovery when it posed such a threat to the attractive vehicle of "me-ness." Why should I choose to pull off my defensive "skins" when I could get by in life, enjoy myself, and probably succeed abundantly in a solid ego? Why would I choose to go on with inner work?

Up to now, inner work had entailed removing the sick skins of a half-formed ego, a less than whole person. But now, if I continued, it would take on an entirely different tone and atmosphere, because the motivation would be to overcome the egoic identity entirely. Whereas before the ego was being built up, now I would be taking it down. The new journey was toward essence, authenticity, and real relationship. My work on the personality had been merely the preparation and groundwork.

My appreciation of this kind of reasoning certainly helped, but what motivated me to go on was simply the conviction that I was following my heart's path—it wasn't really a choice anymore; it was my destiny.

The Bridge of Authenticity

The bridge of authenticity leads you to a place where personal inner exploration reaches its zenith and spills over into a new and expansive experience of reality. This bridge connects our personality with our divinity through the heart.

Connecting through the heart, we sense that the human and the Divine are really one and that this unity is present in us. When we allow growth to unfold, our personal exploration naturally leads us to this core state of unity and authenticity. As we center ourselves in authenticity, we respond to the world, other people, and events in an entirely different way. Beyond the primal motivations of fear and desire, we are no longer constrained by our childhood conditioning or our need to resolve the issues of our early life. Being no longer self-absorbed, we care genuinely, responsively. Our concern and identification becomes more expansive, when we are whole and naturally connected to the world.

The life of transformation is the bridge between the personal and the spiritual—but it is also more. Living authentically empowers us to respond from our center, because we are able to draw on the wisdom of the absolute, as well as on our personal insights and understanding. All our inward searching—the risks we have taken, the trust we have developed, the fearlessness and the sincerity to stay and endure through the ordeal and challenges, the discipline and devotion—has nurtured within us a profound care for our soul. And it has provided us with the deeper understanding of suffering I referred to at the beginning of this chapter. All our pain, confusion, and suffering were a necessary trial, the travail for the birth of our authentic self.

We have reached a point of choice where we will never be the same again, because the change is so fundamental, the reorientation so total. Before we worked from our will, our commitment, hope and faith; now trust and surrender are central. As we approach this point of choice, we know, consciously or unconsciously, that there is no going back. When we shed our historical conditioning and enter into the slipstream of the eternal, personal transformation is inevitable. This is the point that inner work strives toward, the flower of our personal growth. The effects of positive change become irreversible in the depths of transformation. And, with courage, we face it alone.

Alone on the Threshold

We stand by ourselves alone, no longer seeking self-definition in relation to others. The curses of our life have been transformed into blessings. The purpose of our life, which has always been shining within, reveals itself. We stop running and turn and embrace everything we have been trying to escape from.

The way through the threshold of transformation resembles any other breakthrough, except now much more is at stake. But there are dangers: if our courage fails, we can sabotage the threshold by withdrawal, procrastination, or fear.

The journey to transformation is like climbing a mountain. The way is hard and steep. Along the way there are many seductions and temptations to give up and give in to the sleep of unawareness, to adopt a new position that is merely an exchange of bindings, to barter one prison for another, perhaps more comfortable one. The strength of the power of illusion is great, as is our desire to give in to it. But through scrupulous self-honesty, courage, and resolve, we can reach the summit.

Our salvation lies in the knowledge of our inherent capacity. We must respond to this now. Capacity is our innate potential; it shows us how much we have to grow into, how much we have to offer. It gives us a sense of our overall life trajectory and an awareness of where our next challenge lies. Many of us have a realistic sense of our potential. For others it is hidden. What we possess in the inner world and how we possess it lead us to our fulfillment, but we are not all equal. In the world of appearances some have more than others, but this is how we see in the relative world. In reality everyone possesses what is right for them: there is no competition.

Through inner strength, unselfish modesty, kindness to ourself, and clarity, we become conscious of the difficulties we face, allow ourselves to make mistakes, and act responsibly with sincerity and truth to embrace all we are. We should not settle for less than everything—the transformation of the human heart and the courage to demand and bear the responsibility of leading a spiritual life in the world.

A common experience at this time is "holding back the ancestral tide." Our personal story is bound up with the stories of our family and the families that preceded them. They are connected, not only biologically but psychologically and energetically. Something has manifested in our lives in direct relation to our grandfather and grandmother, and to their forebears. Emotional and relationship dynamics in the form of expectations, patterns, beliefs, and fears have been passed down this ancestral line. So when we change on the personal level, we also change in relationship to this momentous stream of life energy—the ancestral tide. One seeker recounts:

My transformation was overwhelming and energetic. I felt this oppressive weight pushing behind me, at my back. With seductions, fear, intimidation, and doubt, it urged me to abandon my inner journey. Sometimes I was almost defeated by the force of it. When I turned and faced this energy, I saw it was my father and mother, their father and mother … back and back, receding into antiquity.

The courage needed to resist the ancestral tide is immense, as is the grief at passing over the threshold. As we embrace the newness of being, we let go and mourn the old self and the old patterns that have protected and sustained us throughout our lives. It is like saying goodbye for the last time to a dear old friend whom we will never see again. Yet we are also saying hello to a stranger we haven't seen for a long time … and the stranger is ourself.

Before the final breakthrough, many of us feel despair before we discover the inner resources to rise to the final challenges. Caught between the impulse to go on and the urge to give up, we must make a last great effort. Fortunately, we have strength in reserve. For our creative spirit rises when we are at our lowest ebb in response to our deep need to try one more time.

And when we do *try one more time*, we cross the threshold of transformation.

The way down the further side of the mountain is in many ways easier because we have overcome a lot and so much is behind us. We are now equipped with an inner certainty, no longer asleep, unaware, or numb to experience. We have a sense of rightness and purpose in what we do.

We need time to process and integrate our inner work and to *feel* deeply. We have reached the end of the known world and life has altered irrevocably. We have grown beyond our fear of change and our attachment to the "known."

Transformation is an act of surrender. Suspended between the known and the unknown, we cannot know how to act now that our habitual ways of acting are no longer appropriate. All we can do is deepen in our practice, trusting that the new way will be revealed. In the meantime, we must wait.

Waiting

The inner journey has its own special rhythm. Our ability to sense and respond to this rhythm prescribes the quality and depth with which our process unfolds. For most of us, the hardest part of the rhythm to respond to is the waiting. Making a deep commitment to the path of transformation brings us to a testing ordeal: the inaction, the surrender, and skillful handling of waiting—waiting to reap the rewards of our work, waiting for change, waiting for the unknown. This is a time for great patience. Nothing *seems* to be happening, but this is a time of deep gestation. Doubt may creep in, but if we falter by being over-eager for the new, we may lose everything. But as we surrender to waiting, being quiet and listening, something miraculous takes place.

In the stillness and the solitariness, the moment waits for our attention; and when we give it undividedly, without expectation or assumption, without even calling it waiting, just becoming quiet and still, we enter into natural elation. Waiting is a time of gathering our strength and replenishing and realigning our energies. We may need to withdraw from active meeting and expression in the outer world, because we need all our energies for ourselves and this inner gestation. If we ignore the challenges of waiting, we are in danger of sabotaging our efforts. Waiting is a time of self-nourishment and inner reflection, when we use it wisely and skillfully.

As we learn to nourish ourselves by waiting, we repel the cycles of frustration and returning to past issues, and allow the mental space that gives us time to integrate, strengthen the body and the spirit, and surrender the will.

Waiting patiently, confidently with assurance, we detach from our conditioning, from the unconscious pursuit of old patterns and desires, and an inner certainty dawns inside us. Watching, taming, beginning to quiet the mind through practicing meditative awareness and mental neutrality, we experience emotions without reacting to them and transcend fear, anger, and negativity. Through harmonizing ourself we reach a sense of inner unity. Patiently pausing and waiting, we allow the mud to settle, and in the clear reflection we see that we embody our worst fears and our most-feared enemies. Like the heroine in a thriller who locks herself in a room to escape her aggressor who is hiding behind the door, our fears and nightmares are locked inside us.

Inner unity requires maturity and commitment. We resolve to follow a course of action, but our success depends on inner resources. Our deepest inner resource is our emptiness. During our waiting we let go into emptiness repeatedly until we are still, peaceful, and timeless ... and centered in our being.

Doing and Being

Being is experienced consciously as a sense of presence. This sense of presence creates our self-awareness. We can say with certainty that we *are* before asking what, who, how, or why we are. The pleasures and challenges of life arise from the simple fact: I am. So isn't it strange that we don't spend more time developing our understanding of our sense of being? Without, at least, an adequate understanding of presence, what can we know of the world—of thought, emotion, physicality, or the realms of the soul and the spirit?

But being is not valued in contemporary Western culture: we are taught that doing is superior. From an early age, we learn to appear active even when we are not, because we have learned to be ashamed of inactivity. People sit in offices or stand on building sites looking purposeful and doing little or nothing. Lying on a sofa in a contented reverie, we grab a magazine when someone enters the room. As the father of a friend of mine who had recently begun practicing meditation remarked to her, "When are you going to get off your behind and do something?"

We are caught in a whirlwind of insane "doing." To pause and reflect on what is behind the outward appearance of things seems to demand rare qualities. But when we practice contemplation and self-reflection we are closer to our being because these tendencies are not superhuman, but intrinsically natural and supremely human. Self-reflection is the unique and distinctive aspect of humanness that provides us with the means to live our potential, fulfill ourselves, and be free. Through conscious self-exploration, awareness reflects back on us, like light hitting a mirror, and in dazzling clarity we see ourselves as we truly are, and the world as it truly is.

Looking inward is often an unconscious act that we do automatically, out of necessity. We solve our outward difficulties by referring inward. The outer world is in many ways the creation of our inner state. This is not to say that our external problems do not exist, but simply that the outer world is transformed through inner inquiry and wise consideration. Before we choose how to act outwardly, we weigh up our actions, consider our thoughts, and evaluate the range of options inwardly.

We put our faith in the ability of our inner resources to deal with outward reality and provide solutions to problems. So how much more potent could it be when we simply choose to look inside and to plumb the inner resources and potentials that we merely skim the surface of when we are in need?

Being precedes doing, having, feeling, or experiencing—it is the foundation of our individual and collective consciousness; it is the spark before the flame, the inspiration before the act of creation. When we have tasted it in its purity, we have an invisible root in the world, an irrefutable place of reference that is unfathomably wise, expansive, and compassionate. We come, as the ancients have advised us to do repeatedly, to know ourselves.

The creative mind is endlessly doing, explaining, and unraveling inner and outer events. Often our thoughts focus on the material things—ambition, development, and outer progress. We are conditioned to focus on the outcome of our actions, and our obsession with results leads to frustration. What we achieve becomes more important than what we do or how we do it.

But "doing" is empty when it is not connected to "being." So often we become lost in the fervor of activity, afraid that if we were to stop and reflect, our actions might seem futile and meaningless. Understandably we may be reluctant to know this, but when we are open to learning it, we discover a key to inner power.

In the Zen monastery where I trained, the monks were building a new meditation hall—the *zendo*. The whole monastic community was intensively focused on this grand project. Sometimes the senior monks worked long into the evening after the rest of us had finished, and we marveled at their ability to endure tirelessly, as we ate our dinner listening to their hammers ringing in the cold night air. Once a month, people from outside the monastery came to attend a silent retreat, and at the end of the day we socialized together under the supervision of a *roshi*. This was the only time we were allowed to talk, and naturally the most frequent topic of conversation was the building work.

One evening, one enthusiastic visitor reported that predicted severe weather conditions were likely to delay the building schedule and even compromise what had already been accomplished. When you are in silence for the whole day, you hunger for drama. This alarmist report concerning the exalted purpose of the zendo construction gave us an excuse for virtuous anxiety. We all began to express our fears and concerns. The roshi listened patiently to our escalating prattle before responding.

"What is important," he said quietly, "is that we do the work of the Buddha." The effect was electrifying, like being rewound from where we had sprung. Everyone froze in a contemplative silent stillness. We were snapped back to ourselves, turned in and away from our desire for results, which was so insidious and insistent that we had spun out of ourselves. The roshi's words relocated us in our beings.

The "work of the Buddha" is alignment with our being. When we are aligned with our true center, being radiates out into action. Action that is transformed by being is effortless, because it has no results, no goal beyond the present moment. Like children we are totally immersed in what we are doing; like sages we find wisdom and heart in all our activities. The work of the Buddha is done as an end in itself, through spontaneous activity. When we are centered in ourselves, we see the changing conditions of progress and setbacks in their true perspective. From the point of view of our inner lives, the events of the external world may be simply grist for the mill.

This inner centering does not mean that nothing gets done. Neither does it mean that we are not appropriately concerned with results or involved with what happens. But curiously the inner release of our attachment to the outcome of our actions makes us more efficient. More gets done when we don't have to carry the weight of anxiety on our shoulders.

You can start this practice now and see for yourself the tremendous difference it makes. At the beginning of your day simply allow yourself five minutes (you may want to add more time later) to center yourself. Now, *breathe*, sitting, standing, or lying down; it doesn't matter which. The essential point is that you quiet yourself inside and *tune in to the underlying sense of being* that supports all your conscious and unconscious processes. Withdraw from the outside world by closing your eyes and bringing your attention wholly inside yourself. Accept and allow thoughts, feelings, and physical sensations in your body, without any interference or resistance, but do not become distracted by them. Now withdraw resolutely into your center and immerse yourself in the experience of space, peace, tranquility, and contentment. Don't mind if it only works a little bit after the first few times; I assure you the practice will deepen over time. Simply be willing, and apply your attention to your sense of being.

Clearing Up Loose Ends

We continue to learn after the completion of our personal journey. Although some loose ends may remain, we are able to deal with them efficiently and quickly.

Our relationship to the small self and our historical conditioning has now altered. However, the small self remains through this second level of deeper personality work and is by no means eradicated. But it has ceased to be central to our psyche; it is no longer the principal reference point or unconscious driving force behind our lives. Now we are centered in our authentic self. The small self resides on the sidelines occasionally behaving mischievously, and we take it much less seriously.

But when we have arrived at a deep understanding of ourselves, the ego can work even more insidiously and dangerously. When we have jettisoned the beliefs, assumptions, and life patterns of our early conditioning, it is all too easy to take on another set of conditions and create a new false personality or "secondary conditioning."

The integration of my own personal inner work took some time to complete, and false pride became a stumbling block. I was in a workshop with the teacher who had guided me patiently and skillfully through my personal process. I had consolidated this work with another guide with whom I worked on issues that seemed to fill in the gaps. I had devoted several years to my personal growth and felt that at last I had "arrived." I came to this workshop with a strong sense of having completed my journey. I was, after all, a successful therapist now and, with all the pride that engendered, I conducted myself confidently as a "somebody." I didn't know that I had succumbed to a secondary conditioning and created a new image for myself, which was just as false as the old one.

What came up for me in this workshop was a deep, historical sense of shame—shame about my family, shame about myself, shame about past actions. It overwhelmed me. It didn't suit my new position of being someone who had resolved his inner issues and found himself. But my guide helped me to drop the pride that prevented me from accepting and letting go of the shame. I surrendered to it, felt it, and let it flow through me. I spoke about it and crumpled and cringed in the experience of it. I finally saw that this shame was now expressed in my new attachment to my identity as a therapist and that in my unawareness, I had allowed ego to fill its boots in my attainment and that felt shameful to me, too. Through gentle, thorough process work, I learned that my façade of successful therapist was the new covering under which shame had hidden, and I shed my "somebody-ness" and emerged in a freer place where I had no need to assume a position. I had held on to this hidden shame for the whole of my life, yet it took me less than an hour to let it go, through trust, willingness, and re-experiencing my emotions and releasing them by catharsis.

Thinking ourselves into a place where we are not, surrendering to self-inflation, allowing our egos to seize the rewards of our hard-won freedom are some of the ways in which we get caught in secondary conditioning. Staying open, remaining humble, keeping aware of our tendency to attachments enable us to steer clear of it.

Inner work on the personality does end—but in its own time. Surrender to the process is paramount, and the process is likely to take longer than we think or hope. We may need to be reminded to stay open and practice continual awareness and self-challenging, to remain free of pride and assuming new positions. The outcome of inner work is not that we become perfect, but that we wholly accept who we are. Loose ends remain, but as time goes on, they become less important as the journey of transformation reveals new and deeper challenges.

We may retain deep, buried traces of patterns and held emotions that stay and linger even after the loose ends have been cleared up. They provide us with opportunities for grounding ourselves long after we have finished our personal work. Jealousy, possessiveness, doubt, and anxiety remain with us through the later stages of inner work. But now they are humbling reminders of our humanness, and we relate to ourselves and to others through, not in spite of, them. Since we judge these conditions less harshly and identify with them less strongly, we can process and heal them much more quickly.

Work on the personality is such a daunting task we may be forgiven for thinking it can never be completed. Today we are chained to lofty ideals and the unreachable goals of perfectionism that resonate with our fear of the inner world. In other activities we may feel that we deserve recognition and status, while still acknowledging that we have more to learn. It is a sensible requirement of our maturity and proficiency that we remain open-minded and humble in our willingness to discover new things. Some of us have experienced the completion of our work on the personality. Others know someone who inspires them with the knowledge that it can be done. For the rest, we must work with faith. Faith enables us to bring something precious into being: the discovery of our self. We need not belittle ourselves or act smaller than we are. We need not compromise or settle for less than everything. Work on the personality is finite, not an endless ordeal, with this one provision: that in inner work we should always remain unprejudiced, receptive, and sincere about what arises to be resolved in our relationships with others and the world, and, when necessary, within ourselves.

Life Transforms

Life continues to provide us with the opportunities we need to enable us to take the next step. One such circumstance occurred in my life when I bought a house just a few miles from where my parents lived. I was in my mid-thirties, and I had practiced therapy and inner work for several years. We fell into a routine whereby they visited me each week and helped around the house, while I gave therapy sessions. In the middle of the day we would eat together.

Sitting with my parents, I felt increasingly uneasy. The incongruity of being an adult, moreover a therapist, falling for the habitual cues of the old family dynamic threw me into confusion and despair. Often I felt like a child. A look, a remark, a single word from my parents could propel me into that familiar small place inside from which I could not escape. Laughter led to humiliation; banter led to pain; anecdotes led to comparisons in which it was inevitable that I would come out badly.

Deeply unhappy about this, I decided to apply the same degree of awareness to my contact with my parents as I did in my therapy work. Immediately I saw how our family dynamic depended on numbing to emotion and adopting a teasing, competitive stance while avoiding serious matters. I began to see how I fell for the cues, walked into the psychological traps, and complied in offering myself up for slaughter.

Gradually I was able to lessen the frequency with which I played the family games and fell into the traps. I began to choose my responses more carefully. I stayed clear, focused, and self-aware, particularly when I was most likely to lose myself. Noticing my tendency to react to negativity with more negativity, I began to respond with neutrality and, occasionally, even genuine positivity. I refused to be led and manipulated, or to compromise myself. Increasingly I stood my ground and oriented myself to what was true for me as the adult I was, and less to what was expected of the son I had been.

I remember the day when my work finally bore fruit. My father had made a remark that would usually have resulted in me losing my self-confidence, feeling humiliated, and reacting defensively. But on this occasion I looked straight at him and remained inwardly centered. I felt solid and real. I could feel the lure of the slippery, sliding slope of my habitual patterns and conditioning, like some stomach-churning fun-fair ride. But I firmly rejected it and it grew fainter. My father floundered, unable to carry on the interaction, and shot a quizzical look at me. Following an uncomfortable silence, he changed the subject and the conversation resumed.

My relationship with my parents was never the same after that. From that decisive moment of contact with my father, I never fell for the family games again. My years of inner searching had at last paid off. I was able to be truly myself. For the first time I felt all-inclusive. I was at once the little boy spending long hours in solitude, inventing games and creating imaginary worlds. I was the eight-year-old with a sense of dawning individuality, scared and apprehensive of death, and behind the mask of death, terrified of life and its awesome challenges. I was the unconfident, wounded teenager trying to maintain a semblance of self in a world that seemed determined to undermine him. I was the young man in his early twenties entering the world of independence, work, money, relationships, hopes, fears, and embarking on the long journey of self-discovery. I was 28 and suffering from indecision and confusion. I was 35, impatient to make a success of my life, and I was 42, discovering the vulnerable, empowered center of my own substance.

Looking back, I now consider my life in its wholeness. Middle-aged, I still feel young. Like the rings of a tree, I contain layers of experience. I feel fond of the younger stages of Richard-ness. I feel a warm glow in my heart when I think of the boy or the young man I once was. I can say, as others have said, that inner work has not changed anything ... and yet everything has changed. While my initial expectations and motivations for beginning self-exploration were the usual ones—to shed my neuroses, to change, to be a better person—what has actually happened is a deep acceptance of myself. This acceptance has come from re-centering my awareness. In psychological terms I have moved away from the defended ego center, which is restrictive and partial, to the authentic center of my whole being. Being whole requires the acceptance of all our selves, the inclusion of likable and unlikable states equally. I am who I am, and I continue to open to becoming more fully myself.

I tell this story about the effectiveness of inner work particularly to people who have become disillusioned. Most people don't see inner work through to this stage of completion. I don't think there was any other way for me to get past the strong repressive dynamics of my family. My personal work started and finished with my mother and my father. My attachment to them was so strong that I would have remained under their influence through their internalized voices all my life if I had not undertaken something as radical as the inner journey to free myself.

In Summary

In this chapter we have ventured further inward than before to the life of transformation and authenticity, and our new, hard-won freedom. Remarkably direct and simple, it was hidden, though plainly visible, and it has only taken dropping our self-delusion to finally see it, and to be seen. Now, before we proceed to heart-centering and compassion in action, take a little time to review and personalize the material with these questions:

1. Relate doing to being: experientially, in routine action, in mental processes, in meditation, from historical example. (For instance, how did your parents relate the two?)

2. What is spiritual enlightenment? How do you understand the human and the Divine?

3. How do you understand the authentic life? What do you think and feel about yourself, your personality, your character, and your emotional-behavioral patterns after reading this chapter?

4. What experiences in your life show that you are revealing and honoring your authentic self instead of playing out old patterns?

8

Responding
from the Heart

Destiny and Purpose

When we have crossed the threshold of authenticity, we discover our true purpose. When we are doing what we should be doing—the activity that resonates with our true nature—we experience a feeling of incomparable rightness.

When we suffer in occupations that do not suit us, we feed our negativity and resentment. We solidify in our small sense of self around a core of frustration. We feel dissatisfied, irritated, and impatient toward others and ourselves. But when we discover our true purpose, we feel such a profound sense of homecoming and belonging that we experience life as a blessing.

Purpose requires surrender. We have to free ourselves from other people's aspirations and let go of our ideas of what we *think* we should be doing. Many of us spend a lifetime trying to fulfill the expectations of someone else, rather than living our own lives.

Anita was an example of someone who turned that around. A professional woman in her mid-thirties, married with no children, she came from an Irish family and had a large number of siblings. She was practical and down-to-earth with a no-nonsense personality. Her profession conformed to the wishes of her parents, and her outward success was bound up with her desire to please them. She had spent a year grappling with inner and outer disturbances. The experiences that led to her crisis were disturbing and spectacular: she felt energies and atmospheres, saw lights, and heard voices. At night she was visited by disembodied beings who asked for her help. Her ways of dealing with these experiences ranged from "pulling herself together" (the no-nonsense approach), to talking to her husband (who favored doctors over therapy), to desperately begging the presences to leave her alone. Anita tried to share her experiences with her husband, but he didn't understand. Increasingly, the two of them grew distant. Her husband eventually decided that she was having a nervous breakdown. By the time she came to see me, she was desperate. With no reference points for what was happening to her, she was living in a state of hopeless terror and despair.

Our work together was fast and thorough. She discovered that her experiences were the projections of her spiritual call onto disembodied beings that she had manifested as a way to handle her inner experiences: the inner disturbances were a call from her deeper self. Besides her inner work, she read widely on psychology and spirituality and began a meditation practice. Her marriage was a casualty of her inner changes, as was her career. She divorced, left her job, and moved into an entirely new phase of life. She took up work with a spiritual, healing focus. Now she writes to me about once a year relating the pleasure of being a healer and her sense of rightness about what she is doing. The merging of her being and her doing has given her a sense of her true purpose.

Purpose resembles what the mythologist Joseph Campbell called "bliss." When he encouraged people to "follow their bliss," it sounded as if he was advising them to seek pleasure. But he was really saying embrace life in all its fullness, whether that is pleasure or pain, happiness or sorrow. Bliss, or purpose, gives our lives meaning, not by altering the conditions of our lives, but by being with those conditions exactly as they are. Illness, the challenges of family life, accidents, pain—all become allies or helpers when we stop rejecting them and embrace them fully. Instead of trying to change our life circumstances, we open to them and they are transformed. Our misfortunes become blessings and point the way to fulfillment.

Our personal task in life may be modest or grandiose, but when we know what it is, we discover how we can express our inner being in the outer world. But our primary purpose is more in-turned; it is the "work of the Buddha" that we discussed earlier, the work that is done as an end in itself, the activity that originates out of our true center and transcends our fear and separateness, and empowers us to realize ourselves.

When we know who we are, we know what we should be doing in the world. We find out who we are when we rise above fear and desire, when we are authentic. Before this we are stumbling blindly, struggling hopelessly. Nothing we "do" will ever fill the emptiness of not knowing who we are and satisfy our need to "be." As inspiration precedes creation and being precedes doing, knowing who we are leads to our life's true purpose.

In my mid-thirties I faced a disturbing dilemma. I wanted to make my living full-time as a psychotherapist, but my practice was too small. So I had to do other work to support myself. I felt psychotherapy was what I should be doing, but I seemed to be thwarted from living my ambition.

So I gave myself a personal retreat, a period of in-turning and inner inquiry. With few distractions, I spent my time meditating, sleeping, and walking. On the third day something extraordinary happened. I was imagining what it would be like to be a full-time therapist. I calculated that I would need sixteen clients each week to make a living. I tried to imagine the whole process in detail: people phoning to make appointments, what they presented in their first sessions, how they looked, how they came in and out of the consulting room... and my fear escalated. When I imagined taking on more than six clients, I began to feel nervous, by eight I felt fearful, and at ten I felt terrified. The physical results were palpable: my heart beat faster, my stomach tightened, my mouth was dry, and my breathing quickened. I felt overwhelmed, because the demands I imagined would be made on me felt too great. Then I had the insight that it was fear that prevented me from realizing my ambition. My fear of being a full-time therapist was greater than my desire. The more I felt into it, the more excruciating it felt.

I saw that I was caught between fear and desire, and I knew that when you want to conquer something you must draw it toward you. For hours I sat with my dreams and fears of becoming a psychotherapist and the hopes it generated, until we became close friends. I allowed the imagined experience, the feelings, and the scenarios to move through me. After five more days I had lived through it all and I felt calm, peaceful, and relaxed, at times even serene. Most surprising of all was that, along with my fear, I had let go of my desire. I was no longer *attached* to being a psychotherapist. I felt strangely content. I returned home and got on with my life.

Within three months my life completely transformed. My modest workshop and individual practice grew rapidly. I created a workshop program of assorted events and scheduled several alternative dates for each one. I expected I would have to cancel most of them, but hoped to salvage some workshops by moving people from the other dates, as usual. But all the events filled to capacity, and virtually overnight I became a full-time therapist and workshop leader. The groups attracted people who wanted to work individually. With a new understanding of the complementary roles of meditation and therapy, I added meditation evenings to my program, as well as an open drop-in group for new people as an introductory event.

In the years that followed, I practiced psychotherapy and it became my career. The power of my personal retreat was undeniable. It had acted as a catalyst, a reservoir of energy, and a source of fearlessness in my life. I had let go fully to fear and desire and gone beyond both. I'd had a transcendent meeting, a communion with destiny. When my therapy practice became established, I had an unwavering sense of rightness about what I was doing.

Whatever work we are destined to do, the purpose is always transcendent of the task itself. This is why Zen teachers are said to exhibit Zen in all their actions, why one can be transformed simply by being in the presence of an enlightened teacher, why a touch or a look from a realized being can awaken the heart instantly. The ultimate purpose of all actions is to realize truth, to flow in the ocean of awareness that is the source of consciousness.

Our attachment to the search for our true purpose may be so strong that we miss it in our seeking. We need look no further than ourselves to find it. In calm, quiet, inner seclusion we hear the voice of our heart telling us what it is. When there is no separation between being and doing, our purpose is ourself. For the purpose of life is simply *itself* and our individual contribution is ourselves.

Inhabiting the Heart: Practicing Compassion

Most of us are unaware of the depths of our emotions, because we don't breathe deeply enough to experience them. During respiration we retain a portion of inhaled breath called "residual volume," so that some air is always left in the lungs even after we imagine we have exhaled completely. When we breathe in again we are inhibited from filling our lungs to full capacity. The result is that many of us live with a chronic background depression: our chest becomes chronically, energetically, and even physically concave, and a full breath into the abdomen and pelvis is habitually inhibited. As a result, our emotions and relationships are merely reactive, since our feelings are mechanical, contrived, and automatic, with little or no emotional spontaneity or authenticity.

Whether it is a result of smoking, lack of exercise, emotional repression, or simply bad habit, bad breathing can be corrected through a number of steps. First, bring your awareness to your breathing. Curiously, this alone may be transformative. Becoming aware of your unnaturally shallow or directed breath may be enough to cause you to take a deeper breath and then begin to change your breathing habits. Directing the in-breath farther and deeper down, through the chest and abdomen and into the pelvis also helps, and, finally, I recommend allowing a full out-breath. When you are really paying attention, give yourself a little restful moment before taking the next in-breath. Try these techniques in any combination to transform your breathing pattern.

When we shift our emotional center into the heart we have a deeper experience of kindness, compassion, and love. The emotional center is usually adapted to memory, early conditioning, and fear. When our heart is governed by these, we cannot really love. To truly care for others, we must truly love ourselves and be aligned with our true center. Only then can we become attuned to the flow of love that expresses itself through compassion.

Compassion is beyond our control, not subject to our will. It is not sentimental, still less can it be manipulated. When genuine compassion arises in us, it has an impersonal quality, because its power is greater than the small self. We inhabit the heart—not our individual heart, but the true heart. Our innate abilities to value, feel, and empathize with others are occupations of the true heart. As authentic beings, caring for another is continuous with caring for ourselves.

When we cannot see the world as it is, we are unable to put genuine caring into action. To act with care involves setting ourselves aside and seeing what the situation demands. A caring action carried out with personal investment is inevitably flawed. It all hinges on *how* we do what we do, rather than *what* we do; the process is more important than the single event.

Deeply genuine compassion requires not merely the individual's lack of investment in the act of compassion, but the absence of individuality and an individual agency. Love today has become an idea, and the idea is usually of a personal love and interdependent love. But love at its highest is truly impersonal or supra-individual. You might say *true compassion is only present when I am not.*

What passes for feeling—our emotional reactions to experience—is often inauthentic and defensive. Real emotion overwhelms us, because it is more real and stronger than the individual self. When we are open and honest, we see the dark in the light, the fire of hate in the passion of love, and the selfishness, however slight, in the "selfless" action. We dare to risk seeing the world "as it is," however scared we may be.

Compassion lies in the dissolving of the ties that bind two together and in seeing that we are connected and ultimately one. In her book *A Wizard of Earthsea*, Ursula Le Guin tells the story of Ged, a young wizard. As a young man, he inadvertently releases a monstrous form in a display of youthful hubris. Ged spends his life fleeing from this monster that follows him wherever he goes. This monster is his shadow. At last exhausted and resigned, he goes out to meet his shadow on a sandbank in the middle of a vast ocean. His shadow assumes the shapes of grim old age, his father, an old enemy, and a terrifying monster with a snout and talons. He embodies Ged's self-hate, his fear, and all the consequences of his past actions. As Ged approaches him and speaks his own name, the shadow speaks his name also. The names, of course, are the same. Ged reaches out to his shadow, the shadow reaches out to him ... and they merge into one.

This beautiful account of the owning of the shadow symbolizes the deep act of compassion toward ourselves that frees us to be compassionate toward others. Compassion arises from accepting and transcending our individual, separate self. When we deny a single part of ourself, our compassion is limited.

With true compassion there is no separation. Compassion is the total acceptance that we feel when we perceive the other in ourself and ourself in the other. Love may be expressed through acts of consideration, care, and kindness. We should not dismiss the day-to-day opportunities for showing love and compassion. When love and compassion are viewed on a grand scale, we may lose sight of the diverse acts of kindness and generosity that can fill our lives and connect us to the world. Interpersonal love can lead to universal love—an experience so overriding and full that all of the manifestation is included. And yet universal love, too, is evident in simple acts of kindness.

Can We Love Enough?

Compassion may be the deepest wisdom and its expression the most profound spiritual act we are capable of, but compassion should never be confused with sentiment or the appearance of love. Genuine compassion cares absolutely. It doesn't need to please or endear when fierceness and challenge are called for. The famous Zen stick, the "encouragement stick," represents a literal symbol of such challenge and it is always administered with reverence.

Sometimes our relationships demand confrontation. When we need to challenge ourselves or a fellow seeker, our compassionate heart rises to the challenge. We are asked to abandon our desire to comfort and truly help by encouraging the other to clearly witness the predicament. It is simply what needs to be done, as it may be in a deep friendship. When we go past the "comfort barrier," the question that arises is "Can I love *enough*?" and we may be stretched to comply with this inner request. It is not so much an issue of loving the person who needs challenging, so much as simply loving. When confrontation comes out of love, it works; when it comes from something else, it fails. A friend once said to me, "When a person challenges you with the truth about yourself, rather than merely offering you superficial comfort, then you know you have found a true friend."

David was another old friend who had learned early on in his life to look happy. Whatever was happening to him and however he was feeling, his face was set with a fixed grin. On one occasion when things were clearly not going well for him, he appeared smiling, while telling me of some sad events that had taken place.

"David," I said, "you are unhappy; you are one of the unhappiest people I have ever known. If you really want your life to change, you are going to have to admit that you haven't been happy for a long time, because only then can you be real and really change." He looked at me uncomprehendingly for a moment, and then his eyes filled with tears.

If you find yourself approaching or inhabiting the second stage of awakening, try this exercise now. Perhaps someone in your life could benefit from your insights and understanding. Perhaps you could have the key to help them take the next step in their inner growth. Ask yourself if you could love them enough to risk their disapproval or anger, and love them enough to challenge them to reach a little further to free themselves and become *more* themselves... and then, if it feels right to do so, *act*!

Inhabiting the heart aligns us with truth and makes us a companion to what is real. Real relationships are characterized by our ability to respond out of caring and compassion. We simply love the other, feel for them, feel with them, and wish the best for them, without shying away from the means to bring that about. Confronting or challenging someone to grow out of love is compassion in action.

In Summary

In this short chapter we have begun to look at the role of the heart and compassion in authentic relationship. Now the other (person, event, phenomenon) is less separate, more thinly divided, and less removed than ever before. Our role now is to relate to the world as ourselves, or to relate to ourselves as if we were the other. Before we go on to the vital process of stabilizing, take a minute or two to consider, through the following questions, the deep integration that may come from reviewing this material:

1. What is your life's purpose? If you aren't sure, what do you find joy in? How were you taken off course? What is the role of being in your doing? How does your essence relate to your ambition and life trajectory?

2. Practice this heart meditation. Focus on the following phrases: "I am the other ... whatever is before me, is me ... we are together with all forms ... arising and dissolving back into Consciousness ... interdependent with each other." Transcend the words and experience their meaning, deepen into the truth behind the words, and throughout the exercise breathe into your heart.

9

Stabilizing
in Transformation

When you reach the second stage of personality work, the transformation into authenticity, you inevitably engage with the world in a healing capacity. You need not be a formal practitioner, but in your speech, presence, and being you experience a deep concern and consideration for others and the world. This concern is not sentimental or superficial, but deeply felt. Your work now is to stabilize in the transformation and avoid egocentric traps.

The Four Stages of Ego

Through the different stages of psycho-spiritual growth we meet the ego in different and appropriate ways. The truth is never fixed; it is always changing. Depending on what stage of awareness and awakening we are in, we have to work with the ego in different ways. There are essentially four stages.

First is the remedial, healing stage. In many of us the ego is either undeveloped or unhealthy because it has never grown sufficiently. Faced with the spiritual notion of "giving up" our egos, we see inside us a tortured, frustrated mass of unfulfilled desires, repressed urges, and unlived dreams, and we feel perplexed. Our spiritual side may be attracted to the idea of giving up the ego. But how can we give up what is not yet fully formed? Our spiritual work in this stage is *strengthening our ego*. This is an integral part of our work on the personality that needs to be done during the process of self-discovery, so when we have crossed the threshold of transformation it is behind us.

The second stage is *offering the ego in service*. We work with our ego and the soul and place them in the right relationship to each other. One spiritual seeker describes this in the relationship between the Pharaoh and his sandal-bearer:

> The Pharaoh works within the realm of the Great Mystery. In his service is his sandal-bearer. Occasionally, the sandal-bearer becomes dissatisfied with the life of service and attempts to carve out his own self-important place in the world. It is at this time that the Pharaoh reminds him that his role is to be in service to the Great Mystery.

When we have developed and healed the ego, but are not ready to surrender it fully, the ego must be *brought into service* to the Soul. Any effort at this point would be fatal. We shouldn't try to let go, because trying is of the ego. We shouldn't hold on either, because that's the ego again. We should steer a course between effort and holding on along a path of non-effort. This brings us up to date, since the task of the authentic self lies between the second and third stages of ego work.

In the third stage we see ego as a process and as an illusion, and, through surrendering and letting go, we begin to detach from it. When we recognize the restrictive self-serving power of ego and slip out of our minds into moments of elation and impersonal freedom, the return to ego-bound existence always feels limiting, because we are liberated from ego. The deep desire to shed the ego becomes a real possibility within our reach, and we work on *shedding our egoic attachments*.

The fourth stage is *transcending the ego* completely. At first it is available only intermittently for short periods. But that can be enough to give us an inner certainty that informs our lives. We begin to feel how we are constantly changing around the unchanging source of our being. This is the challenge of the third level of commitment and intention, the truly spiritual life, which we will look at in the third level of awakening: the Source of Consciousness.

Developing our egos, serving others, and identifying with the Self are the three ways to God described in the *Upanishads*. They correlate directly with the first three stages of ego work. Each of these is a complete way in itself. If we devote ourselves fully to the stage of ego work we are in, we can reach the Soul level. Most of the time, we are flickering between these three levels. One moment we are building or healing ego; in another moment we are serving the Self through ego; in yet another moment we are so far removed from the urges of ego that we are in the state of unity. As we flicker between the levels, we see that—like the lover, the beloved, and love—these stages are not separate but simply different aspects of a single, unfolding event.

When we fight against the ego, we give it credibility and increase its power, since it thrives on separation and conflict. Whenever you fight against someone or something, using like against like, you simply increase its power. To paraphrase Aikido philosophy: move like a beam of light, blend with your attacker, and the opponent disappears. In the same way when we treat the ego with patience and humility, the ego's power weakens and we turn our attention toward the spiritual, while experiencing and witnessing ourselves and the world.

Ego remains with us long after personal transformation. Our task now is to work with the ego and establish a new role for it, in service to others and real relationship to the wider community, through the changing conditions of the outer world.

Aging

Age need never stand in the way of insight and deepening understanding. But as we age we can become more complacent. We may hide behind our seniority, concealing a multitude of ills that we defend with pseudo-awareness. Our changing moods are "justified" in our "knowing" ourselves—"That's just how I am," we might say. Inflexibility, intimidation, and aggression can all be justified similarly. But true awareness implies openness, and openness implies humility. When we develop our humility we become open and available to change—whatever our age.

We should never become so fixed or sure of ourselves that we think there is no more to learn. Although age may grant us the appearance of wisdom and experience, inside we may be resistant to challenge and change. Very often our fixedness, at any age, conceals shame and grief. When shame or grief becomes personalized, it can become overwhelming. Concealment is preferred to revelation and the embarrassment and humiliation that surely follow. But not even a saint will have led a life without learning from mistakes. Forgiving ourselves in later life is crucial. We have more time to think, and we have had more opportunities to make mistakes. If we cannot forgive ourselves we are likely to fall into bitterness, resentment, and self-hate. We contract under the weight of accrued blame and mull over our personal failings.

Old age can be a time when disillusionment hardens into bitterness. It may be that we have spent much of our lifetime in pursuit of money or power; we may have pursued a course that was not of our own making; we may have compromised so much that we look back on a life that wasn't really lived; we may feel that there was much more we could have put in or got out of life ... more love, more joy, more vibrancy, more risk. When whatever we have put our trust in or devoted our life to proves unworthy, we may be left with a feeling of betrayal.

The result is resentment, a sense that life has cheated us. Trust, forgiveness, and surrender all seem to have been denied us, as well as happiness. But if we re-vision this misplaced trust and betrayal, it becomes the fertile ground in which trust and forgiveness grows.

This sequence of trust, through betrayal, to forgiveness and finally transcendence, mirrors the growth of human development through infancy, adulthood, old age, and death. Childhood is a time of great trust and innocence. In adulthood we "betray" this original innocence by becoming more worldly and losing our innate sense of openness and trust. In old age we have the potential to soften and forgive ourselves, others, and life, and honor the joy *and* the suffering it has given us.

Older people who engage in inner work are nearly always models of humility. They are willing, not in spite of their age, but through their experience of aging, to open to learning. Paradoxically, as disenchantment and depression appear, we also deepen in our sense of profound wonder. The wonder we now feel is constantly available in little things. Ordinary existence yields opportunities for re-enchantment in every moment. To notice them we have to pay attention in a new way. We must open the eyes of innocence and experience the world directly. We set aside our long-held, tired judgments, opinions, and insecurities. We are less self-conscious, because increasingly we are no longer centered in our small sense of self, which fades naturally as we age. We are less attached to a position, less attached to who we are. Looking back on our lives, we feel the futility of trying, and yet we sense its appropriateness for a younger age. As we grow into our thirties and forties, we feel that we have to make an effort, to grow and develop. But as we pass into our middle years this effort falls away naturally and we begin to *be*, without effort. As we saw in chapter 5, "Stages of Transition," the thirties and forties are the ages of material ambition, of following the impulse to build up, which we may be released from in our middle years when we turn our attention to the spiritual world.

As we pass middle age, along with the reduction of possibilities, we feel less need for self-aggrandizement because, through a new self-honesty born out of our lack of striving, we at last find self-aggrandizement unconvincing in others and unnecessary in ourselves. We experience the need of others to make us into paragons of virtue or people with advanced abilities as just that—*their* need. It is not always a healthy need, as others are inclined to disown their own positive, as well as negative, character traits through projection. Much as we used to shun the stickiness of our negative image of ourselves, we can see now that excessive positivity also traps us. Often it is even more dangerous than negativity or rejection. Idolizing or making an inner icon of our self-image only adds to the self, and attachment to our egos brings seduction and allure. In old age, our attachment to self naturally fades.

Whether we cling or not will tend to be etched into our facial features over time. Look closely at the face of an old person to see what kind of life they have led. If you have ever been on a meditation retreat, then you know the freedom of not having to create an outward show. Not having to put on a face is deeply liberating. After some days of "facelessness" we can enter the timeless, ageless realm of witness consciousness, where we see events unfolding from our expanded awareness. People who present a strong façade in their facial expression may be quite unrecognizable when caught unaware. They don't have to be unhappy or depressed, but in Western culture a disproportionate amount of stress is laid on facial expression.

As we grow older, we direct our attention more to the inner world. The endless potential and possibilities that were available to us in our youth are tempered by the knowledge that we will not live forever in this present body. This curtailing of our potential can lead to depression. It can be important to treat depression impersonally: like all feeling states, depression will pass and we do not have to cling to and identify with it. Instead of feeling negative about the challenges of aging, we can ask, "What is this a gateway to?" and we may find that the darkness of depression conceals a brighter light. Our disillusionment with our life is the call to a richer existence and a deeper fulfillment. Just as we grew out of our childhood toys in earlier life, we now, if we are open to it, lose interest in the exciting and enticing rewards of adulthood. We open the inner eye, listen with inner ears, touch ourselves deep within. This is the call to the final stages of a lifetime.

When my family and I moved to Andalucia in southern Spain, I couldn't speak a word of Spanish. But I was irresistibly drawn to the old men of the nearby village. A motley assortment of characters, they were united not only in age but also in their common experience of pondering the end of their lives with merely a tenuous hold on the material world. I sensed in them a collective sense of acceptance and completion, as if they felt the gentle relief of lives well spent, well lived, and that they were finished now and uninvolved with the passing spectacle of change. They sat in a line, with some standing on the corner that I unavoidably passed through on my way into the village. I remember the first time I went down and sat with them. I took my place among them to cursory nods and grunts and, when I got over my nervousness that one of them might engage me in conversation, I drew deep breaths and relaxed into the experience. There among these men I felt a great acceptance, as we contemplated some inner stillness, some inner repose, and some appropriate distancing in wisdom from the dramatic narrative of life.

Whether you are old or not, a contemplation of death in life, the meeting of action and stillness, and how the Divine shines through everything in the material world as light and consciousness is a beneficial practice. Blend your inner eye with your outer one now to activate inner vision toward the world about you. You can do this by placing the fingertips of your index fingers gently over your closed eyelids and applying a little pressure for a few seconds only. Now place your attention in the center of your forehead between your eyes and up a little. This activates your third eye, your spiritual eye that brings spiritual vision. Now open you eyes and look outward at the world. You will see everything is brighter, more ethereal, less solid and material. Practice this regularly for a little while, until you witness for yourself that everything is light and everything is consciousness, and all is forms arising in the unity of existence.

Everything is simply an aspect of consciousness, one face of existence. Nothing is more special than anything else. No seduction of the ego can hide this amazing insight and miracle of ordinary life.

In old age we can admit to our weariness with the world and outward concerns. The world becomes our ashram. As we remove the fatigue of worldliness we focus increasingly on the inner life in preparation for the new transition that awaits us. We cultivate neutrality, humility, and desirelessness, as we open to a greater destiny.

Death

Death is intrinsic to life. Our impulse to grow is closely allied to our intuition that death is inherent in life. To live fully we must open, not only to life but also to death. This is both a literal truth, since death inevitably follows life, and a spiritual truth, since the body dies to the spirit. Death and life are inextricably bound. Breathing in, we invite life; breathing out, we touch death. Our lives move between and embrace both. To be truly alive is to be willing to die, because only when we are open enough to give ourselves totally to each moment do we emerge, refreshed, open, and available to the present.

When I was eight I was seized with an overwhelming fear of my mortality, the terrifying specter of death. With no words to express what I was feeling, I crumpled at the top of the stairs outside my bedroom door and whispered to an aunt, "I've got a tummy ache." Even this early on, I understood the need for euphemisms to conceal the feelings that should not be spoken. Death was taboo; strong feelings were taboo; sex was taboo; physical expression was taboo—this obscured most of my life experience, as most of what I was experiencing was forbidden.

In our lifetimes, we have experienced changing attitudes toward what is forbidden and particularly toward death. In my childhood, death was rarely discussed and the fear of it was expressed in the mystification and denial with which it was surrounded and concealed. The day after my grandfather died, I remember being led into his empty, scrupulously cleaned bedroom. The bed linen was turned down and everything was neat and tidy. I was told he had "gone away" and invited to select one of the objects from the top of his tallboy as a keepsake.

Fifty years on, when my father was lying in his hospice bed just days away from his death, I took my children to see him for the last time. Although his head and face resembled a skull cap, and his body was painfully frail and weak, the children were unperturbed. They climbed up onto his bed, lay as close as they could to him, stroked his thin arms and hands, and gazed into his vacant eyes with affection, as the adults sat reservedly on the straight-backed chairs around his bed.

In the bed opposite, another old man lay surrounded by his wife, grown-up children, and in-laws. Clearly uncomfortable with the situation, his relatives were looking around, seeking distractions. When they saw the children draped around my father, framing him on his death bed, and giving him such love and care, one of them exclaimed, "Look at those children; they look just like little angels!" The caring and the love were infectious as they turned to their own dying relative with renewed affection.

The last words my father said to me were, "Look after all those lovely children!" He spoke for us all—for the love that resides in the innocence within us; for the openness in children that provokes our love for them; for the child in him that wanted to be loved and was angry, scared, and sad about being abandoned and rejected; for the adult now for whom it was too late to receive it. And finally for the life that, without him, would never have been born. My children were his legacy, and in them I believe he saw his own hopes and regrets.

From our first gulp to our last gasp of breath, our individual life shimmers like a shard of sunlight for a cosmic moment, before it is gone forever. Passing from life, we are born into the unknown we call death. In our final days perhaps we will look back and ask if there was importance, significance, or meaning to our lifetime. Somehow we may already know the answer—or answers. Our ego may reply with criticism and evaluation, telling us how well we have done in some endeavors and how badly in others. Our expanded self will consider moments of transcendence and selflessness when we pierced through the rice-paper screen of delusion and stood inside Reality.

The Self that is behind and beyond our small self may make no reply. It is beyond concepts and illusion. For the Self, physical death and the end of an individual life make no difference, since consciousness is being and the Self is beyond both being and non-being. For the Self, death has less importance; it is as unremarkable as the changing of the blood and the renewing of body cells. It is a natural process in the stream of life, another step in an endless cycle of changing conditions, while Reality is beyond all conditions.

An elderly spiritual seeker writes:

> I have spent a lot of time reading, listening, and attending lectures, seminars, workshops, growth groups, *satsang* with Indian gurus and monks and Sufi masters and self-styled leaders, self-directed visionaries, psychics, and yogis, and each one has given me their view of *how-it-is*. Some have been genuine and well-motivated, but it has always been their vision of how-it-is, not mine. I have strived to attain a personal vision, an individual seeing, an original point of view of All that is, of life's secrets. The question I ask myself is, how, if at all, has all this reading, thinking, and listening helped me in my quest.
>
> I sometimes wonder: what will I be certain of, lying on my deathbed; what will I actually know; what of all the experiences I have had and of all the inspiring thoughts and feelings I have had will have become a part of me? Will I crave attainment, experience maudlin regret, fear for my lack of faith, bemoan my lack of awareness, or simply yearn for the next breath? It seems to me that what I truly know in my last moments is all that really matters. What I have inside me is all I can take with me, as I cross from life to death.

Life and death comprise a single process. The moment of death is any moment. There are only moments before death and moments after death. So where is death? Death does not exist. It is merely the dark mirror, the empty screen on which we may project our fears. All that scares or attracts us about death is really about life.

What was born will surely die. But what is eternal can never die. What is our true Nature? What is unchanging in us? What survives our individual self and merges into Unity? Intuitively we sense something unchanging, eternal, and undying that bridges the divide between death and life. We may seek this in life and find it in death. We may find it and lose it again. We may doubt it was ever there and yet be certain that it is all there is. We may call it God or Truth or the Absolute. For some it is simply Love.

Love

Love evades all our seeking, because we can never possess or define it. It eludes discovery or understanding, because it is so close to us we may never make an object of it or see it clearly. Ultimately, love is what we "are."

The dancing goddess of Japan, Ogamisama, teaches the refinement of the soul through the practices of prayer and egolessness. In a dance of ecstasy she dissolves self-love and wishing to be loved. Before this dissolution we must begin to understand what love really is; we must undergo a deep self-exploration and experience what love has been for us.

Love is one of the most overused and inaccurately employed words in our language. We say *love* when we mean *need, want, lust, envy,* or *admiration.* Love may be love of self, and even then it may have different meanings. There is narcissistic love where we fall in love with our self-image and become self-obsessed, or there is the kind of self-love where we open to ourselves and grow through self-acceptance.

Love may be reflective, as when we project some part of ourselves onto another. It may be beauty or kindness, human sentiment or maternal warmth, fondness or physical attraction. When we project these parts of ourselves onto another, we are compelled to be with them to be close to the part of us they possess. When we fall out of love we are compelled to take back our projections of ourselves, and our disillusionment makes us and the other a little more real.

Love may be transcendent, like the love of God, and through such love we may expand and meet the Divine in ourselves. Such love is a genuine opening of the heart, a flowering of our spirituality. It involves no other, because there is no separation or projection involved.

As varied as the different kinds of love are, they share a common source. While the source of love is pure and undefined, the many forms of love assume different expressions. Every love seems to want to achieve perfection.

It may be that falling in love is a reflection or even a feature of divine love. However, it is a challenge of inner work to see through illusion and fantasy, or at least to see things for what they are. Therapists frequently play the role of what psychotherapist Irvin Yalom calls "Love's Executioner": the one who penetrates the mystery, dissolves the illusion, and releases us from enchantment.

Perhaps love between two people can be as frail as this, but compare Yalom's point of view with what may be the pinnacle of love between two people—the relationship of the Indian saint Ramakrishna and his wife. Ramakrishna worshipped his wife, Sarada Devi, as the manifestation of the Divine Mother. During worship, he and Sarada lost external consciousness and were united in spiritual consciousness. At Sarada's feet Ramakrishna offered the merit of his spiritual practice.

This worship was not merely the shallow-rooted projection of idealization. The love between Ramakrishna and Sarada had the human qualities of pragmatism, personal challenge, and the growth of intimacy. In Sarada, Ramakrishna saw all women, which enabled him to worship her as the goddess—the Divine Mother. Sarada spoke of her relationship with Ramakrishna in the kind of poetic terms that reflect the natural and involving course of human love.

Love grows in our hearts and seeks to be realized. Love is endless and love is timeless. We can never define love, but we can learn to understand and deepen into—and beyond—our partial human experience of it.

Love is commonly portrayed as a commodity to acquire—through enticement, seduction, material boasting, and manipulation. We believe that we need love, from others, from outside ourselves. We believe we are lacking in love, loved too much, spoiled for love, competing for love, in and out of love. But how different life becomes when we understand that we *are* love and that the flow of love from the deep source of our own heart is unlimited. In Irina Tweedie's book *The Chasm of Fire*, a lovely exchange takes place between Tweedie and her spiritual teacher, when she asks him how great is the capacity of the human heart, and he replies that there is no limit when we are drunk with the wine of the eyes of the Beloved.

When love is no longer a commodity to acquire, give, and receive, the only opportunity love offers is the blessing to love, rather than be loved. We are no more dependent on the object of our desire for love than they are on us. Love is like salt water to a sea fish—it is all around us, we are swimming in it, yet we hardly notice it. Loving, however, is not a personal act, but an impersonal one.

When the Beloved is recognized within us, we become an instrument of love. Scott McPherson's inspiring play *Marvin's Room* was made into a Hollywood movie that explores the nature of love in unusual depth. It tells the story of two sisters, Lee and Bessie, who haven't seen or talked to each other for twenty years. Lee left home to make her way in the world, while Bessie stayed at home to care for their bed-ridden father and eccentric, elderly Aunt Ruth. In a pivotal and touching scene, the two sisters reveal their very different attitudes to love: Bessie declares how lucky she feels to have had love in her life in the form of her father and her aunt. Lee replies that she can see that they love her very much. Bessie says that is not what she means, what she means is that she has been *fortunate to be able to love so much.*

When we seek love outside ourselves, we have difficulty loving. Bessie has discovered love in the opportunity to care for others. She is grateful for the opportunity to love in circumstances in which others might feel resentful, bitter, or taken for granted. When gratitude precedes the act of loving, love is genuine selflessness. When we feel deeply grateful for life, love simply flows out of us.

Seeking to love rather than to be loved is a deep inner quality of our true nature. Being the lover rather than the beloved opens us to the experience of unconditional love. Conditional love is a state of doing; unconditional love is a state of being. For many of us, a sense of merging our being and with our doing is apparent in early life. Later, we re-experience this merging when we "fall in love" with another. Falling in love is involuntary—with our thoughts in abeyance, the usually inhibited life of our emotions overcomes us. The same is true of spiritual love, which lies beyond intellect or reason.

Love is opening. There is an abundance of love, but we keep ourselves protected from it. This abundance may be expressed in an endless variety of ways: in kindness, in compassion, in marriage, in friendship, in genuine caring, and in service. Opening to the abundance of love returns us to our real Selves and the essence of it is giving, rather than acquiring. Love is the deep morality of existence. It needs no acquisition; it is all-pervading and it is what we are: we do not ask for love, we give it.

Giving love is everybody's nature when we are true to our innermost being. The ocean does not want for water; the sun does not want for heat; and the real does not want for truth. What need have we of love, when love is what we are? This is what Ogamisama calls dissolving of self-love and wishing to be loved. And with this comes a deeper motivation, the third level of commitment, intention, and awakening—the impulse to realize ourselves.

In Summary

Even an irreversible depth of human evolution and awakening such as transformation requires the follow-up processes of integrating and stabilizing to strengthen its radical effect on our lives. The next chapter forms a bridge into the spiritual realms and is the last in the second stage of awakening. Before reading on, revert to your inner-work practice and work with these questions:

1. Review the four stages of ego—strengthening the ego, bringing the ego into service to the Soul, shedding ego attachments, transcending the ego—and assess what stage you are in. What are you holding on to? What do you need to let go of? Refer back to this self-assessment when we revisit ego work at the end of the next chapter.

2. How is your relationship with death—the great inevitable? Who dies?

3. In a way an old person is inside us, just the same as a child remains inside us. So, regardless of your biological age, dialogue with the old one inside you and learn to start a relationship.

4. What is your experience of love? Is there a difference between human and divine love? Can love be given unconditionally? After reading this chapter, how do you understand "dissolving self-love and wishing to be loved..."?

10

Ways to Realization

Group Practice, Commitment, and Letting Go

At times a group that is committed to personal and spiritual development is indispensable for our inner journey. In Buddhism the *sangha*, or group of spiritual seekers, is considered one of the three essential conditions for spiritual progress.

A group challenges us to be known by others and act skillfully, responsibly, and compassionately in a community of faith and trust. It tests the depth of our understanding of who we really are and what we have genuinely attained. It supports us in our practice, by encouraging discipline and application. Finally, it allows us to identify with the collective soul through our interaction, cooperation, and relationship with others. A group gives us the opportunity to stabilize in the experience of personal authenticity in ordinary life, by allowing space for the inner being in the outer world.

Those who choose a spiritual path or religion make a deep commitment, but it is still only the reflection of the profound commitment to the true Self. Those who remain in a group will inevitably face the expansion beyond all methods, spiritual appearances, and conventions before they reach their goal. They may choose to retain the appearance of monk, priest, or meditator, but it doesn't matter which costume they wear in the priorities of transcendence.

Many of us are attracted to the outward trappings of spirituality—the *mala*, the robe, the picture of a guru, spiritual statues, a holy book. But none of these things have any spiritual value in themselves. They are of spiritual value only when we internalize the aspect of the spirit they symbolize through practice. If they are not living symbols, they are simply dead. Buddha statues may just as well be models of Mickey Mouse; and malas, cheap trinkets.

Making the mundane sacred is a profound practice. It is pleasant to have devotional objects, but not necessary. Any object can be sacred ... because *life is sacred*. Any clothes can be our spiritual robe and any ornament can be our mala. So long as we dedicate our lives to spiritual unfolding, we need no "special" things.

At the Zen monastery where I trained, intensive *sesshins* were held at regular intervals, and people from all over the world came to participate. As the only resident layperson in the monastery, I felt proud when these inexperienced "outsiders" came in. I loved the precise, devotional, ritualized life of a monk. I was well versed in the monastic routines and rituals, and I felt accomplished in the practices of mindfulness. These included making *gassho*—bowing with the palms of the hands together, fingers just below the tip of the nose, and elbows away from your sides—at each doorway, to the meditation cushion, to our food, to each other, and reciting prayers at the table, in the *zendo*, and even in the lavatory. Washing the dishes was a model of ritualized efficiency: a threefold process of bowl-washing followed by a rigorous process of drying, sorting, and putting away. Going to bed was just as exacting: pulling out our mattresses from under the platform, arranging our bedding, and lying down before a monk carrying a smoking incense stick slowly circumvented the zendo in a closing ritual symbolizing protection. I particularly loved processions and ceremonies when the monks walked solemnly in a hierarchical line, like so many identical Buddhas.

During one sesshin I was working in the kitchens. The kitchens were in a separate building from the dining room, so the food had to be carried up a steep flight of narrow stone steps and across a wide gravel driveway. One particular day was spectacularly windy and blustery. The gusts were so strong that the monks' robes were twisted into knots and lifted, and progress around the monastery grounds was severely impeded.

I wore a layperson's robe consisting of a skirt and a kimono. I was proud of my robe. With a little help, I had cut and sewn the light beige material myself following the pattern prescribed by monastic rules. The full-length skirt was made of several meters of cloth pleated and gathered at the waist. It reached fully down to the ground. My robe was both a source of personal pride and a symbol of forbearance and humility to me. I wore it continually. As with so many monastic practices, it took away the expression of my individuality by removing any possibility of personal choice.

As I approached the steps on my way to the dining room, carrying a large stainless-steel bowl of mashed potatoes, I became acutely aware of several dozen faces staring at me through the low windows across the driveway. Walking in solemn procession at the head of half a dozen monks carrying bowls, being scrutinized by a group of inexperienced meditators, I felt supernally graceful, spiritually elevated. I tried to project flowing movements and a serene expression toward the faces in the windows. Since the retreat participants might not be familiar with the layperson's robe, I fantasized that some of them might think I was a wandering, foreign monk on a pilgrimage or perhaps a visiting abbot from some distant monastery. In mere seconds out of my imagination I had created a narrative, with myself as a paradigm of spiritual virtue eminently worthy of deep veneration.

But the weather conditions distracted me from my delicious daydreaming reverie. With the wind threatening to raise the voluminous skirts of my robe, it took all my concentration to hold the heavy bowl of mashed potatoes firmly between my extended forearms, bearing down with my hips in a futile attempt to counter the uprush. Just as I reached the top step, I trod on the hem of my robe, pitched slowly forward, and with my mouth wide open emitted a high-pitched yelp and fell flat on my face. As I lay spread-eagled, the mashed potato oozed out onto the gravel. I struggled to my feet, fighting against the wind, with my hair, face, and kimono plastered with gravel and potato, only to realize that the retreat participants had observed the whole mishap in minute detail.

When I left the monastery, the world seemed so brash and insensitive that I wondered how I would survive. Then I remembered that I had sometimes felt these qualities in myself—and often projected them onto others—while I was in the monastery. Sometimes I sorely missed the binding power of the ancient rituals and the discipline that had at times felt so restricting when I was there. Now they appealed to me more for the certainty and security they provided. When I recalled the serene faces of the monks, the faces of "ordinary" people seemed disturbed and grotesque. But gradually the gap between the idealized monastery and the rude outside world narrowed. I saw that we are all spirits in form, living, growing, and responding to life as best we can. Finally, I closed the gap by owning my inner spiritual life and retrieving the spiritual projection with which I had clothed the monastery. I understood that my spirit was essentially inner, not "outside"—neither in the monastery nor outside it. By returning it to me, I was free to express it in the world in appropriate ways. I saw that the world and the monastery were not as different as I thought. The world was a monastery, my life was an opportunity for spiritual practice, and the division I had made between the two was the projection of an inner divide, a creation of my mind, not my heart.

Genuine spiritual practice always demands letting go. Any method or practice becomes a trap if we hold on to it for too long. The Benedictine monk John Main likened meditation practice to climbing a hundred-foot pole. He said that as we get higher we are tempted to stop climbing and take in the view. But, suspecting the view will be even better higher up, we carry on climbing. When we get into the clouds, the view disappears. We have no sense of progress, only our commitment to climbing. So we carry on, inches at a time. Then the clouds disperse and the view appears more magnificent than before.

Eventually beyond reason and complacency, purpose and perseverance, we are called to jump: we must abandon the pole. Abandoning the pole takes us into the boundary-less unknown where we are closer to truth than ever before. Where Main leaves us, the celebrated Ch'an master Mumon, in yet another story about a hundred-foot pole, takes up the theme and asks: How do you proceed from the top of the pole? He answers that if you are to avoid danger, your insight must be genuine; your spiritual attainment must be real.

Spiritual practice may be measured in terms of time or even quality, but the realization of spiritual accomplishments cannot truly be measured, because it is only revealed through insight. Without insight we will spiritually perish by plunging into the darkness of ignorance, and our example will lead others into ignorance. But if we are endowed with insight and non-attachment, we may jump with impunity and our example will lead others to freedom. This is the circle that the practice of sangha completes. As we receive help in our spiritual practice, so we are able to give help to others. It is not a question of gaining qualifications or learning skills, but of drawing out the authentic wisdom that is deep within us all.

So, our courage and commitment to begin a spiritual practice must be matched by our willingness to drop it ... when the time is right. Holding on or clinging to a practice is always an expression of fear and resistance. Non-attachment—neither attachment, nor un-attachment—means letting go whenever we are asked to by our inner self. Only when we have relinquished everything we have been holding on to out of fear, can we approach the profoundly intimate relationship with the spiritual, the transcendent, and the divine.

But first there must be lessons in wisdom.

Spiritual Questions and Divine Lessons

Wisdom manifests in the lesson of the present moment. Imagine it this way: wisdom approaches you from a far-off horizon. At first, it appears as silence. As it gets closer it manifests as a murmur, then as a clear answer, and then—close-up now—as the question that can lead you back to the answer, to the murmur, and finally back into the silence. Wisdom is a reciprocal circle. Our life lessons appear to us as spiritual questions and lead us to insight and understanding.

Spiritual questions are like Zen koans—they arise in every moment. One way out of confusion or lack of focus is to ask, "What is my spiritual question?" The question is always present, so to hear it we must also be present. Our spiritual questions change as we live through the answers. Our lives are the answers to our questions.

For example, my present answer is the condition of being a 59-year-old man with a large family who wants time with his wife and children, to practice psychotherapy, and to write about my insights and understanding of personal growth and spiritual practice. This brings many potential conflicts. Should I play with my children or should I withdraw quietly to write? Should I spend time with my wife or take some time for myself? How should I balance my working life with my roles as a father and as a husband? The possibilities for confusion about what is "right" are many. While I am immersed in my life predicament—the *answer*—I have no clear perspective. But things become clearer when I consider the *question* my life is answering.

My present spiritual question is "How is life fulfilled?"[8] and my answer is "Now, in the moment." When I fall out of the moment I become immediately overwhelmed by the demands of life. But when I am in the moment, I can make decisions and fulfill the various roles—father, husband, psychotherapist, author—that my life presents me with. I *live* the answer "now," the constant, eternal, singular moment in which I may transcend the boundaries of duality and the illusion that I am confined by my roles. In each moment life is fulfilled, but that moment and its fulfillment are lost in a single thought. "Now" is the answer to my question "How is life fulfilled?" In any given moment, existence is what presents itself *now*—the swaying branches, the dark mountainside, the yellow seat cover, this glass of water, a crying child, the smell of coffee, the touch of my feet on the earth—this is existence: there are no obstacles to fulfillment.

As we go further in spiritual work, our questions tend to become less spectacular. A senior monk once told me that he was working

---

8. For an explanation of how I arrived at this question, see my book *The Flight of Consciousness* (Ashgrove Publishing, 2002), 9–10.

with "interruptions." At the time, interruptions didn't seem to me to be too profound a spiritual lesson. But some years later, when interruptions constantly pestered me, I understood better. I was forced to look at the question "Who is the 'me' who feels interrupted?" since everything that happened appeared to interrupt "me." Finally, when the interruptions became powerfully overwhelming, I decided that the only way through was to consider all interruptions as spiritual teaching. But now I had to practice my conviction. So each ringing telephone, doorbell, road drill, and unwelcome visitor became a call from my deeper nature urging me to expand my self-awareness. In this way, each interruption presaged a potential revelation, a promise of insight.

Interruptions were my constant learning and my spiritual question until the lesson reached a dramatic climax. One summer I attended a Theravadin Buddhist retreat. For ten days my life consisted of sitting meditation alternating with slow walking meditation, accompanied by the disciplines of fasting after midday, no note-taking, no talking, no worldly distractions, and no vicarious pleasures or vices.

The retreat venue was a large building complex that had been divided into premises for various alternative businesses and organizations. For the first meditation period, the monk who led the retreat entered the large room with his assistant, a junior monk dressed in white robes, who looked like the Buddha himself. The soft footfalls of the monks, the gentle chirping of the birds outside the open windows, the warm summer breeze—all augured an auspicious event.

Two minutes into the first meditation period, the most tremendous commotion broke out. We could hear it through the open window. We all got up to look out and saw a gang of builders who were working up on the fifth-story roof of the neighboring premises. They were throwing boards, bricks, and blocks off the roof into dumpsters placed at ground level. The vibrations resonated through our chests and shook through our entire bodies. But the monk's serenity was unfazed. He said, "Let's use this as a tool. Every time it happens, just let it open your heart." He helped us to work with the situation just as it was … and it turned out to be a blessing. We had to go beyond our prejudices and our models of how a meditation retreat should be. My inner voice said, "I've come here for a nice, peaceful retreat. I don't want this disturbance." So I struggled and resisted openness, acceptance, and surrender. But as we worked with softening and opening, each sound and impact became the thunderclap of the Divine opening our hearts.

Our questions may become less spectacular in progressive stages of spiritual practice, but we need to exert increasingly stringent measures to behave scrupulously. The abbot of a spiritual temple admitted to me that he couldn't afford to make even small mistakes anymore, because the consequences rebounded on his psyche with greater fierceness than ever before. In the secular world it may be the same.

The most unlikely things can help us in our spiritual practice. Any set of circumstances can be used to further our work on ourselves. Our spiritual question is always manifesting in the present moment and revealing our spiritual direction. When we lose it, we lose our focus. But if we maintain our awareness of it, we stay sharp and focused.

As well as individual spiritual questions, we are collectively united in contemporary questions for the collective soul. The question for the group soul binds us together with a common theme. It is the material we share with other seekers. The events of our lives are connected with others through a life curriculum. Our individual spiritual questions are reflections, whereas the group spiritual question is the mirror.

Today, the spiritual questions of the group soul have two essential themes—love and learning. These two themes reflect our spiritual evolution as a collective whole. The first theme is expressed in the question "How can I love?" This central concern of contemporary life may take other forms, which reflect the conditions necessary for love, such as "How can I forgive?" or "How can I rise above my small self?" The second theme is expressed in the question "How can I learn?" Again, this concern may take other forms, such as "How can I open?" or "How can I grow?"

Group and individual spiritual questions reveal our life direction. Whenever we are present, life is teaching us. Without awareness of this we are lost. When a traumatic event or circumstance reveals itself to be a divine lesson, it is our spiritual question that binds the trauma and lesson together.

Beyond Contradiction and Paradox

All things in the manifest world contain their opposites; objects and qualities are balanced by their resistances. So we have day and night, light and dark, good and evil, life and death. Through the dynamic interplay of action and inertia, the relative world of appearances is created and maintained in time and space. It is the ebb and flow of existence, the waft and wane of unfolding events. When we live exclusively in the relative world, we are in a state of contradiction and paradox.

Paradox is the threshold to synthesis and going beyond opposites. We live in a mass of contradictions, expressed in paradoxical thought and behavior. When we look inside, we can see that we are composed of many selves. But we identify with our intellects, and we rationalize and deny these selves to own up to a false self. Our false self is hastily stitched together to give the appearance of unity and substance. The stitching hides the filling—our shame and confusion about who we are, what we are doing, where we are going.

In the early years of the growth movement, I formed a men's group with some friends. One evening we devised an exercise where two of us would go into the middle of the group and respond to each other without any preconceptions whatsoever. The intention was to practice spontaneity, and we called it "exercises in truth." I was paired with Jesse. I liked him for his generosity, his sense of fun, and his openness. But he was also pompous, arrogant, and inclined to hold rigid opinions. To some degree he was the scapegoat of the group for these qualities. He began the exercise with some soulful sharing about himself and his relationship to me. The more serious he was, the funnier I found it. I began to laugh, and the more I laughed the more serious he became, and the more hilarious I found him. As he challenged me and my reaction, he became increasingly offended and I felt a mix of elation and freedom at allowing myself to be contradictory, crazy, and totally unreasonable. The exercise ended with Jesse leaving the room, offended and outraged by my behavior, as I fell about on the floor in hysterics.

What was liberating for me was painful and reactive for Jesse. We had played out the confrontation of contradiction and paradox in a very human scene: reason met unreason, sense met nonsense, sane met insane. When we learn to understand contradiction and paradox, we can make sense of these apparently irreconcilable opposites. We begin to slip through the confines of reason and deepen in the light of insight.

Beyond reason a new and expansive understanding dawns in us. We have been conscious only of a world of shadows. When we release ourselves from our shackles, we are dazzled by the light. The light has cast the shadows that we thought were the real world. Just as the sun illuminates the world, so we appear as shadows of the Divine and our goal is to see things as they really are, prior to their shadows.

The sun is the light that extinguishes the need for any other light. In Hindu literature this image is a metaphor for burning the last desire. Ramana Maharshi said that to see an object in the dark, the eye, light, and the object are needed; to see light, only the eye and light are needed, but to see the sun we need no light, because it will be drowned in the sunlight. Correspondingly, the intellect cannot realize the Self; to see the world or the outward objects that compose the world, we require objects, reflected light, and the mind, but to see the Self, all we need is to turn the mind inward.

So, what we see is partial. Our thoughts, concepts, and experiences are merely relative. To truly see, we must take a leap out of our intuitive heart. The spiritual mapmakers have left behind very clear accounts of "how-it-is"; today we have great knowledge at our disposal. But knowledge alone is not sufficient to awaken us to Truth. That requires a leap of faith: we must turn away from the reflection and gaze at the sun.

Contradiction has created an adversary, and paradox has created confusion. Caught between fear and desire, we have been fleeing from ourselves. Our longing and our terror have been only for ourselves, like Chuang Tzu's story of the running man who feared his own shadow and hated his own footprints. The more he ran, the more footprints he made, and his shadow never left him. So he ran faster and faster until, exhausted, he collapsed and died. If he had stayed in the shade he would have had no shadow, and if he had stood still he would have made no footprints.

Similarly, we have tried to run away from ourselves.

The running man is our small self, our so-called "objective" reality, and the world of common sense is a mere shadow, while the true Self remains quietly in the mystery, a witness to both fear and desire. The Soul is the self-referring subject that signifies the final responsibility: the incorporation of our total projection of reality. Now, finally, outside is inside.

All along we have been a mere reflection, a finger pointing at the moon, a shadow playing in the eye of the Eternal. Like the birds in the Sufi story "The Conference of the Birds," we long to be ushered into the divine presence. Although they have endured many trials in their quest for the magical bird of paradise, the birds are required to pass one final test—total surrender. For those that rise to this challenge, the past is washed away and a new life of peace and detachment begins.

Transcending contradiction and paradox, we become unified and we deepen into freedom. With nothing left to defend, we become transparent to the Soul, and it continually enriches and enlightens our lives. We have asked and attained to live the impossible. All that was merely possible is now behind us. Beyond the curtain of memory and anticipation, spontaneity is within our grasp. Our inner work has led us to a place of profound surrender. We are no longer ourselves and we have never been more ourselves.

We have almost completed this account of the second stage of personality work, the authentic self. Many will remain in this stage, with the sphere of service to others or to the world or both becoming the focus of their commitment and intention. We do not necessarily know, simply by looking, whether a person is living in the first, second, or third stage of awakening. It is quite possible for someone to be working outwardly in social work, for example, while they are inwardly focused on the spiritual life. As we approach the third stage, the deeper challenges of awareness and consciousness, our points of reference are less clear.

Today our spiritual and psychological challenge is to realize ourselves *in* the world, not removed from it. The practice of inner work in the modern world includes the three traditional ways—personal, interpersonal, and transpersonal—and integrates them into a single process of discovery and understanding. Our work on our personalities, authenticity, and spirituality combine, flow together, and create a continuum of revelation—a journey around, and finally to, the Self. As the nineteenth-century philosopher Xenos Clark put it, we journey around ourselves in revelation.

Our inner work has taken us through great and profound depths when we get to this stage of authenticity. Through the museums of our personality, illusion of all kinds, belief systems, and all that was "dead" in us to the flowing waters of our Soul where we find that the Divine is everywhere, the world is our school, and the people in it are our allies and helpers.

Does Inner Work End?

Personal inner work (through the first and second levels of awakening) *can* be completed. It is so difficult that by no means everyone who starts it will reach the end. But however far we travel, we are enriched. Completing personal inner work means that we know enough and are sufficiently wise enough to practice continued awareness of our patterns and our character. In effect, we *know ourselves* in our personality and there should not be too many surprises left. We may reach the transformational threshold through which we may begin (or continue) the transpersonal or spiritual journey to Self-realization. But, even if we don't choose to cross that threshold, we should be empowered to be self-regulating, self-empowered, self-aware, and self-referring.

Personal inner work consists of two stages: the process of self-discovery, which is essentially work on our conditioning, and the transformation into authenticity and living the heart-centered life of compassion. In these two stages we open, explore, and discover the history of the patterns and influences that have shaped our individual lives and created our character. The process of witnessing ourselves, experiencing our feelings, resolving inner conflicts, and revealing ourselves changes how we see ourselves. From identifying with our egos, which are immersed in the drama of our life, we "climb out" of ourselves and identify increasingly with our awareness and authenticity. So we empower ourselves to look inward with growing clarity and attention.

As we shift from seeing ourselves as "subject" to seeing ourselves as "object," we ask, "Who is it that sees, comments on, and tells my story?" We become less identified with our ego-selves and more identified with our awareness. The possibility that there is something "other" begins to dawn within us. Gradually we move out of the ego-center into awareness, and see with increasing clarity. (Please refer back to exercise 1 at the end of the previous chapter, on page 180, and make a further self-assessment now of yourself in regard to this new insight about the ego.)

Each time we complete a circuit around the Self, we grow in knowledge, insight, and understanding. Usually when we have completed the circuit two or three times, we know ourselves well enough and are able to practice awareness deeply enough to see that we are continually making choices about how we live our lives. No longer can we play the "blame game" of attributing our life circumstances to conditioning, other people, fatalism, coincidence, or a range of misfortunes. We reach the point of choice when we can finally take responsibility for our own lives and we are empowered to change if we so choose.

Finally, we move out of self-awareness into simply awareness, and the embrace of this awareness is not only given to ourselves but to all and everything.

Some people do make changes, and in some cases they are sweeping life changes. The shift from victim-consciousness, with its attendant states of self-pity, resentment, and conflict, to an awareness of real choice and power transforms everything, and life is never the same again. For others, there is a peace and groundedness about renewing the relationship to aspects of their lives that they had previously chosen unconsciously. Although outwardly there is little change, the inner changes are nonetheless deep.

This point of choice marks the end of our personal journey. We now have the tools to be empowered, enabled, and self-referring. We have grown out of confusion, alienation, and disempowerment and metamorphosed from a puppet of our conditioning into a psychologically mature adult.

If the psycho-spiritual journey is no longer for us, and we choose to end our inner-work practice here at the conclusion of our personal work, then we may continue living with deeper awareness and inner clarity, knowing what we choose, recognizing what we want, and accepting life's compromises. But if we are spiritually oriented—a life-seeker—the end of the personal journey is the beginning of the spiritual one. Now we know who we are, and we can get on with the task of living and fulfilling a human life, spontaneously and freely. Our inner work now becomes principally spiritual. It is a new perspective, a new way of approaching life in our journey to the Source.

In Summary

We have been on a long journey through the layers and trials of the personality, and into and through the life-processes of transformation and authenticity. Now it is time to take a look back, not only at the previous chapter but also at the first two stages of awakening that we have discussed in this book so far. Before we venture into the spiritual realms per se, consider where you find yourself by answering the following questions for yourself:

1. How has a group or an individual challenged you in your psycho-spiritual development? What attachments to spiritual practices do you need to drop?

2. What is your spiritual question? What is your present divine lesson? How can you love? How can you open and grow?

3. Write your autobiography from the perspective of your spiritual journey, without judgment or criticism.

4. What role has paradox taken in your life? Likewise for intuition, surrender, and spontaneity?

5. Self-assessment time: Where are you in your work on your personality? If you have crossed the transformational threshold, what challenges are you facing? Who witnesses, sees, and is aware of you and your unfolding life narrative?

Stage
THREE

*The Source
of Consciousness*

11

Becoming the True Self

Like the mystical philosopher P. D. Ouspensky, we began by saying, "I …," then time passed while we told our stories and revealed our inner world. Now we return again to "I …," and we find that a transformation has taken place. We are no longer so attached to our stories or our personal definitions.[9] Viewing our biography now from a distance, we can clearly see the limitations it had placed on us. We see ourselves out of a deepening sense of awareness and reality. Our center has shifted, and we are closer to who we really are, now that we have shed the limiting definitions that we clung to out of fear.

As we stabilize in this awareness, the old "I" is entirely transformed from subject to object, and the person uttering the word "I" is likewise transformed from object to subject, from pretence to authenticity, from restriction to freedom. In other words, we can see and include ourselves now in our awareness and in our worldview.

Over time we will see that our truth lies not in who we think we are, but rather in the transcendence of the thought that we are anyone at all. In the silence of "I," we experience the birth and death of the universe, and as the universe is All, so am I. Thus the destination of our journey is to arrive in a place we never left and to become what

---

9. See the "Personal Stories" section in chapter 2.

we have always been, for we ourselves and the whole of existence are One.

Psycho-Spiritual Unfolding: Beyond Being and Experience

In the third level of awakening, our psycho-spiritual unfolding requires the loss of all that we hold dear in order to attain the only thing of value. It is not for the fainthearted or the weak-spirited; the journey takes great courage.

Attaining the true Self puts the role of our small sense of self (and by association, personality, ego, and character) into question. If we realize our true Self, is the small self then dispensable?

Psycho-spiritual development involves a process of unfolding whereby a healthy strong ego may be developed out of attending to the raw material of conditioned upbringing, creating a robust vehicle for our soulful qualities, and offered in spiritual surrender, as and when we are ready to lessen our attachments to the material world. This is spiritual wholeness: developing our ego personality and transcending ourselves as separate individuals *in a single connected process* of human awakening. To be fully human, we have to be not human or divine, but both, and the emphasis on either depends on what stage of life we are in. We can no more separate the developing self from the transcendent one than we can separate the stem from the flower, or the earth from the heavens, because each is an integral part of the whole. Not only is our soul divine, but so too is our humanness.

Speaking of "I," becoming aware of who we really are throws us into a conundrum as difficult as trying to see ourselves. We simply can't do it. Even if we look at ourselves in a mirror, we see only our reflection. The self looking at itself is an impossibility. But in profound meditative silence we drop into the present moment through our persistence, by developing our capacity for inaction and checking our compulsion to wander off in our minds. Being present in this moment makes it possible for us to experience ourselves as we truly are.

Even the personal authenticity we reached through transformation and compassion in the second stage of awakening is merely partial and separate. Beyond this, we can pierce the veil of illusion and discover that we *are* the presence behind the appearance of self, in any guise. The complete fulfillment of a human life is to touch this consciousness, this inner presence. Ultimately the work of the soul is to join the source from which it came and from which it has never truly been separated—beyond thought and concepts, beyond all illusion and separateness; even beyond being and experience.

Let us prepare for these expansive events of transcendence now with a simple but nonetheless extraordinary exercise, which reflects our resistance to the two primary attributes of spiritual illumination: spontaneity and surrender. Take yourself out for a walk. As you walk, become increasingly aware of what you experience—less *what you think you experience* and more *what you actually experience*. Do you notice the separation, like an energetic membrane, between yourself and the world? You experience this separation between the inside and outside of yourself, so that your emotions, your thoughts, your physical sensations, the processes of respiration, digestion, and circulation belong on one side of the separation and outward events—dogs, trees, wind, sounds, other people, houses, cars, and so on belong on the outside. Now the aim of this exercise is simple: bring all your attention to the reality of this separation. Is it not you yourself? Without you yourself, how could this separation exist? So now with this new clarity of focus, walk and meditate on you and this separation between inner and outer.

We will return to the theme of separation and this exercise later on.

The third stage of the inner journey is for those of us who want to know, who want to feel and understand, who are unwilling to settle for anything less than the truth. Awakening to our essential self is the most profound core pursuit for those of us who take deep responsibility for the gift of life. Our inner exploration has awakened us to what is real and precious. We are now open to an experience of life that is deeper and more real than our personality—with its restrictive patterns, models, and concepts—can allow. When we cease looking outside for happiness and fulfillment, and instead look inside, the most surprising events occur. If we persist in self-exploration, we may realize our true Self.

In Summary

So far we have faced many deep challenges. Now we consider inner subjects that are unspeakable, or rather they are very hard to speak about. The words must be understood not as mere descriptions, and certainly not as that which they seek to describe, but as pointers, as traps that we willingly step into to sink into pure meaning. We practice and intend to understand on the deepest level, and submerge ourselves in deeper meaning. A book that expounds inner wisdom cannot tell you anything you don't know already, but it can illuminate the soul and reflect the spirit. Inspiration can lead you to your real nature. These three exercises are appropriate for the tremendous step we are about to take:

1. Meditate on the thought that is "I." What is revealed to you? What do you learn about "I"?

2. A guided imagery: You stand on a great threshold; a gulf is between you and the truth—there can be no escape. You can only return to yourself and to the source of your being-ness, soul, and spirit. How are you? What are you feeling? What do you have to do now?

3. During your life you have forgotten many, many things. But you have never lost sight of yourself. Although you may have been less self-aware at times, "you" have always been there in the background as the "experiencer" of life. Now return to the work you have done on the four stages of ego—the first exercise at the end of chapter 9—and, based on what you have learned from these last two chapters, re-assess your attachment to the ego.

12

Realizing Our True Nature

No longer bound to the senses, filled with a sense of presence, we are liberated from our attachments to the small self. This life, this body, this existence is an opportunity to learn, expand, and live our deepest truth. It is not a matter of getting somewhere, but of *being where we are*. We find ourselves in the process of action and in the quality of being, past reflections of the light, deeper than the echoes of the spiritual, prior to the waterfall's roar in the stillness of our true nature.

Beyond the Shadows of the Divine

Over the course of inner work, we find ourselves to lose ourselves and find ourselves again: in our work on the personality we discover who we are, but we can only go further in moments of deep awareness when compassion and consciousness are manifested *through* us. The self we discover after that transcends definition or labeling.

It is like the story of the poor villager who dreams of a treasure buried under a bridge in a distant city. Overcoming many obstacles and challenges he arrives in the city, where he finds the bridge of his dream. A guard patrolling the bridge sees a man with a shovel acting suspiciously, and when he confronts him, the poor villager confesses everything. "Dreams!" exclaims the guard. "Why, only last night I dreamt that in the house of a poor man in some far-off village, a chest of gold coins is buried under the doorstep. So do I travel all that way to dig up the threshold of some poor idiot's home?" On hearing this and recognizing the description of the house as his own, the poor man hurries home, digs up the threshold to his house, and lives happily ever after on his buried treasure.

Shortly after I had encountered the wonderful magic of inner work through the human potential movement, I met some followers of an Eastern guru. The attraction to their abandon, their lack of inhibitions, perceived freedom, and naturalness was balanced by my wariness, doubt, and a natural aversion toward surrender of the individual self, a being I had not yet fully discovered. Of course I wasn't that clear at the time. The prospect of making my problems spiritual and being healed, not on any physical plane of pain and discomfort but rather along a psychic, ethereal, astral plane of transcendental illumination, was extremely appealing to my young mind.

When my aversion had run its course and yielded to my attraction, I embarked on my journey to the East. Redolent of Hermann Hesse novels, 1970s rites of passage, and clichéd spiritual initiations, this was nonetheless to me a unique event. At the ashram, I meditated, I danced, I chanted, and I meditated some more. This invaluable experience ended when my money ran out and I returned home.

Back home I was shown admiration and castigation in equal measure, but the one person from whom I received the most outright rebuke was my therapist. He openly criticized and belittled me for wearing Eastern dress and beads. In spite of this I persisted with my inner work under his guidance. One day I had this insight: I was divine; within me was the spiritual dimension I was seeking. I had no need to search for it anywhere other than within myself... outside myself it was reflected back to me to remind me, to inform me, and to help me remember. That was it!

This discovery of the inner treasure yields a deeper one. In the all-embracing budding of our true nature, the flower of being opens within us. This flower transcends the individual, separate self and reveals who we truly are. Knowing ourselves, a deep acceptance flows in us and we find that all states and beings are within: we *are* the many-voiced, the many-faced, and the many-faceted, and we understand that *there is truly nothing to do and no one to do it.*

The Taoists tell a story of two friends. One played beautiful music that evoked breathtaking landscapes, vivid colors, splendid varied textures, and a plethora of animals. The other listened and heard the music that outlined, painted, embroidered, and celebrated the world. One day the friend who listened died, and the friend who played the world for him to hear, see, and feel cut the strings of his instrument and never played again. The story expresses life's reciprocity in poignant, poetic symbolism. We create the world out of our interconnectedness. We are the mysterious initiators of existence, both creators and created, both host and guest.

Our true nature lies beyond personality, beyond existence, between love and wisdom, beyond hell and heaven. It is unspoken because it is unspeakable, unwritten because it is un-writeable; we can only say what it is *not.* The best we can do is point toward it. This is why true spiritual teaching is often indirect and confusing, irrational and playful, infuriating and liberating.

Spiritual awakening results from a shock that disturbs our normal points of reference. True spiritual teaching provokes a physical, emotional, and mental revolution, an upheaval, an earthquake, a radical disturbance to the complacent organization of our sense of self. Periods of bliss alternate with painful longing and a deep irritation with ourself and others. As our awareness expands, we become intolerant of the smallest things, as we go through the stress of the changes. We feel helplessness, unworthiness, exhaustion, and self-disgust by turns; grief at the death of ignorance and our old self; rebellions of vanity and eruptions of false pride.

We are shocked into awakening to something we already know and have experienced, it seems, long ago. We are a part of something ancient; we participate in the eternal. So we must practice from our being, with the courage to understand and see ourselves as we are: a point in consciousness, without space or time, drawn into great complexity by the mind's meandering.

Close your eyes now and practice remembering. Allow your imagination to wander. Connect to the ancient path of perennial wisdom; allow yourself to fantasize freely without limitations; be a disciple on the path in any era. Feel what it is like to be a great teacher, an animal you are attracted to, a tree, a flower, and allow yourself to merge with the eternal, the inner essence of all forms appearing in your awareness and in the consciousness of which your awareness is a part.

We are only aware when we are not criticizing or judging. When we isolate aspects of ourselves and label them good or bad, we distance ourselves from others and reinforce our identification with the separate self. But awareness, like the heart, envelops everything in its all-accepting embrace, clears and strengthens us to practice skillfully.

We need to discern what is skillful and appropriate for our spiritual development. How do we stop the mind from creating forms—the shadows of the Divine? What does our interest in others signify, and what does it say about our relationship with ourself? Sometimes our relationship with ourself is so tenuous, our life so vacuous, that the only things that stimulate our interest are outside. Being concerned with someone else's life more than we are with our own signifies that something is wrong.

Criticism or admiration, morbid fascination, and minute attention toward others need to be brought back to ourselves. What are we projecting outward that truly belongs to ourselves in our inner world? Only through owning our judgments and avoidance can we begin to truly see ourselves.

We have shed the attachments to our small sense of self through inner work and empowered ourselves to live authentically. Now we face releasing all our attachments to embrace our true nature. The complete loss of identification with our separate self is the way to our liberation, past conformity, and patterns of any kind. This is how we begin to experience true spontaneity and surrender.

We need to unlearn and purify ourselves, to loosen our attachment to character and form. Nothing less than surrender to conditions *as they are* is asked of us. From now on the inner journey cannot be self-directed, because our goal is the true Self. We grow in wise innocence because only as a true follower, trusting and open, may we approach the no-man's land between the known and the unknown, the place where we may "experience" transcendence.

Experiences of Transcendence

Many people have an experience of "otherness"—the presence of something beyond the personal arises, and we perceive the numinous. For some, the experience is misunderstood, ignored, and finally forgotten. For others, it results in the kind of certainty that informs and guides the remainder of their lives, as it did for this spiritual seeker:

> It was a sublime sensation of bliss. With no loss of consciousness, but an increased intensity of consciousness, I felt vividly the earth beneath me, the air on my skin. I belonged to it; it belonged to me. Everything that was alive was related to me and to generations of birth and death through countless epochs of time. I could feel everything that existed: events, sounds, colors, and tastes, all at once. It was all a part of the bliss. I had the conviction that a most important truth had been spoken, that we are all related—animal, vegetable, and mineral—so no one is alone. I have never forgotten this experience.

These words describe the sort of experience many of us have had, perhaps more often than we remember. It is the deeply spiritual experience of merging with the totality of existence, of resting in unity consciousness. During these moments of transcendence, we pass beyond the usual limitations of life and we are no longer identified with our bodies, confined by space and time, or bound by fear and desire. We are elevated beyond the separate, divisive, habitual creations of our minds.

The spiritual teacher Douglas Harding called it "True Seeing": thinking stops, words cease, personal details are forgotten, humanness drops away, past and future fade and give way to a birth into the present: innocent, new... beyond mind—and all that exists is *now*.

Transcendent experiences involve the loosening of the iron control of normal perception; they depend on the absence of limiting concepts. They occur at a point of non-ordinary ecstasy in everyday life—sharing intimacy with a lover, watching the sun set, sitting by the ocean, listening to music. Or, more ordinarily, something quite mundane, like walking along a street, holding a child's hand, strolling barefoot on the grass. A word, a sound, an atmosphere, a shock: anything may contribute to or provoke a transcendent experience.

Once we have had such an experience, we are never the same. Even if we bury the event deeply in our memories, we can never eradicate the profound sense of inner knowing that comes from a meeting with otherness. A part of us knows that there is more to life than merely outward show, and something lies behind apparent existence. Whether we name that something God, Tao, Buddha Nature, Essence, or Soul is entirely dependent on our beliefs and the interpretations of our minds. But what we *experience* in moments of transcendence is beyond description.

We tend to forget these experiences because they happen outside the constraints of ordinary understanding and create a rupture in our personal narratives. We are quite simply not in our personality; we are, literally, out of our minds. Many hide these experiences in forgetfulness or denial, because otherness challenges the small self and threatens our perceived reality. When we are out of our personality we know that our sense of self is false and that we are not what we think we are. We have been living detached from our true nature. The person we imagined ourselves to be doesn't really exist; it is merely a product of our minds. But with the right stimuli and in the right kind of healing environment, we can reconnect with reality. The following account was written by a student in one of my workshops:

A recurring fear used to overwhelm me when I was nine or ten years of age. The fear was of not existing in the form that I was familiar with. My thoughts would turn to dying, and I could feel my blood running cold in my veins and a sharp, painful tightness in my heart. Fiercely I said to myself, "I would rather spend eternity in hell than not exist."

Twenty-eight years later at one of Richard's workshops, I experienced a wonderful state of being that remained with me for two days. I entered into a state of total absorption with no thoughts or feelings. I went out to walk in the garden. I felt as if I had been in a dark forest and had suddenly, unexpectedly stepped into a sun-filled glade. Every fiber of my being was aglow; my perceptions expanded into infinity; and I experienced a sense of completeness and absolute peace.

When we re-grouped for a sharing session, I tried to describe my experience and newfound perceptions. I clearly remember the look of disbelief and rejection on the face of my friend Anna. She said, "I want you back as you were." By the end of the weekend, I had decided that I would rather spend eternity in hell than give up the sense of myself that I had seen mirrored in Anna's eyes.

Finding our real Self is such a homecoming that all else may seem unimportant. Our desire for friends who need us to collude with them in pretense fades, and, like Anna, such friends may feel threatened by our centeredness and empowerment, and refuse to acknowledge or accept our profound realizations.

Experiences of transcendence give us the certainty that we are, in some way, eternal. We "touch" something everlasting that is beyond belief or reason. Even if we bury the memory deeply, we *know* with absolute conviction that we are more than the small self of our ordinary experience.

Transcendent experiences return us to the source of life, prior to experience and existence. We become a witness to life rather than a participant, and we meet the unspeakable reality that all cultures have sought to express in different ways. It is at once a distance from and a reverence for life, a deep honoring and awed respect for existence.

The great First Nations warrior and orator Crowfoot left us this in his dying words:

> What is life? It is the flash of a firefly in the night. It is the breath of a buffalo in the wintertime. It is the little shadow which runs across the grass and loses itself in the sunset.[10]

Minutely observed and tender, his words read like Japanese haiku or lines from a Shakespearian sonnet. They reach beyond space and time to a point of reference that transcends the normal parameters of space and time and directs us toward eternity.

Dispelling Illusion

Through our spiritual practice, we deepen in our inner inquiry into the very nature of truth, into the relationship of the self to the Eternal Self, and in the relationship of the world of changing forms to the Absolute. Much of our delusion and illusion have now been shed, but the final dispelling of any last vestige of illusion—however slight—is the work we now have before us.

The Truth is so simple that even when we are presented with it in its starkest form we are unable to grasp it. We are a single drop briefly separated from the ocean, and simultaneously we are the ocean masquerading momentarily as the drop. Just as we, as individual selves, have been concealing our divinity, our divinity has been hiding in our individual selves. And what is this divinity that we are? It is simultaneously nothing and everything. It is the total lack of anything happening, as well as the total manifestation of everything that happens—emptiness and fullness.

Theorizing and the functioning of the rational mind only makes this seem more distant. I propose an exercise. Standing, breathing, gently begin to move the upper parts of your body, sway your hips, your knees and ankles, and reach outward in all directions with your

---

10. Quoted in T. C. McLuhan, *Touch the Earth: A Self-Portrait of Indian Existence* (Abacus, 1973), 12.

arms, up and down, back and forward, and to each side, until you find yourself tracing the edges of a great luminous "egg" of energy all around your physical body. Gently extend your fingertips as far as you can and reach all around you to energize this giant egg of energy that surrounds you. Allow this to become a dance ... then when you feel ready to stop, gently sit down in your accustomed meditative posture. Still your mind, and simply experience your energy in, around, and expanding ever in all directions around your physical form. Enter spacious awareness and meditate now for fifteen to twenty minutes. Finally, lie down and rest.

Our usual way of experiencing the world is to perceive it through the physical senses, the cerebral cortex, and conceptualization. But our concepts are conditioned by previous experience. Who can stop their mind from conceptualizing and who can bear the Truth? Who can bear things as they are and the absurdity of habitual, conditioned, mechanical life?

Now we make our choice. Inner work prepares us for this irrational challenge. We become who we truly are and always have been only by letting go of ourselves. We can no longer ignore the wake-up call. All we understand rationally falls away and turns out to be as transient and false as the conditioned concepts that kept us from Truth. The only things that will endure are the unexplainable: what you can express is temporal; what cannot be expressed is eternal.

As our minds convulse in confusion and inadequately attempt to find a rational explanation, we draw closer to Truth. The mind created the nonexistent ego, the great pretender, our small self, but we were unable to understand the simple fact that we are imaginary entities. Our true nature is unutterable, quite other, unexplainable: we are nothing, everything ... and beyond both.

But who will willingly swap certainty for uncertainty, security for fear, solid ground for thin air? And who will exchange themselves for nothing and everything, even if it is their true nature that calls them to do it? We may be searching for the perfection that D. T. Suzuki described when he spoke of losing individuality to the All.

But wasn't it the same Suzuki who said on his deathbed, "I don't want to die"? D. T. Suzuki was celebrated as a great Zen master. He possessed the insightful spiritual wisdom of a gifted teacher. But we can also admire and celebrate his humanness, because not only was he deeply spiritual, he was also profoundly human.

As we dispel the many illusions that surround us, we celebrate our own humanness and spirituality. Throughout our journey we have had to make difficult decisions; we could have given up and fled, succumbed to distraction or to one of the many seductions that tempted us to abandon our inner journey, but we chose to go on. Yet never has our commitment and sincerity been more crucial than now, at this point of choice where we face total reality.

The rare human being who succeeds in completing the journey is not only exceptional; he or she is a testament to naturalness. Just because most people don't take this journey does not mean it is not in their nature to do so. In fact, the opposite is true: it is through the discovery of our true nature that we are finally natural and free. A free human being is a fulfilled one, because freedom is our true nature.

Our freedom lies in the fulfillment and transcendence of our individuality. As individuals we can never arrive here. We have to do more than re-center ourselves in the whole; we *are* the whole and our contribution is essential. Each individual is a part of the total, a note in the symphony, a syllable in the overall message. Understanding this deeply is the dispelling of delusion.

Let's now return to the theme of separation. Remember the walking exercise when you brought your awareness to the separation between your inside and your outside? Now we will take this a step further. This time walking, standing, sitting, or lying—choose whichever works for you best—close your eyes and bring inner attention to yourself. Now becoming aware of the separation, the energetic membrane between you and the outside, existence, the separation that is you yourself, your sense of "I," go further—melt and merge. Let it all become one, with no witness, no "experiencer," no subject or object— just being, consciousness, all-inclusiveness, and unity.

The Divine Nature of Personality

Since we relate to the Absolute, some part of us must be absolute; otherwise we could never be in relationship to it. Therefore, the Absolute is not strictly speaking "other" at all. This is the divine nature of our personality—we are both human and divine. So the personality—temporal and conditional, partial and individual—is also divine. Maya is contained within, and remains at all times and in all circumstances, an aspect of the Absolute, a temporary manifestation of Truth in the field of relativity: time and space. As such, it has the quality of illusion—convincing, charming, involving, but nevertheless illusion—both the appearance and the essence, both sound and the echo, the distant resonance, the seed and the tree, the original impulse and the greatest manifest fulfillment of that impulse. The divine is within and without.

At last we pierce a hole in the veil of illusion and go through the looking glass. This work of gentle demolition (which must be done gently for our healing and our response) exhilarates, frightens, and liberates us. At this stage of the spiritual search we stabilize in the knowledge that there is nothing to search for. But even this is only a new beginning. With our search over, we reorient ourselves and begin again on a new and deeper level.

Our practice now is less an effortful striving for some goal and more the deepening into who we are. We are far more than we think, and this insight leads to a dawning of deep conscience, duty, and discipline. It carries a great responsibility. We must be free to make our own choice without compulsion. This is the prerequisite for what the spiritual teacher Ramesh Balsekar eloquently calls the "final take-off point": our willingness to give up identifying with an imaginary, false self.

The self is the meeting place of the opposites. The self has to mediate between the true and the false within, because it participates in both. As truth, it is the shadow cast by the blinding light of the Absolute; as falsehood, it is the belief in the self as the Soul.

Now we are ready to cross a further bridge—the bridge to spiritual wisdom. Like the coin paid to the ferryman who conveyed the souls of the dead across the river that divided the world of the living from the world of the dead, we have to pay. Only now the price is our self.

The Unattainable Goal

When our human personality meets transcendence, we encounter the quintessential model for heartbreak, futility, disappointment, and unreciprocated love—the preordained drama of incompatibility.

All the love stories, from *Romeo and Juliet* to modern-day paperback romances, express this theme. If you want the partner of your dreams, you won't get them; if you want a good one, you'll get a bad one. After all, tales of love are boring when they end happily-ever-after. In Greek legend, Apollo pursues Daphne, who, determined to remain chaste, flees and turns into a laurel bush; shiny and beautiful, she makes herself unattainable. Similarly, if you chase consciousness you will never catch it. We cannot hunt down our divine nature and possess it; consciousness is unlimited and un-limiting; it is our natural state of liberation beyond separateness.

Conversely, the lovers who are meant to be together are inextricably connected. The damsel of Belle Isle, Odysseus's wife Penelope, and the dying (from lovesickness) suitor of the folk ballad "Barbara Allen" are symbols for the destiny of two becoming one. No effort is needed; all attempts are wasted, because no acts of thwarting can prevent the positive outcome of love.

When we discuss spiritual practice we may say, "I have come this far" and "I've really got to work on this." We use a path-journey metaphor. But it is not only a compromise; it is also incorrect. It puts us into an erroneous place where we are working with duality, which must be transcended. We must watch our language and keep trying to find a way, while using these metaphors. We make the compromise that no seeking is necessary and yet we seek. We make effort to exhaust ourselves, until we realize that none is needed … there is nothing to attain, and no journey to where we are. The journey itself is the destination, and the goal is in the process: we are on the path to *here*.

Your true Self, or consciousness, is simply present without the need for any effort. The true Self is our very essence, so no effort is required for its discovery. Not of the world of appearances, it simply *is*, and any effort on our part only takes us further away.

The spiritual path is beset with the repeated disturbances of the personality on our spiritual "progress." We have to forego egoistic thinking altogether in working toward spiritual "attainment." The ego seizes any opportunity to possess the merit of spiritual "progress." (We are now in the fourth stage of ego, *transcending*, which we discussed in chapter 9.) But when we allow it to do so, it is like picking a lovely wildflower only to find it has wilted by the time we arrive home. The solution is not to become attached to anything, not even to the *thought* of progress. We reach non-attainment by aspiring to be a beginner, since only a beginner is blessed with no thought of attainment.

The mind of the beginner is key because nothing we can do changes any aspect of our spirituality or leads to enlightenment. If our practice is separate from ourselves, we exist in a state of internal division. Our effort distances us from our true Self, and yet we struggle with the idea of making no effort. It seems that we are designed to strive. We try to understand and impose our will, because trying can be stronger than our sense of mystery and our need to surrender.

We need to know when to stop and see through the patterns we are creating and the inner life we externalize. We need to balance creating forms with witnessing the form and formlessness of the Divine. When we stop directing our lives, the Divine enters in.

Here is an exercise that may help you to begin this. Start with small steps, as with any great endeavor. You will need some free time, say a minimum of one to two hours in your schedule, in which you can set everything else to one side and concentrate on this very simple and profound practice. Dress for going out, and take everything you may need with you for a one-to-two-hour period. Pause at your doorway and make a commitment to letting go, to releasing, to dropping thought and anticipation for this short period of meditative action. Now, move mindfully out of the door, and for the next hour or so be open to what happens, without planning, expectation, taking anything for granted, without predetermining anything whatsoever.[11]

You may stumble upon what Lao Tzu gave us—the three elements. The sage Lao Tzu gave three simple keys to help us realize the unattainable. He called them the First Elements and expressed them in these deceptively simple questions: Can you rest where there is rest? Do you know when to stop? Can you stand on your own feet?

We cannot truly rest until we are easy in our hearts, until the unsaid and undone has been said and done. Rest comes into being when unrest is no more. We cannot stop until we are the master of our own mind. The mind creates scenarios and thoughts, expands and spins delicious and fascinating tales into a web of connections outside our conscious control. We cannot "stand on our own feet" until we can think for ourselves, feel for ourselves, be present, and respond spontaneously, knowing that we have everything we need in each moment without effort. Standing on our own feet is not looking outside for the answer, not projecting authority, and not depending on others for the wisdom we already possess in abundance within. Through these straightforward encouragements, Lao Tzu provides us with the building blocks for genuine self-help.

Addicted to life's dramas, we may find these basics too pedestrian to value. But if we can embrace them, we find they are pure gold. The words of Lao Tzu are like the finger pointing at the moon, but the real treasure is in the realization of the words through practice—practice that transcends progress.

The spiritual journey is not a journey after all—so no progress can be made. The journey is simply a metaphor; there can be no journey to where we are already—so nothing can be attained. So is there any reason for spiritual practice at all? Only enjoyment: enjoyment in the simple aspects of life and participation in their arising... and living life, for nothing other than its own sake.

---

11. This practical, spiritual exercise is about trust and surrender, but please do not leave your common sense behind! No walking around with your eyes shut or trying to walk through doors, please!

The goal of spiritual practice is like no other goal, and the destination of the spiritual journey is like no other destination. Spiritual practice is not the way to our real nature; it *is* our real nature. Practicing spirituality is living our enlightenment. It is not "doing"; therefore there is no progress to make. It is not "improving"; therefore there is no getting better at it. It does not respond to effort, because there is nothing to achieve. When we try, all we do is rearrange the components of our worldly lives. This insight brings immediate relief and satisfaction. Being who we are, where we are, and how we are is the unattainable goal we have attained!

Now: Freedom and Fear

Far from being unknown, the future, like the past, is painted vividly by the colors of our present imagination. The future, like the past, is perceived through a filter of fantasy. When we consider a past event and retell it one, two, or three different ways, we see that the past and the future are neither fixed nor definite, but, on the contrary, they reflect the changes in our interpretation. The only place where we can find the living unknown mystery is in the present.

A common dream is the one in which we are taking an exam or standing on a stage in front of an audience, entirely ignorant of what is expected of us and ill-equipped to perform. This reflects the anxiety of our present age, our fear of failure, the threat to our personal survival in a world that requires us to prove our usefulness or value in exchange for acknowledgment and approval. A singer, who participated in one of my workshops, provides an illustration of the same theme from waking life with this vivid account of stage fright:

> I stepped onto the stage in a blinding haze of fear. My name had been called over the house sound system, and the applause of several thousand people was threatening and deafening. I was paralyzed by expectation; somewhere deep inside me I had shut down and folded up and become very small. The guitar looked and felt foreign to me; my hands were like strange appendages I didn't recognize; the coordination of hand and voice that produced

song was far beyond my perception or imagination. I stopped and gazed out at the sea of anonymous faces feeling like the last person on Earth. Terror crawled and convulsed inside me; I was feeble and vulnerable like a newborn child…then just as I felt my most helpless, my energy surged and crashed over the front of my body in a crescendo of waves of light, and I felt absolutely vital and powerful. The surge was so intense, I grew wings of energy out of my taut, tingling shoulder blades. My body was unable to contain them. They lashed and waved around my physical form as I stood inside a fire of intensity and potency. I was fearless…I played and sang like I had never done before, and over the next forty-five minutes I performed without a single flaw.

The inner journey is reminiscent of this singer's energetic meta-morphosis, the transformation of fear into freedom that comes from fully inhabiting the present moment. Fear has no meaning outside the context of the present moment. Whereas personal inner work is concerned with the past and the future, spiritual inner work takes us beyond the spatial-temporal realms into the present. It is here, and only here, that we *are*, and this is where our true healing and develop-ment takes place.

To enter fully into the present, we must go beyond reason and belief to direct experience unhindered by thought. Thought anticipates and tries to protect us from uncertainty and insecurity out of the fear of what is to come. Usually our thinking attempts to preempt all eventu-alities and outcomes, so that we are prepared and defended against life. Life becomes the enemy laying in wait, threatening to ambush us.

I remember spending three weeks on an intensive Theravadin Bud-dhist retreat during which I attained some measure of inner peace and deep contemplation. The retreat ended with a communal meal at which we were, at last, able to talk and behave "normally" as a bridge back to our regular existences. As I was taking my place at the table, some-one informed me that a friend wanted to talk to me on the telephone. Instantly my mind spiraled out of the present and worked through a hundred scenarios of bad news in just a few seconds. My mind's ability to invent these explanations from the mention of a mere phone call was dazzling. In my state of enhanced awareness, I was able to witness the workings of my mind clearly, and see that these creations were usually unconscious and registered as the background anxiety of my character.

Through character and life patterns we are so oriented to the past that we don't notice the present. Our resistance is clear. To sustain ourselves in the illusion of selfhood we cling to the past and the future, knowing that were we to lose our grip we would slip into the unknown, the spontaneous present, the eternal moment. The unknown present is effortless and unpredictable.

Looking into the future we see how we are missing the present through our projections and neuroses. Worries, anxiety, remorse, regret, desire, and fear all project us into the future or the past. But the future and the past do not really exist; they are merely projections of the present. The emotional and mental states that we experience most of the time are unreal. We might say that we are afraid of existence, and to the degree to which we are afraid, we cease to exist. Conversely, when we stop fearing the future and regretting the past, we dare to exist.

Sitting comfortably and quietly, relaxed and alert in your preferred meditation posture, take several deep breaths to center yourself. Now, try this meditation on fear and release. First, bring to mind all your fears, starting with the first, most accessible one and moving through the others. Avoid nothing; allow your deepest fear and your most superficial ones. Don't judge, don't discriminate, just try to bring them all to mind. After a little while it will become harder to detect fears, so then you know that you are getting close to completing.

Second, simply bring your attention to the summation of all your fears; intuit what common threads tie them together and what differences of intensity, scale, tone of feeling, and emotion are associated with them. Wait in this practice of attending to your fears because an insight may occur. Notice that usually you allow your fears to be in the background of your life as anxiety, worry, low-level concern, apprehension, or possibly nervousness. Bringing them to the forefront of your awareness now, you may examine them courageously in detail. Are you afraid of your fears? Now you can take the time to look at them objectively—how terrible and shocking are they in reality?

Third, let the fears go. In reverse of the first stage, from the most hidden to the most accessible, bring your fears to mind one by one and release them. How many are left? How many do you still need to hold on to . . . and why?

Finally, when you have released all the fears you can for now, stop for a few minutes and breathe into the inner space you have created through clearing out those fears. Feel good about what you have done. Feel the inner expansion for as long as you are able, and before you end, take several deep breaths.

Daring to live without fear is the fruit of inner work. And now we take a further step. Since the present we habitually experience consists of the past and the future exclusively, only in the transcendence of the present can we experience what is truly real. Now the present is not what it appears to be: the real present is not definable in relation to the past or the future; it simply *is*. When we look carefully, we see that we are always living in the unadorned, unoccupied present. Our character and our life patterns are all created and enacted *now*. When we look into the future, we see that we are also living in the present through our projections. All of these—both so-called past and so-called future—are the reflections of life and death, the in-breath and the out-breath, memory and anticipation. As we witness this duality, our focus converges on the moment *now*. At first we feel hemmed in by it, limited, and then—if we persist and so long as we can bear it—the moment opens up into unlimited freedom.

This unlimited freedom is the abyss of the moment that we are scared of slipping into or attracted to in practices like meditation and awareness. When we succeed in reaching a sense of profound presence, we lose our personal anxieties, fearful drives, and ego-self completely.

Each of us shares this common intuition of a sense of presence. The source of our presence is absence. We could say that I am only when I am not. In the absence of ourselves, the present moment is all there is. To witness this we must free ourselves of the conceptualizing activities of the mind. When the mind is still, there is emptiness, and that emptiness is the source of all phenomena, including ourselves.

Out of this presence we may enter into pure experience, which is the spontaneous and present-created unknown. Peace, compassion, and unselfconscious love are outside our grasp so long as we are. When our separate self-identity falls away, they all stream in and we exist in the now, fully immersed in the moment without separation, and this becomes our new and true center.

In Summary

Here we are ... now. Your inner work has come to its deepest and most transcendent place in you. These exercises may help to stabilize you in the insights and prepare you for the final chapter of this book:

1. Consider a past event and retell (or write) it several different ways. Notice how the past and the future are neither fixed nor definite and how your changes in interpretation alter the memory of what happened.

2. Breath practice: Breathe in down the frontal line of the body (in at the nose, through the chest and belly, and fully into the pelvis); relax and expand in the different energy centers (throat, heart, solar plexus, abdomen, perineum). Practice as often as possible opening, receiving, and merging with experience.

3. Experience yourself as a point in consciousness, without space or time, drawn into great complexity by the mind's meandering. Where is the living unknown mystery? What is in the present moment?

4. Awareness envelops the mind in its all-accepting field: draw this; write a poem about this; meditate on this.

5. Deeply spiritual experiences, unusual lights and sounds, feelings of merging with existence or of rising above the limitations of ordinary life, unexpected irrational joy, elation, and the complete absence of fear and desire are all characteristics of transcendent experience. Recall and record any such experiences you have had.

13

Perpetual Illumination

What I really am, and what you really are, is all and everything. All and everything cannot describe itself, because to do so it would have to separate itself from itself, from what it is. What we really are can only be expressed through pure, unselfconscious being, and this is what is meant by the true Self that is our original nature. The inner journey has taken us on a spiral around our true Self. Like the sun, we cannot look directly at it and we cannot get too close to it, but nonetheless it is there, and the individual "I" would not be here without our true Self. Each complete circle of the spiral brings us closer to the outer edges of our small self. After some turns around the spiral, we need journey no more; we have arrived at the border of timeless space and being; we have reached the eternal "I."

No Teacher, No System

Ancient and contemporary maps and guides may be powerful resources for recognizing and pursuing the spiritual path. The recorded experiences of others who have passed through a journey similar to our own may help us to chart our course and deepen in understanding. As well as offering guidance and insight, these maps reassure us with the knowledge that others have gone before and point the way to total human fulfillment. In this way spiritual teachers and guides, whether they are in the body or not, may help us through the quality of their timeless presence and the wisdom of their teachings.

But ultimately all the teachings, systems, maps, and methods are merely lovely poetry and beautiful descriptions—art bridging the worlds. Real spiritual insight is not dependent on any teaching or system; it is the result of commitment, sustained practice, and the fruit of the seeds of faith. Plastic beads and false starts, delusion and fake teachings, formulas and instruction books may proliferate and adorn our way, but eventually we attain the jewel beyond price that was always in our heart.

While in a transcendent, altered state, P. D. Ouspensky experienced some great understanding. So he sought a formula, a key to his insights, so that when he returned to a normal state he could remember his insights. He wrote down a short sentence summing up his understanding, so that he might rejoin his exalted state anxiety-free. On the following day he read the sentence: "Think in other categories."

The beautiful, sparkling pebbles we bring back from the beach always look dull when we get them home. No attempt to describe the numinous can ever do it justice. In a world with no boundaries and perfect freedom, thinking in any category is no longer possible. Ouspensky was bound by thought, and he took systems of transcendent thought as far as anyone could. Finally, disenchanted, at the end of a life devoted to finding a "system" for the Divine, he lurched inebriated onto a lecture stage and announced to an astonished audience, "There is no system."

Ouspensky had stumbled upon the futility of thought. He had made the error of reading and gathering all the information, without spending enough time reading his own heart. Even the greatness of a spiritual luminary like Bhagawan Nityananda, who never wrote a book or devised a system, was not enough for his disciple Muktananda, who appeared before his guru with a book under his arm once too often, prompting Nityananda to declare, "Where is your own mind? Throw away the book and meditate!"

Throwing away our books means releasing our attachment to the idea that we will somehow gain the wisdom we lack through acquiring knowledge. Searching for the spiritual, we eventually discover that the divine has always been within. We learn this through practicing what Muktananda later called "uninterrupted awareness." This kind of awareness is broken when we appeal to a book or a teacher for the wisdom that we already possess. A fifty-five-year-old meditation student told me:

> As I grow older, words that I thought I understood become real for me. Before, these words acted like signposts pointing the way. I knew what the words said and I thought the words were true, but they were not yet my words. I knew that the words were somehow within me, but I couldn't reach them. Now, I have grown *down* and dug deep inside to find them in me. I learn more from inside myself now than I do from outside myself.

The objections to external teachings and spiritual groups are well known. First, religions and cults are inherently competitive as a result of their exclusivity. Choosing one religion over another assumes that one is preferred and implicitly superior to the others. Second, religions are usually based on the belief in certain doctrines and practices, which masks the fear of uncertainty and doubt. The lives of the mystics who had the courage to step outside of established religion show us that uncertainty and doubt are indispensable aspects of the spiritual path. Third, committing to an established religion tends to close us to questioning and inquiry and destroys faith, which is built on the openness and willingness to face the unknown—the spiritual path of non-attachment.

Authentic spiritual practice refers us back to ourselves. Gurus, teachings, methods, and systems are simply devices. We need not dwell on the road once we have reached our destination. Regardless of which spiritual teaching and method you choose from the many that are available, the most important point is non-attachment. In the end, you must let go completely.

Time and again we learn that Self-realization is ordinary participation in the world. A young physician went to see Zen master Nan-in to overcome his fear of death. Nan-in said, "Zen is not a difficult task. Treat your patients with kindness. That is Zen." In the twelfth-century scripture the Ten Bulls, the Self-realized being wanders through the world responding lightly and spontaneously to all that arises. There is no teacher and no system that cannot be discarded eventually. Life is our teacher, and if we are able to surrender unselfconsciously to what life asks of us, then life is also our liberator.

Reading the book of your heart is an exercise you can practice anytime and even eventually *all* the time. But as a formal practice, simply sit in your preferred meditation posture, breathe, center yourself in your heart chakra, and be receptive to love and wisdom.

Who "I" Really Am

What is the essence of the great teachings? What is it that binds them all together—into the very *core* of spirituality? When we sacrifice our character, history, feelings, thoughts, and experiences on the altar of Truth, what is left and who are we?

In my early life I already *knew*. I would lie in bed on dark evenings awake and wrestle with myself, my environment, my family, this life. Alongside these reflections was a sense, I later came to realize, that something was perceived, not by senses or thought, any neurological pathway, or even intuition of "other" or of the numinous. An indefinable shape, a distant memory, haunted my inner world; an unimaginable dimension of human existence whose presence could not be sensed or grasped by my senses or any rational framework. With it came a strong feeling of longing, of nostalgia for something wonderful, ecstatic, and heavenly, some place of bliss where I belonged. The world and this life awaited me; I was not yet ready for the answer. But my whole life prepared me for what I already knew as a child: "I" am in this world or the world is in me; they are the same thing, and simultaneously "I" am reflecting into this world from beyond.

In the Hindu tradition this is called the *Mahavakya*—the great saying of the ancient Upanishads, Tat Tvam Asi, *I Am That*: the revelation that the human and the Divine are one and that the Self is identical with ultimate reality. This is our liberation into present reality and cannot be understood, still less experienced, through the senses, thought, or any worldly knowledge.

We are everything and nothing. We are the world we see and we are none of this. Beyond our cloak of character and selfhood we are the eternal Soul, undifferentiated and unnameable. I Am That is the trinity of Self, Not Self, and Being: it is all One. This is who we are— inexpressibly conscious and beyond consciousness. Now, how are we to wear the cloak of our humanness and live this truth? How are we to live the complete spectrum—eternal and temporal, absolute and relative, nowhere and everywhere?

The passage that follows is taken from my inner-work notebooks. It is an account of a guided imagery, a spiritual journey, and it illustrates the inner meeting of my small self with the Eternal, of the human with the Divine.

> I am walking up steps. There are two places to go and I have to choose one. Silently I ask, and I know *immediately* that I must choose fear, the unknown. The way is into the sky. I take a last step before I leave the earth. There is only sky. I am floating in the vast blueness. Nothing is happening. I think of Michelangelo's image of God in the Sistine Chapel, the arm reaching out ... there are no things ... like unconsciousness ... nothing solid ... just floating. I am only consciousness. Not even a cloud. I move through colors with no form. It's like going through a rainbow: red, orange, yellow ... When I grab a color it turns into something else ... something abstract. I feel the motion slowing down. I have the impression a meeting is going to take place. I have a feeling of a sense of me, and this sense of me resists the meeting.
>
> I have a weird physical sensation: I am huge, too big, a huge glob that is like a false sense of size, which refuses to accept the

meeting and pushes everything away from me. So I ask how to change it, and the answer comes, "Think small." Now I see my body from a distance. It is very tiny in the big blue sky. I see how small I am. I join that small me in the sky, an image of the huge me on the right hand and the tiny me on the left hand—three bodies, and we are flying upward by a lot of redness. A strong triangular shape with something shooting out of it passes across from left to right. I am resisting the meeting, feeling incredibly blank.

I see a vision of a vast hall. I am looking down it, and my body has gone up somewhere. The hall is huge with great big pillars to left and right. I cannot see the far end. Everything is gold and silver, for miles, with arches, a roof, a vast floor of diamond shapes, all bright—even the dark is bright!

I feel fed up about it; it is all so much. I am not in the least bit awestruck, and I am slouching. I ask and the answer comes back straightaway, "Get up to the other end." So I start walking. I have a weird sense of the sides closing in. It feels narrow, like it is bearing in. My footsteps echo, everything shining like glass, pillars like marble, all bright. I don't know what is beyond the pillars or where I'm going and part of me doesn't want to go.

I feel seduced to feel fed up. It doesn't feel real, but like some inflated self has taken over. It's difficult to resist, but it is a false self in the way of me, preventing me from worshipping. At the end are steps. I go up them. They are very wide, and made of a lot of gold. It's easier to go up in worship than to feel fed up. I am walking up with a straight back, not slouching now, because I can worship. I climb the steps in a slow meditative rhythm.

I have a cloak on now, a gold cloak, straight and hanging down. I have arrived, but I don't want to look. I hang my head facedown, ashamed. I hear the words "What took you so long." I am crouched down, worshipping. A voice says my name. I say, "I want to hear. I want to see." The voice says, "You *can* see."

I realize that this big hall is hidden in the sky. Like it is in another dimension and I was flying in it all the time. If you can see, you can see it all the time at another level—this big golden hallway.

I sense that I must return, and that my stupidity is being tolerated good-humoredly, since it is only my character. It's me who doesn't love my character. But now I am here, I don't want to go. I know what I have to do: *teach people to see*, and I am actually always here in this golden hall, so I don't really have to leave.

I remind myself that I am on these steps, worshipping. I don't feel worthy; I feel like the poor relation. Without a seat, I am just standing there. There is just the one seat; it's almost gaudy. I can hardly look. I feel poor. I had a golden cloak on, but it has become a grey cowl. It might have turned grey because it's so bright. This is the light, sitting in the throne. I would almost like to make it into a person. I call out to it and there is a voice couched in gold. I am small, insignificant, not really meant ... "You and I are the same," the voice says.

My hands reach up toward the light. I am ready to come down. I realize that of the two places at the first steps where I had to choose, the other place was ordinary: a forest with earth, grass, and leaves. I am in both places, and they are entirely different. I have to see the earth with the eyes of the golden hall.

True understanding is not intellectual but direct appreciation that is felt in every pore and cell. It is so momentous that we must respond to it lightly. Enlightening understanding should always be received lightly. It is not burdensome; it implies no duty or responsibility—we are, and have always been, utterly free.

Now take your own spiritual journey. Try this guided imagery. You will have either to record the words or have a friend read them to you, carefully attending to the pauses denoted by "..." for at least two or three breaths, and sometimes more. Let's begin.

Sit or lie comfortably and take several breaths to bring yourself to a relaxed, alert state. Relax tensions in the body and allow your heart and mind to become receptive, open, and as empty as possible. When you feel ready, begin.

Now ... visualize yourself walking on a path ... be aware of the sights, sounds, and fragrances around you. Be aware of the air on your skin and any other sensations as you walk ... You are walking to a meeting ... a divine meeting. Now you come to a fork in the road ... you have to make a choice ... when you have made your choice, follow where you are led, where you have to go. Remember everything that happens to you ... (long pause ... while the journey and meeting unfolds in yourself or the person you are guiding) ... (very gently) Now it is time for you to return ... from where your journey has taken you ... Take three deep breaths ... and gently come back into the room.

Tell the story of your journey to someone who can write your experience down so you can refer to it later. Take a little time to lie down and rest.

Freedom surrounds and permeates us like air or sunshine. We merge with the ocean, like the falling drop. We burn in the fire, like a flying flame separated momentarily from the blaze. We are on the earth, but not of it. We are one with life, yet also we transcend it.

We do not need to try; we do not make effort. We do not need to think, play, dance, or create anything; it is all done. No creation or destruction ever takes place, since the world, as we perceive it, has never existed. When Brahman opens his eyes, a world comes into existence; when he blinks, it disappears. Like Plato's cave of shadows, Shakespeare's "fleeting world," or the maya of Vedanta, worlds appear and disappear over and over in the blink of an eye.

Ultimately we are "other." So the very experience of "otherness" that we resisted, forgot, and denied in experiences of transcendence is nothing but the Self, the I AM of existence, and our soul is All Souls which are one. Now we have returned to our source, beyond all desire and fear. With nothing to do, nowhere to go, we simply *are*. Nonexistence is the shadow, the doorway, or prelude to existence and I AM THAT.

As we reflect and comment, draw subjective pictures of our lives, giving form and content to our abstract and meandering course through a succession of living moments, we feel the truth of the statement "'I am not I." The question is "Who am I?" The answer is, simply, "I am." Beyond that there is only silence.

Spontaneity and Surrender

We have passed through many resistances, points of choice that could have led us away from our path. Now we have arrived at the end of the journey. In chapter 1, we discussed the *floor of shifting patterns*, one of the many ingenious ways in which we can avoid ourselves out of fear. In this stage, the floor, the ground of being, is transformed forever—and all it took was courage.

Our doing blended with our being, no longer separate or split, our wounds healed: this is where we have arrived, in unity with life, beyond subject and object. No longer is there a purpose to anything outside of itself; we do what we do *for its own sake*. No longer are we invested in lack, for we are complete in ourselves. No longer do we drag around the heaped baggage of our conditioning, because we are now free. At last we live in truth and whatever life presents us with; we accept deeply, for we see it is only ourselves in new forms.

The later stages of inner work are distinguished by their ordinariness. However spectacular or miraculous our experiences have been, they have faded now. What remains is the continual flow of life out of which all our experiences have come and gone. We have processed the unresolved, the limiting, the fearful, and the suffering inside us, until we are finally at peace. We sought resolution, release, and liberation, the experience of wholeness and reality to touch the ground of being. Now we dwell serenely within and flow between life's events, changing conditions, feelings, experiences, and truth from our true center. We are attached, ever lightly, through our humanness, and unattached, ever deepening, through our divinity. We seek no posture and no special identity and find always that the way is invisibly between two opposites.

The end of our search is also a beginning—the beginning of the life of spiritual transformation. Nothing is stale or rehashed, as it was when we were constrained within the patterns of mind and emotion. We wear our identity loosely now and reside in the present, at one with the totality of existence. Gently, patiently, courageously, we have arrived in the reality of transcendence and ordinariness. We are continually enveloped in secret and mystic silence that is beyond knowledge or concept, beyond all veils, reason, or opposites.

We have searched for a reason, something outside ourselves, for definition and meaning. We have strived toward a goal that can never be reached, because we were happier to be in pursuit of our life than in receipt of it. But that has changed now.

A woman came to visit me. She was traveling around the world "to find God," she told me. We explored the concept "God": God is the Absolute, nothing and everything, and therefore beyond location, time, and space. These definitions provide flawless "proofs," but to communicate them truly to another we must be strongly in our true hearts, vulnerable and transparent. She wrestled with her investment in the search, in not finding anything, in never ending. Eventually she realized that her search was futile. God is here, now. So, she left and carried on with her odyssey, but with God as her constant companion rather than as her distant goal.

I had learned this lesson when, as a young man, I traveled to India in search of God. I learned then that traveling to find God as another person in another place denied the divinity in me. Today I learn this lesson in ever subtler but powerful ways. Whenever we miss the moment, get "caught" by our thoughts, distracted from our awareness, lose our center; every time our minds go before us and we are caught up in the results of our actions, we are lost again. When we throw the imaginary destination ahead of us, life ceases, because we are no longer living in the present. Whatever gifts life offers us, we are unable to receive them when we are not present.

We must go to where the life is, to where the joyous music is play-ing. Existence offers no certainty or security, but letting go, being flexible, surrendering, we return to the great flow at the border of timeless space and being: the river has remembered and returned to the ocean. We have discovered that we really are unconditional, abso-lute Being. We have remembered our real Self now that we have jour-neyed round ourself in revelation. At last we are undeceived and we have stopped creating a world and populating it. We know now that there is no journey to where we already are.

We are, after all, awareness, the Eternal subject. We no longer exist in separation, but participate fully in the world in blessing and con-tentment. Now we can embrace life and truly experience, and the essence of real experience is spontaneity and surrender. We don't per-sist; neither do we resist. With no separate self as agency, no striving to a goal of desire out of fear, we do what we have always done ... for happiness ... and true happiness is within us.

The love, the peace, the wisdom we sought turns out to be within, too. The truth was so obvious, so present, so near us that we were unable to see it. We were looking so hard, traveling so far, that we never took the time to stand still and witness or understand it. Now, in this precious awakening, we know who we really are, and we are, of course ... even if we wanted to ... unable to speak of it.

Afterword

Today we human beings have grown away from our true nature, from our essential selves. Inner work is needed to bring us back to ourselves, to the naturalness that has been lost, to our inner wisdom, and to our true purpose. Evolving human consciousness must become the prevailing focus for humanity if we are to avert the impending spiritual, ecological, heartbreakingly human, and global crisis of the twenty-first century. Inner work must become commonplace, routine, and universal among people, rather than merely the concern of a relative few.

Overcoming our fear of the unknown to be all we are, to be true to our innermost being, is crucial: it connects us with Nature and the rest of existence. As more people awaken, the quality of our lives will change. So it is both personally and globally vital that we foster an authentic love for creation, a deep empathy with existence, a strong attitude of tolerance and cooperation toward the outside world, and that we strive toward enlightenment as our life's goal. The inner journey liberates, fulfills, and releases our potential into the world. Denial and repression of our shadow and inner darkness result in outward projections of prejudice and evil into the world.

It is my hope that this account of the magnificent journey of awakening to your essential self has informed, inspired, and encouraged you to begin, continue, or complete your inner journey. *You are a divine being.* This is, ultimately, what we human beings have to awaken to—the divinity of the self. The paradox is that to become as natural as we are, we suffer and struggle with inner conflicts, confusion, and resistance, when our awakening is as natural as fresh air, as a gentle breeze, as the waves crashing on the seashore, as the majestic movement of the planets through the vast cosmos.

May you and I fully awaken.

May all beings fully awaken.

May all of existence fully awaken.

Bibliography

Balsekar, Ramesh S. (Revised and ed. by Sudhakar S. Dikshit). *Pointers from Nisargadatta Maharaj*. Durham, NC: The Acorn Press, 1990.

Bolen, Jean Shinoda. *Ring of Power*. New York: HarperSanFrancisco, 1992.

Campbell, Joseph. *The Power of Myth*. New York: Doubleday, 1988.

Coelho, Paulo. *The Alchemist*. London: Thorsons, 1995.

Foundation for Inner Peace, and Helen Schucman. *A Course in Miracles: The Text, Workbook for Students and Manual for Teachers*. London: Arkana, 1985.

Harding, Douglas. *On Having No Head: Zen and the Rediscovery of the Obvious*. London: Arkana, 1986.

Harvey, Richard. *The Flight of Consciousness: A Contemporary Map for the Spiritual Journey*. London: Ashgrove Publishing, 2002.

Heilpern, John. *Conference of the Birds: The Story of Peter Brook in Africa*. New York: Routledge, 1999.

John, Da Free. *The Knee of Listening*. San Rafael, CA: Dawn Horse Press, 1973.

Johnson, Robert A. *HE: Understanding Masculine Psychology*. New York: Harper and Row, 1977.

Krishnamurti, J. (Luis S. R. Vas, ed.). *The Mind of J Krishnamurti*. Bombay, India: Jaico Publishing House, 1971.

Lao Tzu (C. H. Wu, trans.). *Tao Teh Ching*. Boston: Shambhala Publications, 1990.

Le Guin, Ursula K. *A Wizard of Earthsea*. New York: Houghton Mifflin, 1968.

Lorca, Federico Garcia (Jerome Rotherberg, trans.). *Selected Poems*. London: Penguin, 1997.

Maharshi, Sri Ramana (David Godman, ed.). *Be as You Are: The Teachings of Sri Ramana Maharshi*. London: Arkana, 1985.

———. *Talks with Ramana Maharshi*. Carlsbad, CA: Inner Directions Foundation, 2000. (Originally published in India by Sri Ramanasramam.)

Main, John. *The Way of Unknowing*. London: Darton, Longman and Todd, 1989.

McLuhan, T. C. *Touch the Earth: A Self-Portrait of Indian Existence*. London: Abacus, 1973.

Miller, D. Patrick. *The Complete Story of the Course: The History, the People and the Controversies Behind a Course in Miracles*. London: Rider, 1998.

Muktananda Paramahamsa, Swami. *Bhagawan Nityananada of Ganeshpuri*. New York: SYDA Foundation, 1996.

———. *Play of Consciousness (Chitshakti Vilas)*. South Fallsburg, NY: SYDA Foundation, 2000.

Nisargadatta Maharaj, Sri (Maurice Frydman, trans.; Sudhakar S. Dikshit, ed.). *I Am That: Talks with Sri Nisargadatta Maharaj*. Durham, NC: The Acorn Press, 1988.

Ouspensky, P. D. *In Search of the Miraculous: Fragments of an Unknown Teaching*. London: Routledge & Kegan Paul, 1950.

Ramakrishna: The Gospel of Sri, Originally Recorded in Bengali by M., a Disciple of the Master (Swami Nikhilananda, trans.). New York: Ramakrishna-Vivekananda Center, 1942.

Ray, Paul H., and Sherry Ruth Anderson. *The Cultural Creatives: How 50 Million People Are Changing the World*. New York: Three Rivers Press, 2001.

Reps, Paul. *Zen Flesh, Zen Bones*. London: Penguin, 1972.

Rilke, Rainer Maria (M. D. Herter, trans.). *Letters to a Young Poet*. New York: W. W. Norton & Co., 1962.

Shah, Idries. *Exploits of the Incomparable Mulla Nasruddin*. London: Picador, 1973.

Somé, Malidoma Patrice. *The Healing Wisdom of Africa: Finding Life Purpose Through Nature, Ritual, and Community*. London: Thorsons, 1999.

Spirit of the Upanishads; or, The Aphorisms of the Wise. Chicago: The Yogi Publication Society, 1907.

Suzuki, Shunryu (Trudy Dixon, ed.). *Zen Mind, Beginner's Mind*. New York: John Weatherhill, 1986.

Tweedie, Irina. *The Chasm of Fire: A Woman's Experience of Liberation through the Teachings of a Sufi Master*. Shaftesbury, UK: Element Books, 1979.

Watts, Alan (ed. and adapted by Judith Johnstone). *OM: Creative Meditations*. Berkeley, CA: Celestial Arts, 1980.

Yalom, Irvin D. *Love's Executioner and Other Tales of Psychotherapy*. London: Penguin,1991.

Index

To Write to the Author

If you wish to contact the author or would like more information about this book, please write to the author in care of Llewellyn Worldwide Ltd. and we will forward your request. Both the author and publisher appreciate hearing from you and learning of your enjoyment of this book and how it has helped you. Llewellyn Worldwide Ltd. cannot guarantee that every letter written to the author can be answered, but all will be forwarded. Please write to:

Richard Harvey
℅ Llewellyn Worldwide
2143 Wooddale Drive
Woodbury, MN 55125-2989

Please enclose a self-addressed stamped envelope for reply,
or $1.00 to cover costs. If outside the USA, enclose
an international postal reply coupon.

Many of Llewellyn's authors have websites with additional information and resources. For more information, please visit our website at http://www.llewellyn.com.

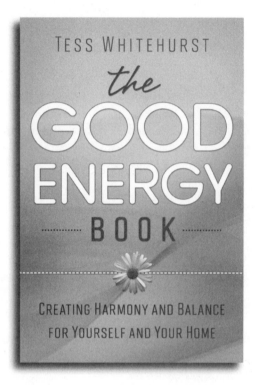

TESS WHITEHURST

the

GOOD ENERGY
BOOK

CREATING HARMONY AND BALANCE
FOR YOURSELF AND YOUR HOME

The Good Energy Book
Creating Harmony and Balance for Yourself and Your Home
TESS WHITEHURST

Free yourself from negativity and create positive energy in every facet of your life.

Energy is all around us, and it can hold positive or negative influences. If you're filled with the negative, the positive can't get in. Get rid of the bad and bring in happiness and success with *The Good Energy Book*. Learn how to:

- Clear negativity from people, objects, and places
- Keep your energy clear and positive
- Activate your intuition
- Perform highly effective space-clearing and protective rituals

This book will positively change your life! It will give you proactive and holistic tools and techniques to establish powerfully positive conditions in your mind, body, home, and affairs. Practical and down-to-earth, this book is the indispensable guide to energy work.

978-0-7387-2772-1, 240 pp., 5³⁄₁₆ x 8   **$14.95**

Garden of
Bliss

Cultivating the Inner Landscape
for Self-Discovery

DEBRA MOFFITT

Garden of Bliss

Cultivating the Inner Landscape for Self-Discovery

DEBRA MOFFITT

Garden of Bliss begins on the French Riviera, where author Debra Moffitt, despite her glamorous European lifestyle, is unhappy. Realizing that financial success doesn't necessarily equate to happiness, she looks inside herself and decides to make some changes.

The message of her journey is simple: bliss is a destination that exists within all of us. Using the metaphor of a secret garden, Moffitt encourages her readers to manifest this space in the physical world and connect with the Divine Feminine through nature. *Garden of Bliss* can be read as a stand-alone book or as a companion text to Moffitt's award-winning debut, *Awake in the World*.

978-0-7387-3382-1, 288 pp., 5³⁄₁₆ x 8   **$16.99**

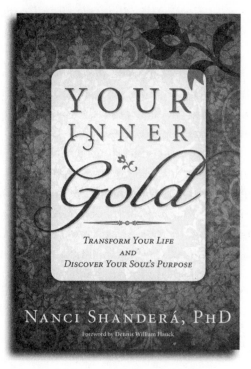

YOUR
INNER
Gold

Transform Your Life
and
Discover Your Soul's Purpose

NANCI SHANDERÁ, PhD

Foreword by Dennis William Hauck

Your Inner Gold
Transform Your Life and Discover Your Soul's Purpose
NANCI SHANDERÁ, PHD

Create positive personal life changes, free yourself from fear, and open your heart to the shining philosopher's stone of your inner gold. This alchemical guide presents a comprehensive model to help you discover your true self and its relationship to your soul's purpose.

Transform yourself with the seven basic stages of spiritual alchemy: calcination, dissolution, separation, conjunction, putrefaction-fermentation, mortification, distillation, and coagulation. Whether you're new to spiritual practice or an advanced seeker, this useful guide will help you apply each principle to your life through meditations, exercises, and other creative techniques. Learn how to overcome what holds you back, how your soul speaks to you, how your soul's pre-birth agreements affect your life challenges, and much more. Even though you can't remove any aspect of yourself, you can transform it with spiritual alchemy.

978-0-7387-3601-3, 240 pp., 6 x 9   **$15.99**

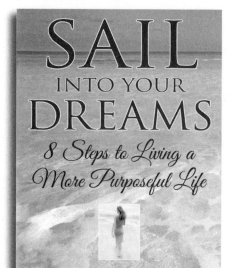

Sail into Your Dreams
8 Steps to Living a More Purposeful Life
KAREN MEHRINGER

Sail into Your Dreams is the perfect book for anyone who has ever asked, "Is this all there is to life?"

Unsatisfied with her busy life in Seattle, Karen Mehringer embarked on a six-month, life-changing ocean odyssey to Australia, Indonesia, and Fiji. Most importantly, she journeyed toward the joyful, fulfilling life she had always wanted.

You don't have to leave land to make your dreams come true. Karen shares the wisdom and practical tools she learned on her ocean odyssey, showing us how to focus on what truly matters. Journal entries and inspiring stories from Karen and others highlight how to slow down, nurture yourself, connect with others, and tap into your life force energy—the source of infinite possibilities.

This eight-step program will help you assess your life and eliminate toxic relationships, emotional trauma, physical clutter, and debt—making space for new experiences that awaken your passion and spirit.

978-0-7387-1053-2, 240 pp., 5 x 7   **$13.95**

To order, call 1-877-NEW-WRLD
Prices subject to change without notice
Order at Llewellyn.com 24 hours a day, 7 days a week